RADICAL

POLITICAL THEOLOGY

INSURRECTIONS: CRITICAL STUDIES IN RELIGION, POLITICS, AND CULTURE

SLAVOJ ŽIŽEK, CLAYTON CROCKETT, CRESTON DAVIS, JEFFREY W. ROBBINS, EDITORS

The intersection of religion, politics, and culture is one of the most discussed areas in theory today. It also has the deepest and most wide-ranging impact on the world. Insurrections: Critical Studies in Religion, Politics, and Culture will bring the tools of philosophy and critical theory to the political implications of the religious turn. The series will address a range of religious traditions and political viewpoints in the United States, Europe, and other parts of the world. Without advocating any specific religious or theological stance, the series aims nonetheless to be faithful to the radical emancipatory potential of religion.

COLUMBIA UNIVERSITY PRESS   NEW YORK

CLAYTON CROCKETT

RELIGION AND POLITICS AFTER LIBERALISM

RADICAL
POLITICAL THEOLOGY

COLUMBIA UNIVERSITY PRESS

PUBLISHERS SINCE 1893

NEW YORK   CHICHESTER, WEST SUSSEX

Library of Congress Cataloging-in-Publication Data

Crockett, Clayton, 1969–

Radical political theology : religion and politics after liberalism / Clayton Crockett.

p.   cm. — (Insurrections)

Includes bibliographical references (p.) and index.

ISBN 978-0-231-14982-2 (cloth : alk. paper)—ISBN 978-0-231-14983-9 (pbk. : alk. paper)—

ISBN 978-0-231-52076-8 (e-book)

1. Religion and politics. 2. Political theology. I. Title. II. Series.

BL65.P7C75   2011

201'.72—dc222010012341

c 10 9 8 7 6 5 4 3 2

p 10 9 8 7 6 5 4 3 2 1

Book and cover design by Chang Jae Lee

Cover image © Gallerystock/Harry Weber

To my parents, Becky Crockett and Bill Crockett

CONTENTS

ACKNOWLEDGMENTS

Some of the material from section II of the introduction is drawn from my chapter "Jeb Stuart's Revenge: The Civil War, the Religious Right, and American Fascism" in *The Sleeping Giant Has Awoken: The New Politics of Religion in the United States*, ed. Jeffrey W. Robbins and Neal Magee (London: Continuum, 2008). Jeffrey W. Robbins coauthored an initial draft of chapter 5 with me, which was presented at a session of the American Academy of Religion Annual Meeting in November 2007, and he graciously allowed me to rework it and use it in this book. Some material from chapter 8 is taken from my foreword to Catherine Malabou, *Plasticity at the Dusk of Writing*, trans. Carolyn Shread (New York: Columbia University Press, 2009). I want to particularly thank Malabou for her insights and conversation, and especially for her willingness to collaborate with me on an article that served as an earlier version of this chapter, "Plasticity and the Future of Philosophy and Theology," published in a special issue of *Political Theology* (10, no. 4 [2009]), "The Continental Shift," edited by Creston Davis.

Most of all, I would like to acknowledge and thank my coeditors and editors with Insurrections and Columbia University Press, Jeff Robbins, Creston Davis, Slavoj Žižek, Wendy Lochner, and Christine Mortlock for their support, encouragement, and camaraderie.

Next, I want to thank Catherine Keller, Ward Blanton, and Jeff Robbins for their care and commitment in reading the book manuscript and offering insightful and constructive feedback. Thanks to Danny Finer for compiling the index—semper fi!

For all my friends and colleagues whose conversations and discussions helped me as I worked and thought through these issues, I am extremely grateful. In addition to those already named above, these include, but are not limited to: Noëlle Vahanian, Catherine Malabou, Jack Caputo, Keith Putt, Sharon Baker, Michael Wilson, Natalie Zimmerman, Kevin Mequet, Sara Galvin, Mason Brothers, Sara Harvey, Mary-Ruth Marotte, Phillip Huddleston, Charlie Harvey, Jim Shelton, Peter Mehl, Jesse Butler, Julie Butler, Philip Goodchild, Bob Spivey, Oz Lorentzen, Malik Saafir, Aaron Simmons, Jay McDaniel, the late Edith Wyschogrod, Thomas Altizer, Lissa McCullough, Charles Long, Gavin Hyman, Santiago Zabala, Mary-Jane Rubenstein, Ludger Viefhues, David Loy, Danny Finer, Wilson Dickinson, Jeremy Vecchi, Francis Sanzaro, Dan Miller, Craig Martin, Andrew Saldino, David Miller, Alan Richard, Gabe Gentry, Jo Anne Stephens, Jeff Kelly, Matt Chiorini, Brian Campbell, Vic Taylor, Carl Raschke, Joshua Delpech-Ramey, Arvind Mandair, William Robert, Jim DiCenso, Dori Parmenter, Ananda Abeysekara, Brad Johnson, Adam Kotsko, Anthony Paul Smith, Nicole Ferrari, Aaron Barraza, Jairo Barraza, Amanda Wallace, Greg Chatman, Ashley Mathews, and Matthew Creswell.

Finally, I want to thank my family for their love and support—especially my wife, Vicki, and my children, Bryan and Maria, as well as my brother, Clint, and my grandmother, Tollie Spivey. This book is dedicated to my parents, who not only gave me the gift of life but were also my first teachers. Here is a product of their labor.

RADICAL
POLITICAL THEOLOGY

INTRODUCTION

THE FREEDOM OF RADICAL THEOLOGY AFTER THE

DEATH OF GOD

I

IN THE *ANALECTS* 13.1, CONFUCIUS IS ASKED, "IF THE RULER OF WEI were to entrust you with the government of the country, what would be your first initiative?" His response: "It would certainly be to rectify the names."[1] What would it mean to rectify names like law, justice, and democracy today, if it is not already too late? If a thing does not correspond to its name, does it not create disorder and confusion, and make virtue impossible? One way to characterize the postmodern world that we live in is the determination that things no longer correspond to their names, that names float freely, without anchor, just like monetary currencies. I believe that there is no simple solution, that names cannot simply be rectified in a traditionalist manner. I also fear that we may be entering into another Period of Warring States, and while I am not a *junzi* (a sage or a virtuous person, sometimes translated anachronistically as "gentleman"), in this book I want to reflect theoretically on the current crisis of the name and state of political theology, including concepts like freedom, sovereignty, democracy, law, power, God, and the messianic.

1

Religion has returned, famously and controversially, to human thought and culture, and this return is a political (re)turn. I argue that the resurgence of determinate forms of religiosity today represents a crisis of modern liberal capitalism. Liberal modernity is constituted by excluding determinate religion from public life, creating a secular nonreligious space. This distinction between religious and secular is breaking down, so that it is no longer possible to consistently and rigorously separate and oppose the sacred and the profane. Religion and secular spheres and concepts deconstruct, to use Jacques Derrida's language.

At the same time, the recent and continuing deformation of the line delineating the religious and the secular also demonstrates that it has never been possible to strictly separate the two, although a large part of what we call Western modernity has been predicated on the possibility that religion and secularity can be kept apart. The ideology of secularism is concomitant with liberalism, because liberalism imagines a neutral, value-free space in which a free market can work. By liberalism here, I am referring to classical liberalism more so than to contemporary liberalism, the latter of which is largely a nostalgic vestige of the former. Economic neoliberalism represents the ideological triumph of free-market capitalism at a time when the scarcity of cheap energy, as well as the enormity of public and private debt worldwide, challenges assumptions of indefinite growth.

If religion and secularity cannot be neatly separated, we cannot fully separate or distinguish political philosophy from political theology. In a postsecularist environment, we possess no absolute or certain criterion by which to claim that any phenomenon is theological as opposed to nontheological. Here theology means theoretical reflection about religious phenomena in general rather than a specific tradition or set of truth-claims. This book on political theology analyzes some of the nature and stakes of this inseparable intertwining of religious and secular by attending to the conceptual stakes of this return of religion. A contemporary political theology grapples with important concepts such as sovereignty, democracy, and the role that they play in our current postmodern intellectual and cultural situation. But, this is not simply a book about political theology; it is a book advocating a radical political theology. For me, radical political theology means the attempt to sketch out a constructive theology that is neither liberal in a classic sense nor conservative or orthodox in any way, whether politically or theologically. Many critiques of contemporary secularism as well as the ravages of corporate capitalism are traditionalist insofar as they rely on premodern values and religious or theological expressions to counterpose to the ones that currently reign. I suggest that many thinkers are caught within a liberal-conservative binary, where the only way to oppose liberalism is to become conservative or neoconservative, again whether in political or theological terms. But, this binary opposition masks the radical alternative, which is post-Marxist (not anti-Marxist) in a broad sense because it relies upon a critique of capital that has been obscured in many ways by contemporary postmodernism and cultural-humanistic studies. What would a radical political theology look like? While this book does not provide a systematic or comprehensive answer to that question, it does open up concepts and analyses that allow us to understand what is at stake with such a radical political theology. These chapters and readings are not merely descriptive overviews, therefore, but consist of creative interventions onto the theoretical landscape of theological ideas, which is why there is no clear and clean separation of descriptive analysis and imaginative intervention.

In this introduction, I want to engage the discourse of radical theology and show where it links up with political issues and ideas. Radical theology links up with discussions of Continental philosophy and ultimately political theory over the last decades of the twentieth century. Before taking up radical theology explicitly, however, I want to briefly consider the context and nature of the Religious Right in the United States over the past several decades. After this more contextual political analysis, I will engage with the tradition of radical theology in the United States as a potential counterweight to the intensification of the conservative Christianity. As part of an elaboration of radical theology and its significance for political theology, I will focus theoretically upon the concept of freedom, which is both a theological and, I am insisting, a political concept. Human freedom in light of divine omnipotence is a classical theological topic, and modern humanism and existentialism emerges by opposing human freedom to divine power. Today, both of these alternatives—either divine freedom and power or human freedom and self-assertion—are too simplistic in a postsecularist context. Freedom is the freedom to think anything at all, which also concerns the ability to do anything at all, and as liberty becomes a fundamental modern political concept, during the course of modernity we discover more and more how we are not free in any pure or absolute terms. One of the main themes of twentieth-century Continental philosophy is the notion of potentiality, and I am suggesting that "potentiality" is a good contemporary postmodern name for freedom.

II

Radical political theology seeks to understand religion's role and significance today, in cultural, economic, and political terms—one cannot understand religion without taking into account these political, cultural, and economic factors. One of the most powerful expressions of religion in American culture is the rise of the Religious Right over the past three decades. To understand the significance of the Religious Right in the United States today, we need to see how it is not only obviously religious, but also and perhaps even more importantly, how it is driven by *other*—less obvious—political, economic, and cultural phenomena. We need such analytical tools to be able to discern the ideological elements of the contemporary Religious Right.

In some ways, the current situation of religion in American politics and the rise of the Religious Right can be related to the aftermath of the U.S. Civil War, when the South lost its military and political attempt to secede from the Union and form a new nation. My claim is that while the South was defeated in the Civil War, the contemporary resurgence of conservative political religion represents a dangerous victory for the South. While the division over states' rights and the continued presence of slavery in the South were obviously crucial to the conflict, an often overlooked, though equally if not more important, issue was how the extension of the practice of slavery to new territories and states as the Union expanded west in search of its Manifest Destiny had certain economic and political effects. The rise of maritime capitalism in the Northeast in the early nineteenth century created a competing economic paradigm with Southern plantations, and in fact free factory workers toiling for low wages proved more efficient than the "free" labor of slaves. The majority of interests in the Northern states, with the exception of a small but vocal group of radical abolitionists, were content to contain Southern plantation slavery but would not allow its expansion to new western territories. The Southern states recognized that their lifestyle could not flourish politically or economically if they were overshadowed by an industrial capitalist North and West, so they made a desperate attempt to dissolve the Union.

As we know, this attempt failed, slavery was eventually abolished, and the Union was reestablished. What is important in a religious context is that religion was not necessarily as significant for the American South prior to the Civil War as it was elsewhere in the United States. The waves of religious revivalism that swept across the United States in the early nineteenth century occurred mostly along the frontier of the original thirteen colonies and included upstate New York's so-called burnt-over district. This movement was called the Second Great Awakening, to distinguish it from the first Great Awakening of the 1730s–1750s.[2] Although religion was sometimes used by whites to justify slavery, religiosity in the South was not especially intense compared with other parts of the country, with the exception of the African Americans themselves, who were stripped of their African religions and later embraced Methodist and Baptist forms of Christianity.

After the Civil War, white Southerners took refuge in religion and created a nostalgic picture of antebellum life, ignoring or downplaying the brutal aspects of American plantation slavery. In many ways, this turn to religion constituted a repression of other, more explicitly political desires. This repression was enforced by Northern military power as well as the postwar Reconstruction. All of the major Protestant churches split prior to the Civil War. Some of them eventually reunited but only after the Civil War religion was irrevocably split between North and South. As the historian of American religion George Marsden explains, the incredible emphasis upon Southern religion was "an integral part of the southern glorification of the lost cause in the half century after the War Between the States. Although Southerners had lost the war on the battlefield, they were determined to win the war of ideas."[3]

The Southern postwar struggle was not just a war of ideas. The Southern states, overwhelmingly Democratic in opposition to the Northern Republicans, evolved a system of segregation between blacks and whites that allowed Southern whites to maintain their economic privileges and sense of cultural superiority. This system was accommodated by the rest of the country in the course of its ascent to the position of a dominant world power. After World War II, however, segregation was increasingly difficult to justify and to maintain, both politically and economically. In the 1950s and 1960s, desegregation and the civil rights movement functioned to dismantle the institutions of segregation and inflicted yet another defeat upon white Southern pride. The civil rights movement, starting with the Supreme Court decision of *Brown v. Board of Education* in 1954, and culminating with the Civil Rights Act of 1964 and the Voting Rights Act of 1965, was experienced by Southerners as a repetition of the Civil War.[4]

From the ashes of this defeat emerged the movement that became known as the Religious Right, which managed to co-opt most strands of evangelicalism and fundamentalism in the United States after World War II. During the civil rights movement, a more liberal Christian evangelicalism prevailed, particularly among the major activists and leaders of the movement, including the Southern Christian Leadership Coalition, cofounded and led by Martin Luther King Jr. Democratic party politicians at the national level promoted and enforced civil rights, which led to a backlash on the part of white Southerners. Although Lyndon Baines Johnson won the 1964 presidential election over Barry Goldwater in a landslide, Johnson also remarked upon signing of the Civil Rights Act, "I think we just gave the South to the Republicans."[5]

From the ashes of its political defeat in 1964, the Republican party, historically the party of big business and corporate interests, made an alliance with white Southerners that eventually propelled them back into power.[6] The Republicans cultivated Southern anger and frustration over perceived wounds to their culture and pride, and began to adopt the religious language of Southern, white Christians, which culminated in 1980 with the Reagan Revolution, closely tied to Jerry Falwell's Moral Majority and Pat Robertson's emergence as a national religious figure. The Religious Right became visible in the 1980s, seemed to peak in 1988 with the failed presidential candidacy of Pat Robertson, but reemerged at the grassroots level in the 1994 congressional elections, and finally cemented its central place in American political and cultural life in the controversial election and reelection of George W. Bush.

This is not simply a history lesson. I am analyzing the history of religion in the United States to propose a mechanism for understanding the development of Southern religion as a response to the outcome of the Civil War, as reexperienced in the context of the civil rights movement. Southern religion is the place where repressed political and cultural aspirations are consolidated. The civil rights movement is experienced as a repetition of the Civil War, but this defeat is far less traumatic; and with the help of the Republican party, it produces the Religious Right as a "return of the repressed," to apply a Freudian term usually understood in terms of individuals to a broader historical and social process. According to Freud, individuals repress traumatic experiences from consciousness, but they reemerge later and elsewhere, often in a destructive way, in what he calls the return of the repressed.[7] In this case, the vanquished South represses its cultural and political desires and conflates those desires with Southern Christianity. And today we are seeing a return of the repressed, touched off by the civil rights movement and its aftermath.

During the Reconstruction following the Civil War, as well as the early part of the twentieth century, religion provided a space separate from contemporary culture, and American Fundamentalism in particular was a movement that set itself apart from and judged a sinful, secular society. In many cases, Southern white Christianity rejected the entire social and political process, and focused more on its own religious purity and salvation than on saving the country at large. What changed after the civil rights movement, however, is that now this Southern Christianity positively attempts to remake and reconstruct American society along its religious lines. In other words, rather than setting itself apart from sinful, secular society and remaining a largely apolitical religious movement primarily concerned with the saving of individual souls, Southern evangelical Christianity has become politicized.

For example, one of the most significant, if not very well-known, movements that emerged in the 1970s and 1980s is Christian Reconstruction. Christian Reconstruction is a form of Calvinism that reaches back to eighteenth-century Puritan optimism in its attempt to refashion society, as well as its emphasis upon the Old Testament. Christian Reconstruction, as expressed by Rousas John Rushdoony, asserts the universal applicability of the Biblical Law of Moses.[8] There is no suspension or revocation of Mosaic Law by Jesus, and furthermore, Jesus will not return until all nations, led by the United States, institute and follow this biblical law. According to Rushdoony's son-in-law, Gary North, "Christian Reconstruction is the only Bible-affirming movement on earth that offers an uncompromisingly biblical alternative."[9]

This emphasis on the Bible is not just a matter of belief, but a practical—and political—blueprint for transforming society. Christian Reconstruction is a form of Dominionism, which appeals to the first book of Genesis for warrant that God gave humans, and by extension Christians, dominion over the earth. Faithful Christians must exercise dominion first over the United States, and after setting up a theocracy there will spread Christianity and God's government throughout the world. Although the Christian Reconstruction movement split as a result of North's rejection of Rushdoony's contention that the U.S. Constitution is the Word of God, Dominionism has flourished at the extreme edges of Christian fundamentalism.[10] This Dominionism accompanies and sometimes inspires the primary transformation of what I am calling Southern Christianity during the 1960s and 1970s, which shifts from a standpoint of pessimism to optimism in its attitude toward American society and its political and economic possibilities.

The transformation of white Southern Christianity from pessimism to optimism, from defeat and nostalgia to victory and patriotic American nationalism, and from personal piety to politics coincides with its alliance with the Republican party in the late 1960s and early 1970s. In many ways, this alliance appears to be a bizarre and unholy alliance, because it weds American nationalism and free-market capitalism to Christian evangelicalism and fundamentalism. Ultimately, this Southern Christianity is at least in part a façade behind which dangerous forms of authoritarianism, wealth consolidation, and militarism thrive and grow. At the same time, religion is a necessary catalyst for these processes because religious passion allows a cultural and political legitimization for many of these forces, which would not have been as acceptable or as successful without this religious cloak. The forms of Southern Christianity that have become so pervasive are both powerful and sincere, but they have also been appropriated, enflamed, and directed by other financial interests.[11]

My argument is that the Republican party, which has historically been the party of big business, co-opted white Southern Christianity and used its energy, its anger, and its pathos as cover to advance its own interests, even as it in turn has been shaped by these religious ideas and beliefs. At the same time, more subtly, corporate capitalism in the form of multinational companies has used both nationalism and religion as a smokescreen to advance its own global and financial interests, which often are in conflict with both national and Christian interests and values. These three phenomena are bundled together in an uneven and highly dangerous fashion, and together they threaten to bring about an apocalyptic catastrophe in the form of financial depression due to overextended debt, environmental devastation due to irreversible climate change caused by emissions from burning hydrocarbons, economic collapse due to the increasing scarcity of fossil fuels, and a military conflagration due to conflicts driven by energy needs and other economic forces.[12]

During the last thirty years or so, the same time period covered by the rise of the Religious Right in the United States, a new, virulent form of corporate capitalism has evolved, which Naomi Klein calls "disaster capitalism."[13] Inspired by the economic prescriptions of Milton Friedman and his disciples at the University of Chicago, disaster capitalism thrives on crises. Friedman advocates radical free-market reforms that cause a tremendous amount of pain and suffering for people who undergo them, and he recognizes that people will not choose to do this voluntarily. Therefore, a crisis must be either precipitated or exploited to realize these reforms. Klein traces the development and implementation of this new form of free-market capitalism from Chile to Eastern Europe to China to Iraq to Great Britain and the United States.

Although Klein does not treat religion in her book, she does expose the dangerous link between the political and military events of the last few decades and the economic policies of the "Chicago Boys" that helped promote and exploit them in ways that have increased wealth disparity and have impoverished millions of people at the expense of wealthy corporations. Klein analyzes a corporatist system and shows how "political and corporate elites have simply merged, trading favors to secure the right to appropriate precious resources previously held in the public domain."[14] The shock of a crisis induces paralysis and disorientation, which provides an opportunity for introducing radical free-market reforms. Peoples and countries suffer these shocks as torture, and Klein chillingly connects the torture of peoples using methods developed by the C.I.A. with the torture of countries using methods developed by the Chicago Boys and implemented by the I.M.F. and the World Bank. Although "free markets and free peoples have been packaged as a single ideology that claims to be humanity's best and only defense against repeating a history filled with mass graves, killing fields and torture chambers," in fact the application of "the contemporary religion of unfettered free markets" has had a very different result. At least in Latin America, where it was first applied, "it did not bring democracy; it was predicated on the overthrow of democracy in country after country. And it did not bring peace but required the systematic murder of tens of thousands and the torture of between 100,000 and 150,000 people."[15] According to Klein, the shocks of September 11 offered new opportunities for the application of corporatism in Iraq and in the United States.

Whether or not the United States has shaped the War on Terror to pursue its own militaristic and financial ends, at the very least the proliferation of disaster capitalism along with other concerns such as oil, energy, the state of the dollar, geopolitical interests, and even the conflation of war and violence with Biblical Revelations and predictions of the Apocalypse and the Second Coming of Christ suggest that something is deeply wrong at the heart of the American Empire. For Southern religion, the irony is that the defeated Confederacy gets its revenge on the politics and culture of the United States, but this revenge ultimately leads to national if not global defeat and collapse. Due to the takeover of Southern Christianity by nationalist militarism and corporate capitalism, we have an unsustainable economy and immoral way of life. This time, in a repetition of the Civil War, the whole country loses. The question is how much of the rest of the world we take with us.

III

What is radical theology, and how does a radical political theology represent a discourse capable of helping us grapple with these urgent political, economic, and social crises? Radical theology emerges in the wake of the death of God. However strange or incoherent the Death of God theology that emerged in some quarters of the U.S. academy in the 1960s appeared, it gave rise to a radical theological vision, one attached to the academy to be sure, but detached from ecclesiastical or pastoral commitments and concerns.[16] Radical theology, in the work of Mark C. Taylor, Charles E. Winquist, Carl A. Raschke, and others, welded these insights into the death of God and the poststructuralist philosophies being translated from France in the 1970s and 1980s, fashioning an American postmodern theology.[17] What was missing from this early American postmodern theology, which was more preoccupied with aesthetic, epistemological, and cultural concerns, was an explicitly political focus, as Jeffrey W. Robbins has observed. In an essay on "Terror and the Postmodern Condition," Robbins examines American radical and postmodern theology, and charges that while its interests "were characteristically broad and far-ranging, moving seamlessly from philosophy and theology to literature, psychoanalytic theory, art and architecture, the political was marked by its absence."[18] Robbins calls for "a truly radical political theology," one that "puts both the political and the theological order in question."[19] He claims that postmodern theology has not met this task, and neither have two other contemporary forms of theological thinking, liberation theology and process theology. According to Robbins, liberation theology, "while effectively integrating a Marxist critique and programmatic into an already-established theological framework, whether it be Catholic, Protestant, or Islamic," it "never went so far as to put the established theology into question."[20] In a footnote, Robbins argues that process thought "still operates almost exclusively within a Christian confessional framework," and due to the overwhelming influence of Alfred North Whitehead's speculative theology, sometimes turns Whitehead's "famous image of speculative thought as the 'flight of an aeroplane' into, at times at least, a rigid system of Whiteheadian dogma."[21] I sympathize with Robbins's criticisms, although I also think that there is important and vital political theology being done in both liberation theology and process theology. But I am working more explicitly in a radical postmodern theological tradition and want to take seriously Robbins's challenge for a radical postmodern political theology without dismissing other forms of theological thinking.

This political element was partially restored to postmodern theology by the emergence of British Radical Orthodoxy in the 1990s, which combines a radical social theory with important political implications and interventions, and a more conservative, or orthodox, theology. By crossing a radical political critique with a theoretically informed, postmodern version of Christian orthodoxy, Radical Orthodoxy, associated primarily with the work of John Milbank, Graham Ward, Catherine Pickstock, and others, became popular and influential in intellectual, academic, and seminary environments in the early 2000s. My problem with Radical Orthodoxy is that it is not radical enough, however, and it lacks the creative force of earlier American radical theology. Essentially, Radical Orthodoxy desires to effect a restoration of a neotraditional orthodoxy, which is a triumphalist Christianity that was broken with the emergence of a nontheological secular sphere at the start of European modernity. Radical Orthodoxy appropriates postmodern insights and critiques about the nature of the European Enlightenment and modernity but then sublates these problems with a beatific vision of Christian harmony that appears both naïve and incredible. At the same time, Radical Orthodoxy provides a strong and important critique of contemporary liberalism and capitalism and offers nonmodern resources that function as alternative sources of value and meaning.

Unfortunately, the political project of Radical Orthodoxy is based on a medieval vision of Christian empire that eliminates democracy as a viable political form in its critique of liberalism in general. Part of what makes my project distinct is that it articulates a political theology that criticizes liberalism not to salvage orthodoxy but as an attempt to save democracy in the form of a radical democracy, which is the topic of chapter 6. The attention given to social and political issues by Radical Orthodoxy, then, provides an opening and a challenge to develop a radical political theology that would be neither orthodoxy theologically nor conservative politically. My book, unlike more conservative theological projects, takes seriously the breakdown of the secular-religious opposition without simply reducing the secular to the religious.

A recent volume that provides important resources for thinking a radical political theology is *Theology and the Political: The New Debate*, edited by John Milbank, Slavoj Žižek, and Creston Davis. Most of the explicitly theological essays, however, are inspired by some version of Radical Orthodoxy, and many of the more secular, nonorthodox essays eschew the word "theology."[22] This situation institutes a cleavage or a break that reinforces the irreconcilable split between theology and philosophy, secular and sacred. Many of the most influential philosophers of our time have taken up writing about religion in important ways, including Slavoj Žižek, Giorgio Agamben, Alain Badiou, Antonio Negri, Jean-Luc Nancy, Gianni Vattimo, and of course the late Jacques Derrida. The problem with the orthodox theological framework is that it can only appropriate these philosophical insights and critiques for the purposes of a preestablished Christian agenda rather than read them as already profoundly theological in a way that challenges the strict separation between philosophy and theology without subsuming one into the other. The encounter that *Theology and the Political* stages between a radical political philosophy and an orthodox theology that embraces radical social theory opens up a space for a radical political theology, but it does not explicitly name, announce, or pursue this possibility as such.

At around the same time that Radical Orthodoxy was emerging upon the theological scene, a Continental philosophy of religion was taking shape, influenced by the religious implications of the work of Derrida, Emmanuel Levinas, and Jean-Luc Marion, and associated with philosophers such as John D. Caputo, Merold Westphal, and Richard Kearney. Influenced more by phenomenology, these theorists mostly dismissed theology as ontotheology, following Heidegger, although Caputo has recently published an important book of theology, *The Weakness of God*, which I will consider in chapter 3. Although these thinkers have been interested in political questions, until recently such political concerns were secondary to phenomenological and religious questions.

We now need a radical theological thinking that is at the same time radically political. Radical theology is here the freedom to think God without God, liberated from the weight of traditional formulations that constrain its creativity in dogmatics and sap its vitality in apologetics. Radical theology in the wake of the death of God is freed up to engage in constructive political thought and challenged to create a radical political theology, which is its urgent contemporary task. The political stakes of radical theology are enormous, because what is at stake is the world, which is all that is the case, including whether we can continue to have one.

With his parable "The Madman," Nietzsche famously announces that God is dead: "God is dead. God remains dead. And we have killed him."[23] What Nietzsche pronounces philosophically, theology internalizes almost a century later. In the infamous Death of God theology of the 1960s, God is finally killed in his own name, which became somewhat of a fad and a media event despite the theological sophistication of many of its proponents. Contemporary religion, including many forms of Western monotheism, is currently living off the remains of God's corpse. Traditional faith in a rational, benevolent, and omnipotent deity has become incredible and has been replaced by reactionary forms of evangelicalism and fundamentalism.

In the early twenty-first century, we live in a period of counter-Enlightenment. The European Enlightenment and its universal ideals have been rendered questionable at best despite urgent attempts to resurrect them.[24] Our era, the Latin term for which is a *saeculum*, is one of postmodern revivalism. Evangelicals are just beginning to realize how conducive postmodernism is to their project.[25] At the same time, however, some aspects of this religious revivalism stink of big business, no matter how heartfelt and sincere its adherents may be: "Gods, too, decompose."[26] The resurgence of neotraditionalist forms of religion in thought and culture threatens to overwhelm critical thinking if we are not careful. Witness all the evident religiosity; we are saturated by it, even drowning in it. But again, it reeks: of corporate capitalism and its gospel of wealth and financial prosperity. According to Mark C. Taylor, the resurgence of religion since the 1970s coincides with the explosive growth of global capitalism: "Global capitalism, in other words, is inseparable from a global religious revival."[27]

The resurgence of more conservative forms of religion represents a reaction to the expansion and hegemony of global capitalism. At the same time, as Taylor points out, there is "a critical difference in the relation of religion, politics and economics within and beyond the US borders."[28] For many people outside the United States, conservative religion "often becomes a strategy to resist global capitalism and all it represents. In the United States, by contrast, conservative religion is commonly used to promote the spread of global capitalism."[29] Taylor equates religion and economics, claiming that both are confidence games that rest upon nothing other than the faith of their true believers. He correlates the Death of God theology of the 1960s with the abandonment of the gold standard by the Nixon administration in 1971, which signaled the end of the 1944 Bretton Woods arrangement.[30] After the end of the gold standard, currencies were left to float, revealing their true nature as virtual. As already discussed above, the unholy alliance between global capitalism and conservative religion gave rise to the Religious Right, with its continuing influence upon the cultural and political situation in the

United States. Taylor outlines the ways in which the economy becomes ever more complex and defies the assumptions of market fundamentalists, who ironically become more fundamentalist in light of this growing complexity. Both religious and economic fundamentalists dream an impossible dream of a world of simplicity in which complete redemption is possible, overseen by a rational and dependable God.[31]

The more we pursue God, the more we are forced to recognize God's complicity in the human projects of economic moneymaking and political domination and that these projects often produce immoral and brutal results. Another way to express this is to recognize that the death of God is the result of a genuine theological yearning for God, not simply a cynical and self-serving pronouncement. In the third essay of his *Genealogy of Morals*, Nietzsche poses the enormous problem of the ascetic ideal. He argues that "all great things bring about their own destruction through an act of self-overcoming."[32] Christian morality brings about its own destruction precisely through its own intensification, and in this process it follows the collapse of Christian dogma. "In this way Christianity *as a dogma* was destroyed by its own morality," Nietzsche writes; "in the same way Christianity *as morality* must now perish, too: we stand on the threshold of this event."[33]

If the death of God is the self-devaluation of the highest value, this is due to the radicalization of these very values, which ultimately turn against their origin and betray it in its name. Nietzsche names this radicalization the will to truth, which itself in turn becomes questionable. The devaluation of the highest values is called European nihilism, and it is an inherently ascetic process that ultimately denies and sacrifices life for the sake of truth. The point here is that just as Nietzsche offers a genealogy in which our belief in truth breaks down precisely under the intensity of our will to truth, I am suggesting that the death of God is the result of radical theological interrogation. At a certain point the will to truth, to be faithful to the "truth" is forced to admit that there is no truth or that truth is a lie, or to discover that the will to truth is in fact a will to power. In the same way, radical theology is forced to sacrifice traditional belief in God for a thinking about divinity "that does not disappoint," as Charles Winquist puts it.[34]

In response to the death of God, we can envision at least three distinct possibilities. The most natural response is simply to discard theology as a viable mode of intelligible discourse. A great many self-conscious, thinking intellectuals have taken this option, including philosophers, historians, and sociologists of religion. Recently, the widespread cultural and political power of the Christian Right as well as neofundamentalist forms of Islam have produced a new secularist reaction by scientists such as Richard Dawkins, intellectuals such as Sam Harris and Daniel Dennett, and journalists such as Christopher Hitchens.[35]

Why adhere to a way of thinking that does not make sense because it lacks a credible referent, especially given the violence that religious adherents have promoted? The problem with this response lies in its inherent superficiality, because by jettisoning theology such thinking lacks a discourse in which to think or discuss ultimacy. Of course, ultimacy can be treated in other languages, including philosophy, ethics, mysticism, and naturalism, but these languages themselves are ungrounded precisely in the same way that theology cannot be grounded in a traditional belief in God. That is, questions of ultimate concern are theological issues, to use Paul Tillich's language, but they are ungrounded insofar as they possess no certain or stable foundation. Much antitheological discourse seeks to dispense with questions of ultimacy because of the dangers of arrogant fundamentalism. This move is purely reactive, and in fact any attempt to eliminate religion would have to become at least as violent as religious fanatics are purported to be.

I argue that religion is universal, that it is part of the nature of being human, and even though phrases like "ultimate concern" are vague, there is no escaping the questions that are raised, whether or not the answers can possess any credibility. I endorse the definition of the historian of religion Charles H. Long, who defines religion as "orientation in the ultimate sense, that is, how one comes to terms with the ultimate significance of one's place in the world."[36] Even if conventional reality is completely identical with ultimate reality, the determination that this is the case would be implicitly a religious conclusion. Because we are animals who can think in symbolic representation, we are capable of imaginative flights of fancy as well as incredible efforts of technical understanding, and religion appears to be coextensive with human culture.

The second possibility is the one that most obviously passes for theology today, but unfortunately it is also the most conservative. Here a desperate attempt is made to resurrect the God who is dead, to restore God as an object of belief. This move amounts to propping up a corpse. While this is certainly a harsh conclusion, as I mentioned above in reference to Taylor's work on global capitalism, this effort at resuscitation is sometimes undertaken for the most cynical and manipulative of reasons despite the evident sincerity of most believers. In a radical, Nietzschean sense, there is a lining of bad faith that necessarily accompanies this project, though it is often understandable and undertaken with the best of motivations. It is natural to resist the declaration that God is dead, which on the face of it is an absurd claim; but the truth of God's death remains in its very questionability. That is, the questionability of God "is" the death of God, and this cannot be undone. Once one learns to question God, or breaks the link of self-evident authority whereby it is possible to not believe in God, God "dies" in terms of absolute transcendence and can only be recovered or restored, that is, shored up. The freedom of the death of God means the freedom to think theologically with and without God, that is, without presupposing that God is, God exists. Finally, to take the empirical resurgence of religion in the contemporary world for evidence of God's resurrection confuses the issue, because these conservative forms of faith called fundamentalist or neofundamentalist constitute a reaction against the death of God, a refusal to accept this reality, and an intense repression that breaks out in virulent and deadly ways.

Finally, the third possibility is to substitute for God other names in a complex metaphorical or dialectical interplay of meanings and significations. Some of these names, most of which are human, ethical, or naturalistic, are reinterpreted in such a way that they pass under the Name of God. Here, theology retains in part the form of a traditional religious language, but God is reinvested with new meanings. This project is sometimes straightforward about what it is doing, and other times more ambiguous, in using the word God to designate, capture, and activate concepts such as goodness, suffering, life, justice, being, compassion, love, the universe, order, meaning, reason, logos, death, univocity, uniqueness, complexity, information, and freedom. In an autobiographical account in the essay "Circumfessions," Jacques Derrida claims that for him, "the constancy of God in my life is called by other names," such that he can "quite rightly pass for an atheist."[37] Here, theology would be the obverse of Derrida's description, because God would be used either along with or instead of these other names, such that one could rightly pass for a theist.

My constructive suggestion is a variation upon option three, and I suggest that such a passing could be called an *intercession*. Intercessions are not simply pastoral prayers, but in the course of a radical political theology, pragmatic interventions into contemporary theoretical thinking about the intersections of religion and politics. Specifically, in this introduction I venture to name freedom as that which now passes for divinity in the wake of the death of God, even if the rest of the book explores the theoretical resources of other names. Freedom also metonymically names the freedom of theology to think matters of ultimate concern—political, moral, existential, cosmological—without the constraint of tradition, authority, or the presumed certainty of dogmatic answers.

IV

Freedom does not simply substitute for God, but in a formal sense captures the possibility of thinking God as well as thinking anything at all. In this sense, a formal theological thinking would attend to what makes concepts available for understanding and articulation. Concepts such as God here refer to the passing, the passing for, and the passage among thing, image, and word that is also an impossible passage, what Derrida calls an *aporia* following Aristotle. Despite its impossibility, such passings occur, and freedom is a name for these passages, even though freedom, like God, does not exist as such.

What is the possibility for a radical theology without asceticism, one that does not sacrifice the intellect or meaning and value in pursuit of a thinking of God when God is dead? God is nothing, and this is the triumph of nihilism. And yet, there is the freedom to think God theologically.

Freedom undergoes a similar devaluation during the course of European modernity. The more intellectuals pursue scientific, political, philosophical, and religious freedom, the more they discover how unfree we really are. It is the desperate struggle for freedom that dialectically reveals the state of bondage of human beings, which is tied to or determined by nature, causality, physiology, and evolution, and deluded by individual desires, as well as social, political, and economic interests. In *Beyond Good and Evil*, Nietzsche analyzes the problem of free will and destroys its classical formulation, although this understanding had already been unsettled by Kant.

Kant provides the modern philosophical articulation of the problem of freedom, specifically in the third chapter of *The Groundwork of the Metaphysics of Morals*. For Kant, the idea of freedom accomplishes the transition from a metaphysic of morals to a critique of pure practical reason. The positive concept of freedom is an *a priori* idea that is necessary to sustain the principle of morality, which consists in good will. A good will must be characterized by freedom, so we have to think the moral will as free even though we can never experience freedom in nature under the rule of causality. We must presuppose freedom "if we wish to conceive a being as rational and as endowed with consciousness of his causality in regard to actions," but "we have been quite unable to demonstrate freedom as something actual in ourselves and in human nature."[38]

Freedom is necessary to have morality, but it is not possible to experience this freedom in nature. Kant sets up an antinomy between the idea of freedom supplied by reason and the experience of causal necessity given by the understanding. He then resolves this antinomy by positing a distinction between the sensible world and the intelligible world. Kant explains that "as regards mere perception and the capacity for receiving sensations he must count himself as belonging to the *sensible world*, but as regards whatever there may be in him of pure activity . . . he must count himself as belonging to the *intellectual world*, of which, however, he knows nothing further."[39] The grounds of this distinction are ultimately Aristotelian, because Kant associates passivity with the sensible world and activity with the intellectual world. Furthermore, even though we know nothing determinate about the intelligible world, Kant claims that "the intelligible world contains the ground of the sensible world and therefore also of its laws"; it is self-legislating.[40]

The will must be thought according to physical laws of causality by the understanding insofar as it is an object of experience, or a thing that appears. But, the will must be posited as free in itself by reason according to the idea of freedom. Freedom cannot be experienced or explained but must be posited to salvage morality, because only a moral law that is self-prescribed is ultimately valid as duty. In conclusion, Kant affirms that "while we do not comprehend the practical unconditioned necessity of the moral imperative, we do comprehend its incomprehensibility."[41] Of course, Nietzsche is highly critical of the separation Kant makes between sensible and intelligible world to resolve the antinomy between freedom and necessity. This is the Kant whom Nietzsche describes as "a fox who loses his way and goes astray back into his cage. Yet it had been *his* strength and cleverness that had *broken open* the cage!"[42]

Nietzsche collapses the distinction between sensible and intelligible worlds, between nature and freedom, which he claims has only served to devalue life. Discussing the will in *Beyond Good and Evil*, Nietzsche argues that what we call free will is simply a strong will and its opposite, the unfree will, is only a weak will. "The 'unfree will' is mythology," just as much as the "free will";

"in real life it is only a matter of *strong* and *weak* wills."[43] Nietzsche sets aside philosophical prejudice to examine the will phenomenologically. He says,

> let us say that in all willing there is, first, a plurality of sensations, namely the sensation of the state "*away from which*," the sensation of the state "*towards which*," the sensations of this "*from*" and "*towards*" themselves, and then also an accompanying muscular sensation, which, even without our putting into motion "arms and legs," begins its action by force of habit as soon as we "will" anything.[44]

Present along with these sensations is thinking, and furthermore, "the will is not only a complex of sensation and thinking, but it is above all an *affect*, and specifically the affect of a command."[45] According to Nietzsche, the will is divided between a part that commands and a part that obeys, and our experience of freedom occurs when we identify ourselves with the commanding part, whereas our experience of unfreedom results from identifying with the obeying part.

This is how Nietzsche reduces Kant's antinomy between freedom and nature to a duality between strong and weak wills. Nietzsche rejects the absolute nature of Kantian morality and replaces the opposition good and evil with that of good and bad, where humans generally associate strength with being good and weakness with being bad. At the same time, Nietzsche preserves a shadow of Kantian freedom in his writing when he affirms that the philosophers of the future "will be free, very free spirits."[46] That is, they will have to freedom and the courage to think difficult and dangerous thoughts, even the thinking of their own bondage to drives and wills and their enslavement by an illusive morality or a deceitful grammar.

I want to capture this very paradoxical Nietzschean freedom in my discussion of radical theology: that the more we freely seek freedom the more we discover our own enslavement, or that the more we seek to adequately comprehend divinity the less credible God becomes, which is not simply due to the weakness of our own ability to conceive God. At the same time, our world becomes more and more unbearable, that is, we desperately need God precisely because we know that God does not exist, and we desperately require freedom even as we recognize that our postmodern society is relentlessly shutting down any and all spaces of freedom from capitalist, bureaucratic, or military control, often in the name of freedom or democracy.

In twentieth-century Continental philosophy, the problem of freedom transmutes into the problem of potentiality, and potentiality is gradually dislocated from actuality. Freedom becomes a possibility, but possibility is no longer subservient to what actually exists. According to Derrida, God refers to "a structure of conscience" within the human being, which is the possibility of keeping a secret: "God is the name of the possibility I have of keeping a secret that is visible from the interior but not from the exterior."[47] Beyond the metaphorics of inside and outside at work in this definition, God is here associated both with possibility or potentiality and with secrecy, the possibility of keeping a secret, which is connected with Nietzsche's examination in *The Genealogy of Morals* of the tortured process through which human beings became creatures who could keep promises, that is, tell the truth or keep a secret. For Derrida, the Name of God still encapsulates this potentiality though he rightly passes for an atheist!

The potential to keep a secret testifies to the division or divisibility of the self, because "once there is secrecy and secret witnessing within me, then what I call God exists, (there is) what I call God in me, (it happens that) I call myself God."[48] What is the secret of God here? That Derrida is a closet believer? Not necessarily, or at least, not simply. The gift (of death) that connects me with others concerns "the infinite sharing of the secret," which generalizes and thus in a way destroys the secret as a secret, since it is infinitely shared, as least potentially.[49] Taking up the side of potentiality, which is a postmodern term for freedom, here is the potential for a radical rethinking of God as secret and as shared, as gift and as death, which is what God means. God is this potentiality.

Potentiality is the locus of freedom because it is divorced from a necessary connection to actuality (the secret is shared before it is said, the gift is given prior to any actual distribution), and this understanding of potentiality is sometimes called "virtual." I want to indicate that the notion of potentiality or the virtual is a thinking of freedom in the thought of Giorgio Agamben, Gilles Deleuze, and Antonio Negri (each of whom, along with Derrida, is an important influence upon this book), although I defer more detailed discussions to later chapters.

The distinction between potentiality and actuality goes back to Aristotle. Aristotle is also the philosopher who privileged actuality over potentiality, and this bias persists throughout the Middle Ages into European modernity, to the extent that St. Thomas Aquinas can define God as pure act, *actus purus*. In the twentieth century, Heidegger's engagement with Aristotle provides a breakthrough for Heidegger's understanding of Being and time. Furthermore, Heidegger rereads Aristotle's discussion of potentiality and actuality in the *Metaphysics* and reverses the significance of these two terms.[50] According to Heidegger, the potentiality of Being to be is the highest power of Being, not its actualization in particular beings.

The Italian philosopher Giorgio Agamben was a student of Heidegger, and he further develops the significance of Heidegger's reversal. In some of his most important essays, Agamben wrestles with the concept of potentiality and shows how it connects with the notion of impotentiality. For Agamben, potentiality is closer to the original Aristotelian definition, whereas impotentiality is the "potential to not do," which is a refusal of actuality and a higher form of Being because it is a kind of freedom.[51] Impotentiality in Agamben is closer to Heidegger's understanding of the potentiality of Being. Impotentiality is also close to what Derrida calls "impossibility" in his claim that deconstruction concerns both the conditions for possibility and the conditions of impossibility of actual phenomena.[52]

I suggest that the concept of sovereignty is deeply problematic in both political and theological terms, and I will engage with this notion in chapter 2 with a more developed discussion of Agamben's ideas of potentiality and impotentiality. I will also consider recent theological emphases upon weakness as opposed to strength and power. I will also return to Agamben's work, but more explicitly his political thought, in chapter 6, where I will engage his significant book *State of Exception* and apply his reading of Carl Schmitt to our contemporary crisis of faith in law.

Another name for potentiality, a more postmodern name, is virtuality. In his books *Bergsonism* and *Difference and Repetition*, Deleuze provides a thinking of the virtual that approaches Agamben's understanding of potentiality. Deleuze does not use the term "potentiality" because he wants to find a way beyond the constraining opposition between potentiality and actuality in its Aristotelian formulation. The virtual is not what is possible, because possibility connotes something that has less reality. For Deleuze, the virtual is contrasted with actuality, but both are understood to be fully real. The virtual becomes actualized in a process of differenciation.

I am suggesting that Deleuze's notion of virtuality converges with Agamben's concept of potentiality and that both are essentially tied up with the idea of freedom. They free potentiality or virtuality from its traditional subordination to actuality. I will discuss Deleuze's idea of the virtual in more detail in chapter 3, in connection with Spinoza and Negri. In chapter 6, I will connect Deleuze's thinking of the event to Agamben's work and, in chapter 7, to the contemporary stakes of a reading of the apostle Paul.

Theologically, God does not exist in actuality; God is dead. But, the idea of God remains virtually or potentially significant, although to think God as virtual and as potential, following the logic of Agamben and Deleuze, constitutes a perversion of the traditional notion of God as well as a de-formation of orthodoxy. In addition, assimilating radical theology with freedom understood as potential or as virtual possesses immediate political implications, as Antonio Negri's work demonstrates.

Although Negri was not a student of Deleuze, in many ways Negri is the most significant contemporary philosopher influenced by Deleuze. In the wake of Deleuze's treatment of Spinoza in *Expressionism in Philosophy*, Negri writes an important interpretation of Spinoza's work, *The Savage Anomaly*, in which he develops a distinction in Spinoza between *potentia* and *potestas*. I will spell out this distinction further in chapter 3, where I will conduct a radical theo-political reading of Spinoza with Deleuze and Negri.

In their coauthored works, particularly *Empire* and *Multitude*, Negri and Hardt sketch out a political ontology based on the *potentia* (potential power) of the multitude, which is opposed to the *potestas* (actualization or instantiation) of sovereign power that currently takes the form of empire and expresses itself in global war, even though these two terms are not explicitly used in *Multitude*. The theoretical background of these political works becomes manifest in the context of Negri's own philosophical works, including *The Savage Anomaly* and *Time for Revolution*. I am suggesting that the political and the theological problem of our time is that of freedom, which takes the form of potentiality in Agamben, the virtual in Deleuze, and potentia as constituting power in Negri. Freedom is a political project, not merely a theoretical one. Radical theology's epistemological and political task is to think freedom, which means to think the death of God, especially since the idea of God traditionally grounds sovereign power and serves as its highest instantiation.

V

This book constitutes a sketch for a radical political theology, which is not a systematic theology in any way but takes the form of discrete but related interventions, or intercessions. *Radical Political Theology* is an effort to grapple with the politico-theological stakes of contemporary theoretical and cultural forms. Chapter 1, "The Parallax of Religion," reads religion as a parallax, following Slavoj Žižek. A parallactical perspective shifts from one perspective to another but affords no synthesis or unity. I argue that religion can be seen as a parallax divided between ideology, on the one hand, and theology, on the other. In chapter 2, "Sovereignty and the Weakness of God," I will consider the deconstruction of traditional notions of sovereignty and argue that sovereign power must be seen as political and theological at the same time and must be countered theologically and politically. The coincidence of the religious and the political in the constitution of sovereign power is profoundly ideological, and I will address the deconstruction of sovereignty in Derrida's and Agamben's work, following a brief discussion of Hobbes as a founder of modern sovereignty. I will also take up the contemporary postmodern theologies of Catherine Keller and John D. Caputo, along with the distinction between weakness and power, and argue that weakness is not simply the opposite of power but a resource of potentiality to challenge theo-political forms of power. Finally, Judith Butler's interpretation of Walter Benjamin's influential essay on "The Critique of Violence" will show what it means to align divinity with impotentiality rather than actual violence.

The middle of the book, chapters 3, 4, and 5, constitutes a complex engagement with issues of political theology as they are formulated in Spinoza and Carl Schmitt. This discussion attempts to work beyond both thinkers in order to preserve a more Spinozist perspective and oppose a more Schmittian one, even while learning from the force of Schmitt's critique of modern liberalism. Chapter 3, "Baruch Spinoza and the Potential for a Radical Political Theology," expands upon my reading of Negri above and elaborates on the potential for a radical political theology in the wake of Deleuze's and Negri's interpretations of Spinoza in a postsecular context. Potentia as understood by Negri is seen as a supplement to Derridean possibility and Agamben's conception of potentiality rather than a substitution. Chapter 4, "Carl Schmitt, Leo Strauss, and the Theo-Political Problem of Liberalism," directly engages with Carl Schmitt's conception of political theology and compares his thought with Leo Strauss, another influential and controversial intellectual. I seek to learn from Schmitt while disagreeing with him, as well as Strauss, and I suggest that we must understand what both Strauss and Schmitt criticize, which is liberalism.

Liberalism is seriously compromised by its entanglement with industrial capitalism, as the work of Karl Polanyi demonstrates. If liberalism is dead, or replaced by neoliberalism, and capitalism is triumphant but savagely immoral, then what about democracy? In chapter 5, "Elements for Radical Democracy," I articulate the idea of a radical democracy that sets the problematic up within the terms of Spinoza and Schmitt but then opens up beyond this horizon by considering the work of Michel Foucault, Jacques Ranciére, and Catherine Malabou.

Chapter 5 raises the most important question of this book and risks thinking a radical democracy beyond liberalism and capitalism. Chapter 6, "Law Beyond Law," turns to the question and current crisis of law and suggests that we are seeing a breakdown of our faith in law and that, in part, the neofundamentalisms of both Christianity and Islam, as well as other religions, can be seen as reactions to this situation, a desperate attempt to invoke a literalistic, divine law. I use Agamben's thought in *State of Exception* to frame the problem, which is also an urgent practical problem in the context of the defiance and dismantling of United States and international law, partly with executive signing statements. Then, after briefly passing through Lacan and the post-Lacanian political thought of Alain Badiou and Žižek, I develop a post-Lacanian idea of unconscious law that I then relate to Deleuze's notion of a productive event. Law is unconscious; it is not simply there (just as God does not simply exist) but rather is produced unconsciously, that is, before and beyond simple conscious, instrumental thought, by an event. This is a complex and constructive reading and leads in chapter 7, "Radical Theology and the Event," into a further elaboration of the event by reading Deleuze into the current theoretical discussion of the importance of St. Paul raised by Badiou and Žižek, among others. Paul becomes a Deleuzian saint by reading Deleuze against the grain of his own antipathy to Paul but in a way that raises significant questions about the event of Christianity, the Resurrection of Christ Jesus, and the political stakes of our era.

Finally, the last chapter, "Plasticity and the Future of Theology: Messianicity and the Deconstruction of Christianity," notes the messianic tone that pervades postmodern theology and philosophy of religion but also critically questions whether this messianism does not represent a desperate stratagem to preserve the hegemony of the West, by tying Western modernity so closely to its religious (Christian, or at most Judeo-Christian) identity. Here I draw upon the work of Catherine Malabou and her conception of plasticity to think a different configuration of theology, one that is more focused forward than backward, one that may be freed somewhat from the bonds of tradition and the responsibility for an oppressive and suffocating past. Plasticity is a new form of potentiality, but one that is immanent to form rather than transcendent of it. Plasticity can be viewed as a kind of immanent freedom in material terms. In a brief conclusion, I will summarize the claims of the book by articulating six theses of political theology.

1. THE PARALLAX OF RELIGION

THEOLOGY AND IDEOLOGY

A DISCUSSION OF THEOLOGY NECESSITATES A CONSIDERATION OF religion. As mentioned in the introduction, radical political theology possesses a freedom to engage the current crisis of the names and concepts of religion and theology without simply accepting the traditional or conventional meanings of these terms. In this opening chapter, I will provide a constructive understanding of religion that links two apparently opposing terms, theology and ideology. Ideology attends to the political power plays inherent in religion and religious practice and discourse, while theology here indicates the inherent and irrepressible desire that religion do some good. Much contemporary discussion of political theology *either* purifies theology of complicity with ideological manipulation and power play *or* completely identifies theology with such ideology. My understanding of religion and theology here acknowledges the significance of ideology but refuses any simple either/or.

In this chapter, I will attend to some of the political contexts of religion as a term and as a phenomenon. In addition, I will offer a constructive way to think about religion, employing Slavoj Zizek's use of the word "parallax."

Religion can be studied in parallactic terms as ideology or as theology. Ideology refers to the necessary implication of religion in problems of political power, while theology attests to an irreducible desire for religion to do good. Here, theology is understood broadly as an open-ended discourse about value and meaning in an ultimate sense, which I will call "secular theology" later in the chapter, rather than a narrow, confessional, or apologetic discursive practice.[1]

The classical origin of the term "religion" is generally understood as indicating a process of binding or gathering and may indicate what is sometimes called a tradition, although its modern use dates to the European Enlightenment. The concept of religion emerges as an independent notion out of Christianity in the seventeenth century and gradually encompasses non-Christian faiths and practices. As Wilfred Cantwell Smith explains in *The Meaning and End of Religion*, an intellectual concept born of the Enlightenment becomes historicized during the nineteenth century: "the static quality of the Enlightenment's rationalism was filled out with an increasing knowledge of, and presently sense of, history."[2] Smith refers to the genealogy of the notion of world religions in the late nineteenth century, a process that Tomoko Masuzawa treats in more detail in *The Invention of World Religions*.

Masuzawa offers a fine-grained account of the development of the idea of world religions out of a more theological and confessional Christian orientation during the nineteenth century. She shows the surprising and disturbing continuities between traditional theological approaches and supposedly more academic, scientific, and objective approaches to the study of world religions. In her conclusion, Masuzawa argues that

> we have good reason to suspect that the discourse of world religions came into being precisely as a makeshift solution to the particular predicament that confounded European Christianity at the end of the nineteenth century, that is to say, as a covert way out of the profound conceptual difficulty confronting Europe and its imperial subject position.[3]

Part of this construction is a geo-political aim, which is still operative today in the discourse of world religions, that is, the "strong drive to hellenize and aryanize Christianity" and the need to demonize and "semitize Islam."[4] Masuzawa shows that the concept of religion is neither innocent nor neutral.

The term "religion," then, is a modern, Western construct that is imposed upon widely diverse phenomena and should be seen as an essentially political and contested term. Postcolonial critiques have challenged the applicability of religion to non-Western practices and phenomena, and postmodern analyses have deconstructed the essential autonomy of the concept of religion.[5] Religion as it has been constructed and wielded is marked by its origin in Christian theology, and this mark has not been able to be erased. The formation of religion is a political production, and its usage today is no less fundamentally political.

In this context, the contemporary resurgence of neotraditionalist and fundamentalist expressions of what is generally called religion renders this problem even more acute for the modern disciplinary conception of religion, because it attests to the politico-theological struggles that are occurring both within and outside of the academy. Scholars of religion benefit from a more emphatic awareness of the importance of religion in the world today. At the same time, academic scholars who pursue social-scientific methodologies are threatened by the rise of what is sometimes called a postsecular orientation. One response of scholars like Russell T. McCutcheon who desire to establish the study of religion as a legitimate scholarly enterprise is to exclude theology as a confessional approach, turning theologians into natives who supply data and banishing any work that betrays any theological residue or affirmation of religion as a sui generis affair.[6] The hope is that if we can finally banish any and all confessional theological residue from religion, then we can study it objectively and scientifically, and it will become a legitimate discipline. On the other hand, the work of scholars like Masuzawa suggests that there is a deeper problem. At the end of her book, Masuzawa questions the adequacy of excluding theology from religious studies:

> And if and when we will finally manage to round up sundry varieties of crypto-theology scurrying in the tribunal of science, will we then apprehend the right suspects? Or are we failing to see a much larger, systemic network of discursive organization, of which the ones in custody are but low-level functionaries? Is the effort to prosecute these "theological assumptions" for illegally traversing and thereby downgrading the science of religion, then, not like an attempt to punish some unknown evil still at large by burning a host of effigies?[7]

I agree with Masuzawa here. Eliminating the intentional affirmation of religion and religious phenomena in the form of theology by scholars is insufficient and may make understanding the political issues related to religion more difficult to perceive, because these political problems are not only situated at the level of conscious belief or affiliation but also pervade the "systemic network of discursive organization" that shapes how we conceive religion.

In a postcolonial as well as a postmodern context, scholars of religion find it increasingly difficult to simply assign or ascribe the term "religion" to given practices and beliefs. If the designation of an activity as religious is a political act (for example, the naming of various systems of practices and ideas that are seen as originating on the Indian subcontinent as religion under the aegis of British colonialism and of the reaction to British colonialism as the assertion of an indigenous religion), then the academic study of religion is also a political activity. Postcolonial and subaltern studies have largely focused on India and South Asia, where the profound critique of Western modes of thought and practice has accompanied a commitment to a methodological secularism that in part reflects a third-world, Marxist orientation as well as the secular orientation of the Indian state. For instance, in *The Politics of the Governed*, Partha Chatterjee pushes readers to grapple with new models of political activity and interaction, complex zones of paralegal practices that exist between governmental functions and community institutions. At the same time, these provocative and experimental aspects of what Chatterjee calls "political society" are limited to a "different modality of secular politics."[8] Chatterjee cautions readers that based on his experiences he is wary of possessing "rosy ideas about any sort of innate secularism of the Bengali people, whether Hindu or Muslim."[9]

While postmodern thinkers may uncritically adopt Western and Eurocentric modes of understanding, postcolonial correctives may too quickly adopt secularist perspectives. As Dipesh Chakrabarty suggests at the conclusion of his groundbreaking work *Provincializing Europe*,

> historicist narratives by secular and rational scholars have produced either harshly judgmental or sympathetic accounts of subaltern social groups' tendency to treat gods, spirits, and other supernatural entities as agential beings in the worlds of humans. But, sympathetic or not, these accounts all foreground a separation—a subject-object distinction—between the academic observer-subject and the "superstitious" persons serving as the objects of study.[10]

Provincializing Western modes of discourse, as Chakrabarty calls us to do, also requires the provincialization, rather than the straightforward universalization, of Western secularism.

The danger of the theory and practice of a complete provincialization, however, is that it threatens to obscure the universal nature of capitalism, or at least its global effects. From a certain theoretical perspective that I will call "twenty-first-century global capitalism," the resurgence of religious phenomena in thought and culture indicates the convergence of post-colonialism and postmodernism with a certain form of postsecularism.[11] Rather than simply celebrate or deplore the so-called return of religion, I suggest that its phenomenal occurrence demands a theoretical framework or perspective that I am calling, provocatively, political theology. In his introduction to the substantial volume *Political Theologies: Public Religions in a Post-Secular World*, Hent de Vries claims that "there is no more urgent project, therefore, than to ask in what sense the legacies of 'religion' disarticulate and reconstellate themselves as the elementary forms of life in the twenty-first century."[12] If de Vries is correct that there is no more urgent project, then political theology would name such a mode of inquiry in a broad sense. For me, political theology names an unstable but critical discourse, one in which the political and the religious imply each other, although this discourse does not necessarily adopt a confessional theological (or political) standpoint.

In this chapter, from the viewpoint of an academic political theology, my constructive theoretical proposal is to think religion as the concept that names the link between ideology and theology. If religion deconstructs or devolves into ideology and theology, this division could open up a productive tension, if scholars resist exclusively choosing one over the other. The term "religion" would continue to be employed, but this analysis would render the concept more transparent, weakening the term somewhat along the lines of Gianni Vattimo's conception of weak thought.

According to Vattimo, "weakening" refers to a nondestructive nihilism thought in the context of Heideggerian Being. The weakening of Being means the opening toward a radical hermeneutics, because we cannot presuppose certainty about our ideas and their conformity to the world but are always caught up in contested interpretations. In an essay on "Nihilism and the Post-Modern in Philosophy," Vattimo argues for a *Verwindung* of classical metaphysics. *Verwindung* is a Heideggerian term that means something like convalescence, a "going-beyond that is both an acceptance and a deepening."[13] *Verwindung* is contrasted with *Überwindung*, which is a more straightforward overcoming. According to Vattimo, metaphysics is not something that we can simply get away from, but "rather, it is something which stays in us as do the traces of an illness or a kind of pain to which we are resigned."[14] In some of his later books, Vattimo assimilates the history of metaphysics to the development of (Christian) religion,[15] although I am suggesting a more direct application of Vattimo's notion of *Verwindung* to religion here. When Vattimo tentatively offers a translation for *Verwindung* at the end of his essay, he suggests the term "secularization." He writes that "secularization/*Verwindung* would describe the course of history not as a linear progression or as decadence, but as a course of events in which emancipation is reached only by a radical transformation and distortion of its very contents."[16] Here, secularization is not simply the opposite of religion, but a process inherent within it that empties it or weakens it of its strong, foundational manifestations.

That is, instead of a strategy of intensification or escalation, which de Vries opposes, we could weaken or dilute our concepts, in this case religion. Furthermore, this weakening or secularization of religion as a concept is a work against the escalation of religion and religious sovereignty in the form of violence. In *Political Theologies*, de Vries attends to what he calls "the geographical and demographic-sociological base of physical struggle inspired or at least verbally legitimated by religion," and looks for ways to de-escalate this manifestation of religion in its more forceful guise.[17] An academic political theology, according to de Vries, "might well become the discipline of studying and eventually mastering such 'escalation,' that is, the excesses of sovereignty and their violence."[18] The key here is both the relevance of something like what Vattimo calls weakness or weakening and the fact that for de Vries the problem of political theology occurs in a postsecular world, that is, a world in which it is not possible to simply oppose religion with secularism. In fact, the opposition between secular and religious breaks down in a postsecularist context, which can be seen in the work of Talal Asad and William Connolly.

In his book *Why I am Not a Secularist*, Connolly argues that the idea of the secular needs to be refashioned, away from the straightforward opposition between secularism and Christianity, or the "Judeo-Christian" tradition. He supports a more open "public ethos of engagement" that is deeply pluralistic.[19] Connolly thinks beyond the limits of secularism as it is expressed by many thinkers, including Habermas and Rawls, because this version of secularism inconsistently attempts to contain religious passions and expressions within the private sphere. Connolly appeals to the thought of Gilles Deleuze in advocating for a rhizomatic micropolitics that is radically pluralistic. Connolly writes:

> In an age of globalization and the accentuation of speed in so many domains of life, a cultural pluralism appropriate to the times is unlikely to be housed in an austere postmetaphysical partisanship that purports to place itself above the fray. The need today, rather, is to rewrite secularism to pursue an ethos of engagement in public life among a plurality of controversial *metaphysical* perspectives, including, for starters, Christian and other monotheistic perspectives, secular thought, and asecular, nontheistic perspectives.[20]

A postsecularist perspective is not necessarily theistic, but it allows for a more pluralistic and agonistic understanding of the public sphere. Secularism, however, falls into a simple either/or and excludes religion from the public realm, which both trivializes and neutralizes vital life and political engagement.

In his book *Capitalism and Christianity, American Style,* Connolly analyzes the spiritual ethos that informs the contemporary "evangelical-capitalist resonance machine" and offers a counterethos that neither privileges nor excludes theistic and confessional faiths. Connolly affirms the resources of "open theism" (the notion that God is not omnipotent in a classical manner but can listen and change, expressed in reference to the work of John Sanders) from a nontheistic perspective that is both tragic and meliorist (combining Frederich Nietzsche, William James, and Gilles Deleuze). Rather than simply opposing religion with a renewed commitment to antireligious secularism, as commentators like Richard Dawkins and Christopher Hitchens do, Connolly draws upon diverse forms of existential faith to envision an "interim future" beyond the hard edge of Right-wing capitalism.[21] I am less hopeful than Connolly, who "retain[s] the basic capitalist axiomatic" but suggests micropolitical experiments and reforms that "taken together, may launch eco-egalitarianism within capitalism."[22] Even if I am more pessimistic about the possibilities of reforming capitalism, I appreciate both the validity of Connolly's analysis, as well as his interim vision and his avocation to a deep pluralism. Finally, I agree with Connolly that we need to fashion better theoretical tools to think across the theistic/nontheistic or religious/nonreligious dichotomy.

In fact, the completely autonomous secular sphere that Connolly critiques is also at least in part a religious conception and creation, as Talal Asad demonstrates genealogically in *Formations of the Secular*. Asad argues that the exclusion of religion from public life is a political work undertaken by modern European thought. He challenges the self-evidence of the conclusion that "the secular" emancipates human life from the "controlling 'power' of religion."[23] In fact, "the secular" is part of the doctrine of secularism that Connolly criticizes and desires to refashion. Asad traces the genealogy of secularism and concludes that "in the discourse of modernity 'the secular' presents itself as the ground from which theological discourse was generated (as a form of false consciousness) and from which it gradually emancipated itself in its march to freedom."[24]

As Asad demonstrates, the secular is not simply the emancipation from religion; it emerges also as the religious emancipation, or the establishment of the true, rational religion of the European Enlightenment. The secular is not simply the replacement or the denial of religion but a kind of displacement or rearrangement. "The secular, I argue," he says, "is neither continuous with the religious that supposedly preceded it . . . nor a simple break from it. . . . I take the secular to be a concept that brings together certain behaviors, knowledges, and sensibilities in modern life."[25] The secular emerges as a distinct orientation to religion that later becomes conceptualized as a nonreligious secularism for the purposes of governing diverse nations of people. The supposed generation of enlightened and tolerant religion occurs in the context of modern nationalism and the nation state. Nationalism is a complex phenomenon, composed of religious and nonreligious elements, but it depends upon an ideology of secularism to mediate a transcendental identity among its adherents.

In any case, questions of political power permeate both the secular and what we call religion, in distinction from the secular. Asad carefully shows how this fundamental opposition is untenable by drawing attention to how the distinction becomes constructed in modernity. Both the religious and the secular are shifting, noncoincident but overlapping terms that indicate distinct forms of life that Asad looks at anthropologically. Secularism, however, is an ideology of the modern liberal state that governs political strategy. Secularism homogenizes human beings into a governable society by transcending "particular and differentiating practices of the self that are articulated through class, gender, and religion."[26] Secularism does not replace religion but regulates it within political and civil society.

Asad concludes that "the categories of 'politics' and 'religion' turn out to implicate each other more profoundly than we thought, a discovery that has accompanied our growing understanding of the powers of the modern nation-state."[27]

If the concepts of religion and the secular are deeply implicated by each other, and implicated politically and for reasons of political power, then we cannot simply resolve the "problems" of violence and injustice in our contemporary world by reinforcing secularism and restraining religion *or* by abolishing the secular and reestablishing religion. Again, all of our concepts are politically charged and contested; there is no safe and neutral space from which to arbitrate religious or secular disputes. Although I am strongly impressed with Asad's analyses, I would like to follow Connolly in affirming a place for the secular divorced from the ideology of secularism in a postsecularist world, that is, a world in which the secular can never be completely divorced from nor completely assimilated into what we call religion.

My suggestion, then, is not to give up the term "religion" but to argue that we need a more complex understanding of religion and that, in some ways, viewing religion as a parallax might help. In his book *The Parallax View*, Slavoj Žižek talks about a "constantly shifting perspective between two points [between] which no synthesis or mediation is possible."[28] Every perspective, including even the notion of perspective as such, exhibits this character of parallax. Any duality or polarity attests not to a dualism, or a twoness, but to a "gap which separates the One from itself," which Žižek calls "parallax."[29] Žižek claims that there are a "multitude of parallax gaps," but he focuses on "three main modes: philosophical, scientific, and political."[30] Žižek understands parallax more broadly and generally than my application of his work here and does not explicitly treat religion, although he does advocate a materialist theology in relation to the first, philosophical or ontological, mode, a notion to which I will return at the end of this chapter. I think that it is useful here to apply his understanding of parallax to the mode of religion without excluding or discounting the other modes Žižek discusses at length in his book.

In this case, religion can be seen parallactically as either theology or ideology. A division of religion into two parts or shares, the ideological and the theological, reconstructs religion as a political theology, but not a substantial political theology, because ideology and theology are always kept apart, at least slightly, which is the goal of de Vries in his conception of a de-escalating political theology as well. As a parallax, religion names the gap between the ideological and the theological, between religion as ideology, which completely explains religion, and religion as theology, which completely subsumes it. Together, however, both offer resources to better comprehend religion.

First, as ideology, a post-Marxist (but not anti-Marxist) analysis of capital can be deployed. According to Louis Althusser's Marxist understanding of ideology, "ideology represents the imaginary relationship of individuals to their real conditions of existence."[31] Ideology in the form of ideological apparatuses summons the subject into being through a process that Althusser calls "interpellation." The subject becomes a subject to these ideological apparatuses that determine the subject in its very being. He claims that the category of the subject is constitutive of all ideology "insofar as all ideology has the function (which defines it) of 'constituting' concrete individuals as subjects."[32] Ideology is imaginary, however, in contrast to a real that can be discovered with science, and Althusser considers Marx to be the founder of the science of history.

Althusser utilizes Lacan's terms "imaginary" and "real" to distinguish ideology from (Marxist) science. In a more orthodox Lacanian sense, though, the real as such recedes and cannot be captured in a science, which means that ideology pervades not only the imaginary but also the symbolic. Ideology is radicalized to such an extent that we cannot simply delimit or demarcate its field and functioning. Religion, in one of its two modes, is coextensive with ideology. For Christian religious ideology, Althusser explains, in the Scriptures, particularly in the case of Moses, "God thus defines himself as the Subject par excellence, he who is through himself and for himself ('I am that I am'), and he who interpellates his subject, the individual subjected to him by his very interpellation, i.e., the individual named Moses."[33] Religion interpellates human subjects in ideological terms, summons them to see themselves as subject to a belief that determines their material, social, and political practice, and masks the real workings of these practices and beliefs. The problem, however, is that there is no nonideological space outside of ideology from which to critique ideology. The only frameworks possible from which to engage in ideological critique are those constituted by other ideologies.

Althusser insists that ideology, like the unconscious, is eternal; but at the same time, he suggests a historical link with capital, which is the historical relationship that Marx forged and which distinguishes his work. What are the relationships between religion and capital, and how does religion function to serve capitalist ideology as well as provide opportunities to expose and critique it? The works of Immanuel Wallerstein, Ellen Meiksins Wood, and Antonio Negri, among others, help us better understand the ideology of capitalism. From books such as *Marx Beyond Marx, Time for Revolution*, through the celebrated works coauthored with Michael Hardt, *Empire* and *Multitude*, Negri develops a counterideology to capitalism that describes the multitude as the biopolitical subject constituted in the "singular event of the decision upon the common" based on love and living labor.[34] The multitude is a production, a generation that escapes being captured in a determinate state-interpellated subject. I will elaborate upon Negri's political reading of Spinoza through Marx and its implications for a radical political theology in chapter 4.

In her book, *Empire of Capital*, Ellen Meiksins Wood shows the intrinsic links between capitalism and imperialism, including war and military force. She states that "what makes class domination or imperialism specifically *capitalist* is the predominance of economic, as distinct from direct 'extra-economic'—political, military, judicial—coercion."[35] Capitalism is able to detach and deploy primarily economic force, but it must be supported or backed up by more conventional forms of power, and this "extra-economic power is today, as before, primarily supplied by the state."[36] The nation-state, far from being dissolved into a postmodern empire, as Negri and Hardt seem to imply, still functions to maintain these fundamental and invidious economic relationships. At the same time, perhaps the devolution of the most powerful state, the United States, from an apparently predominantly economic power to a more explicitly military power points to a crisis or a weakening of capitalist relations, because the state is forced to resort to more conventional forms of coercion.

One way to read the shift of American imperialism from an economic to a military emphasis after September 11, 2001, is to see it as symptomatic of a breakdown of capitalism. Immanuel Wallerstein analyzes the development of capitalism in modern Europe in his important two-volume work *The Modern World-System*.[37] In a later book, *The Decline of American Power*, Wallerstein argues that "the period 1450 to today . . . marks the life-cycle of the capitalist world-economy, which had its period of genesis, its period of normal development, and now has entered into its period of terminal crisis."[38] Wallerstein identifies "three major secular trends that are approaching their asymptotes" and contributing to the terminal crisis of capitalism.[39] The first is the rise of real wages relative to costs of production. Although in the

United States, real wages have generally been stagnant or falling since the 1970s, the rise in real-world wage levels has spurred corporations to desperately seek areas around the globe where they can pay lower wages. The second secular trend that is approaching a real limit involves the cost of material inputs. One reason that materials are becoming more expensive is that natural resources are becoming scarcer, making it is much more difficult to externalize costs. A major issue here is the ecological and environmental situation, including the growing awareness of large-scale climate change. Businesses and governments are forced to reckon with and calculate some of the effects on the environment, however insufficiently or ineffectively this works in practice. The final secular trend involves the difficulty of taxation despite the popular demands for services such as "educational institutions, health facilities, and guarantees of income across the lifetime of individuals."[40] As these services are demanded more insistently, social pressure increases the level of taxation, but "at a certain point, such redistributive taxation reaches levels where it interferes seriously with the possibility of accumulating capital."[41] The capitalist response has been to attempt to rollback or dismantle the welfare state, but this contributes to rising poverty and social unrest.

My point is that if Wallerstein is correct in his assessment that modern capitalism is entering a state of terminal crisis, and one effect of this development is the increasing militarization of the United States, then another symptom of this crisis may be the resurgence of more traditionalist forms of religion. My contention is that in many ways, the resurgence of religion must be read ideologically in relation to the spread of global capitalism and symptomatically as evidence that, despite its expansiveness, global capitalism is far from well. Capitalism is reaching real limits to growth, and it is not clear whether capitalism can continue to function in the absence of economic growth. The resurgence of religion is an important political phenomenon in its own right, but it is also related to the breakdown of global capitalism.

The British philosopher of religion Philip Goodchild makes important links between religion and capital in *Capitalism and Religion*, where he demonstrates how faith in money replaces faith in God in the modern world and calls for an alternative form of postcapitalist piety based on attention to human suffering.[42] Furthermore, in his subsequent work *Theology of Money*, Goodchild develops his understanding of the sovereignty of money, including the relationship between money and energy and between money and debt. As capitalism runs up against the real limits of energy, ecology, and natural resources, the bubble of economic growth collapses, leaving us swamped by debt. According to Goodchild, capitalism is "the social system in which capital is measured as an accumulative quantity in terms of exchange value," which means that capital can only be valued as monetary profit.[43] It is currently more profitable in the short term to consume the means of production of capital itself than to preserve them for the production of future capital. Since capitalism cannot simply grow without cheap energy inputs, it is consuming the means of production itself in a desperate attempt to generate ever-diminishing amounts of short-term profit. Goodchild proposes new methods of evaluation and credit that subvert and exceed the sovereignty of money as absolute value, though perhaps these are only thinkable because of the desperate situation in which capitalism finds itself.

Although less explicitly academic, Kevin Phillips's book *American Theocracy* brings together religious and political with economic and financial phenomena. Phillips argues that oil has fueled the rise and maintenance of American power and prosperity, and that recent military operations in the Middle East including the Iraq war are driven by the need for oil. This drive for control of global oil production is even more acute given the evidence that world oil production is peaking or will peak within the next few years.[44] This drive for oil is masked by a radicalized Southern religion where a cynical Republican party manipulates religious ideology to provide cover for its corporate capitalist interests, as treated in the introduction. Theocratic cultural expressions are useful because they distract people from the underlying economic causes of military intervention, and they supply an apocalyptic orientation that does not emphasize preserving the world or natural resources in light of an imminent end of the world.[45] Finally, Phillips analyzes the explosion of debt at all levels of American public and private life, and draws parallels to the decline of previous empires such as Spain, Holland, and Great Britain. The increasing financialization of the American economy indicates an unstable imbalance that will most likely lead to a long-term decline, if not a short-term crash, and his analysis has been validated by events of the last few years. First, we saw the bursting of the housing market bubble and the turmoil that enveloped financial institutions beginning in August 2007 that led to massive bankruptcies and bailouts, the run-up of oil prices to almost $150 a barrel in summer 2008, and finally the steep downturn of the stock market in fall 2008 that touched off a global recession.

In the context of these interwoven phenomena of oil, debt, and radical religion, religion functions ideologically as a smokescreen for deeper economic processes. Religion and culture mask material situations, such that the so-called clash of civilizations between Western Christianity and a barbaric Islam can be seen as a manipulated spectacle to distract from military struggles over energy resources. If world oil production is peaking, then the fight to control oil supplies in the Middle East and Central Asia becomes extremely significant, even if oil is broadly dismissed as *the* reason for American military operations. Furthermore, a financial analysis that understands how oil is linked to the U.S. dollar becomes significant for understanding why an exchange such as the Iranian bourse, which sells oil in currencies other than the dollar, threatens U.S. hegemony, taking into account that Saddam Hussein declared that he would sell oil for euros rather than dollars shortly before the U.S. invasion.[46] So long as observers and academics accept only the superficial religious explanations that are offered, they risk being duped by mediatized processes that work against understanding.

The critique of ideology is not sufficient, however. There is no neutral, objective space for ideological analysis, just as there are no neutral explanations. All terms are contested, and although the term "theology" seems even more problematic than religion, one advantage of deploying the term is that it might make naiveté more difficult. A strategy for legitimating the discipline of religious studies has been to exclude theology. However, the work of Masuzawa and others shows how religion continues to be infected and affected by a theological or quasitheological agenda.

My constructive suggestion is to think theology as the alternative mode of the parallax of religion. Theology indicates a commitment to certain values, whether these are identified, acknowledged, intended, or deployed. These values may be more traditionally religious or more secular, but we should keep in mind the difficulty of fully distinguishing the two terms. Using the term "theology" would pressure scholars of religion to reflect upon their own commitments, principles such as freedom, ethics, dialogue, liberation, and understanding, and certain aspects of particular academic, religious, or political traditions. Every intervention into a state of affairs alters the state of affairs; even observation is not neutral. And every scholarly study is also an intervention, including interventions that take the form of cautioning other scholars not to intervene. For instance, Connolly in *Capitalism and Christianity, American Style* not only exposes the Christian-capitalist assemblage and its workings, he also envisions his book as an intervention, a counterassemblage and counterethos, and he affirms his own nontheistic but nondogmatic existential faith in a nonreductive naturalism.[47]

Secular theology paradoxically names a nonconfessional and nondogmatic theology in a postsecular context that is not chained to secularist ideology. Playing upon the equivocation between the religious and antireligious connotations of the Latin *saeculum*, I suggest that a secular theological thinking is possible that is open-ended rather than committed to a particular institutional, dogmatic, or ecclesiastical orientation, and this could include varieties of open theism as well as nontheism. Secular theology confronts the impossibility of rigorously separating religion and religious concerns from secular and nonreligious ones, which is connected with the use of the term "postsecular." Postsecular does not mean antisecular, anymore than postmodern means antimodern. Secular theology indicates that we cannot avoid questions of meaning and value, even those of ultimate significance, in our theoretical understanding of religion. If theology is not necessarily confessional, which is one legacy of the tradition of radical theology influenced by the Death of God theology in the United States, then theological commitment may be viewed in more formal and minimalist terms or in more substantial and maximalist ones. Traditional views of theology are generally viewed as maximal and substantial by proponents and opponents of theology and religion. At the same time, I suggest that there is formally an ineliminable minimal commitment to some sort of "good" in every study, including the most objective academic ones, which is also implicated in and shaped by political processes.

Every particular commitment to making things better, in religious, humanistic, political, scientific, and ethical terms, is at least in part the expression or effect of an ideological formation. At the same time, theological commitment as such, the pure desire to do good, or to make better, or even to stop desiring to make things better exceeds ideology as such, even as it is coextensive with ideology.

Theology for me names what Derrida calls an "originary possibility," or a "religion without religion," rather than a determinate theology, which would necessarily take the form of ideology. In his essay "Faith and Knowledge," Derrida analyzes the two sources of religion as belief and the sacred or holy, and he claims that these two sources can be deployed in a positivistic manner to create "something like a religion," understood as "an instituted apparatus consisting of dogmas or articles of faith that are both determinate and inseparable from a given historical *socius*."[48] This determinate religion conforms broadly with what I call ideology above. At the same time, with the same conjunction of the sacred and belief, we can think "the most originary possibility" of religion as such, which I call "theology," although Derrida does not use that word.[49]

An understanding of theology in Derridean terms as the "originary possibility" of religion implies that such a theology is a radical theology. Radical theology etymologically refers to a *radix* or root, the rootedness of theological issues and questions in religious experience, practices, and traditions. Radical theology names this originary possibility at work in the constitution of religion, before and beyond all dogmatic assertions about the nature of divinity and humanity. Originary possibility concerns potentiality, as discussed in the introduction. By linking theology with ideology, across a gap, I am also suggesting that a radical theology is necessarily a political theology. That is, radical theology necessarily finds itself informed and engaged with political conflicts and cannot simply appeal to a transcendent entity to escape or trump human social and political conversations and contestations. There is an irreducible gap between the originary possibility, understood here as radical theology and the instituted apparatus that takes ideological form, which is what Žižek calls a "parallax gap."

Theology always takes the form of ideology. There is never theology without ideology, but there is also no ideology or critique of ideology without a liberative theological component. There is always a gap between ideology and theology, and religion is this gap, the link between the two. And the gap is also a parallax gap. Most of the time theologians want to operate solely at the theological level, which risks avoiding, obscuring, or neglecting the ideological aspects of religion, including the beliefs and practices of theologians. Sometimes scholars and scientists avoid or obscure their own theological desires, because it would be "bad" if they were seen to infect or corrupt scholarly or scientific work. At the other extreme, religion is viewed by some scholars solely as ideology because theological aspects are deemed invalid and excluded, but this solution restricts scholars from reflecting upon the ideological implications of their study, as well as their intense and unacknowledged theological commitments. Presumably, nobody could justify education or scholarship if it does not produce some good, in some way, in some form, for at least some people, a fact that is dangerously naïve to ignore.

In *The Parallax View*, Žižek invokes a materialist theology, although he does not distinguish religion and theology in same the way that I am doing. Žižek refers to Kierkegaard's distinction between the aesthetic and the ethical and says that for Kierkegaard "the Religious is by no means the mediating synthesis of the two, but, on the contrary, the radical assertion of the parallax gap."[50] In another essay, Žižek explains the strange nature of the atheist belief that accompanies materialist theology. Atheist belief is, strictly speaking, unbelief, which is "the pure form of belief deprived of its substantialization."[51]

For Žižek, materialist theology is another name for religion because it names and spans the parallax gap, which presupposes the recognition of ideology and the desire for the real as well as the profound implication of the two. Materialist theology is a way to name the gap for Žižek, whereas I am using the term "theology" to indicate one irreducible pole of what we can call religion, which can be slightly confusing. But, I think it is worth the risk to illustrate a constructive theoretical understanding of religion. Religion names the parallax gap and devolves into ideology, on the one hand, and theology, on the other.

This parallactic understanding affords a more nuanced understanding of the historical and contemporary context of the resurgence of conservative forms of Christianity, or the Religious Right, and its unholy alliance with corporate capitalism as discussed in the introduction, which Connolly analyzes in *Capitalism and Christianity, American Style*. In the next chapter, I will take up the issue of sovereignty, which is a form of religio-political ideology, and show how the deconstruction of sovereignty in the philosophies of Derrida and Agamben, as well as the theological work of Catherine Keller and John D. Caputo, provide crucial resources to recast notions of divine and human power.

2. SOVEREIGNTY AND THE WEAKNESS OF GOD

WHAT IS SOVEREIGN POWER, OR WHAT DOES IT MEAN TO THINK OF sovereignty as power, as traditional theology and political theory have consistently done? The complicity of political and religious power is extremely dangerous. In the introduction, I discussed the emergence of the Religious Right and its complicity with global capitalism. As Jeff Sharlet shows in his book on *The Family*, however, a more secretive and elite form of theocratic fundamentalism emerged in the wake of the Great Depression and the Second World War, which co-opted Christianity to serve the interests of American power. Founded as the Fellowship by Abraham Vereide, this organization formed links to powerful politicians and businessmen, impelled by the vision of ministering to the elite. It was, Sharlet claims, "the most ambitious theocratic project of the American century, 'every Christian a leader, every leader a Christian,' and this ruling class of Christ-committed men [were] bound in a fellowship of the anointed, the chosen, key men in a voluntary dictatorship of the divine."[1] The only public event sponsored by the Fellowship is the National Prayer Breakfast, inaugurated by president Eisenhower in 1952 and held annually.[2] Renamed the Family by Vereide's successor, Doug

Coe, this movement has gone underground to the extent that it does not advertise or publicize its activities, and it does not advance a determinate theology, but rather the vague claim of "Jesus plus nothing."[3] Its main tactic, pioneered by Vereide, has been the employment of prayer-cells, small groups in which members can talk and pray together. Forged in the heart of the Cold War, "the Family's faith is not that of a walled-off community but of an empire; not one to come but one that stretches around the globe, the soft empire of American dollars and, more subtly, American gods."[4] Sharlet claims that America has always had a theocratic strand, going back at least as far as Jonathan Edwards, and that to ignore its presence throughout its history is to misunderstand what the United States is and represents.

As Sharlet explains in his important study of this underground but well-connected Christian movement, the slogan proclaimed by its leader Doug Coe, "Jesus plus nothing," opens onto a void:

> Let J stand for Jesus. J + o = X. Is X a body of cells, or a social order, or a vision? Yes. All three. X = a vision. The vision isn't the Sermon on the Mount; it's not the beatitudes; its so simple it hurts . . . : the vision is total loyalty. Loyalty to what? To the idea of loyalty. It's another M. C. Escher drawing, the one of a hand drawing the hand that is drawing itself. The Communist Party, plus Jesus. The Nazi Party, plus Jesus. The Red Guard, plus Jesus. What is the common denominator? Jesus? Or power? Jesus plus nothing equals power, "invisible" power, the long slow building power of a few brothers and sisters. J + o = P.[5]

Who doesn't want power? And what country would be worth anything without military, political, and economic power? How could anyone worship God if God is not all-powerful? "Sovereign power" names existing power, and the question is whether positive sovereignty is unavoidable, which is another way of asking whether might makes right. That is, if sovereignty is necessarily thought of as power, then there is only the choice of what power reigns, legitimately or illegitimately. We could oppose the sovereign political power of the monarch or the people to the sovereignty of God, and vice versa. One way to call into question the powers-that-be is to assert another power, a stronger and more effective power that renders the powers-that-be relatively impotent.

But what if sovereignty is divorced from power, or at least actual power, and thought rather along the lines of Agamben's impotentiality, Negri's *potentia,* or Deleuze's virtuality, as suggested in the introduction? Sovereignty has been deconstructed, and the question is whether or not it can and should be reconstructed, and in what way. This chapter will briefly survey modern notions of political sovereignty, paradigmatically founded by Thomas Hobbes, and then examine Derrida's deconstruction of sovereignty in one of his last books, *Rogues.* Then I will turn to two theological attempts to think divinity without power, in the work of John D. Caputo and Catherine Keller. Finally, I consider Judith Butler's reading of Walter Benjamin's essay "Critique of Violence." I argue that we must resist positive sovereign power in both political and theological terms. Sovereignty, if it can still be called sovereign, will be seen as the "power not to," the ability to resist exercising positive power.

In modern political philosophy, The *Leviathan* of Hobbes founded the modern liberal state by denigrating religious claims to sovereignty for royal, monarchial, and national sovereignty. Here, the absolute power of the monarch replaces the sovereignty of the Church as God's representative. I want to consider Hobbes as founder of modern sovereignty in this chapter, although in the next chapter I will shift to Spinoza for an alternative to Hobbes. They prefigure my discussions of Strauss and Schmitt, liberalism, and democracy in chapters 4 and 5. Spinoza, however, is strangely absent from Pierre Manent's influential book, *An Intellectual History of Liberalism.* According to Manent, liberalism emerges out of a "bitter struggle against Christianity, and particularly the Catholic Church."[6] Manent's genealogy locates the origin of modern liberal politics in Machiavelli, and he devotes later chapters to Hobbes, Locke, Montesquieu, Rousseau, Constant, and de Toqueville, but leaves out any chapter or specific reference to Spinoza.

According to Manent, Machiavelli provides the initial formulation of what later becomes modern liberalism, but Hobbes provides the clearest instantiation of it. Manent says that "the nonreligious, secular, lay world had to be organized under a form that was neither city-state nor empire," and this political form of liberalism is essentially "absolute or national monarchy," of which later popular sovereignty of representative democracy is merely a derivation.[7] Hobbes opposes the legitimate political power of the sovereign to "the Kingdome of Darknesse" of the Roman Catholic Church, claiming that the ecclesiastical power of the apostles "is but the power to teach," because "the Kingdome of Christ is not of this world."[8]

Hobbes begins empirically with the human senses and builds up a social contract out of human fear and impotence in the face of nature. Ultimately, the law of nature and human civil law mirror each other, even though civil law requires a unitary sovereign: "the Law of Nature, and the Civill Law, contain each other, and are of equal extent."[9] Sovereignty, in contrast to the multiplicity of nature, is predicated upon unity. "A Multitude of men, are made One person, when they are by one man, or one Person, Represented," Hobbes writes.[10] The commonwealth is formed when the many become one, and are represented by one sovereign power:

> The only way to erect such a Common Power, as may be able to defend them from the invasion of forraigners, and the injuries of one another, and thereby to secure them in such sort, as that by their owne industrie, and by the fruites of the Earth, they may nourish themselves and live contentedly; is, to conferre all their power and strength upon one Man, or upon one Assembly of men, that may reduce all their Wills, by plurality of voices, unto one Will.[11]

The sovereign does not have to be one person, an individual monarch, but whatever comprises the sovereign power must by a unity.

In this way, "the Multitude so united in one Person, is called a Common-Wealth, in latine Civitas."[12] The formation of a commonwealth or a state comes about by uniting the multitude into one person, whether a single individual or a representative assembly: "And he that carryeth this Person, is called Soveraigne, and said to have Soveraigne Power; and every one besides, his Subject."[13] The sovereign corporate person is the soul of the commonwealth, and all of its members are subject to this power. The idea of God is retained by Hobbes but distanced from human affairs and relegated to an otherworldly power. Ultimately, "the End of Worship amongst men," which is the concern of public worship or civil religion, as opposed to a purely private worship of God, "is power."[14] Hobbes fashions a concept of modern sovereignty by limiting ecclesiastical power and reproducing theological power in the civil sphere.

Later, in the work of Locke and Rousseau, this sovereign person becomes a general will, and the sovereignty of the monarch devolves in modern democracy into the notion of the people. Popular sovereignty is derived from absolute, monarchical sovereignty because it is the unitary will of the people that is sovereign, not the individual whims of the multitude. Today, political power is mediated and mediatized in complex ways that render the will of the people impotent and irrelevant to the will of corporations; sovereignty can be seen as divided between a more naked military force and a more subtle sovereign wealth, or money.[15]

If modern political sovereignty is seen to issue from medieval forms of theological power, which is a complex transition,[16] then one way to read contemporary forms of liberation theology is to see the sovereignty of God reasserted over human powers and principalities. If there is no alternative to sovereignty in a positive sense, then the question is which power, who is to be king? But what if sovereignty is deconstructed? What if God can be thought without or beyond the concept of divine power? And if this is possible, can a God without power be mapped onto the political sphere, into a dislocation of political power? A radical political theology does not simply replace one power with another but calls into question all power, including that of God.

I suggest that the sovereign power of God is intrinsically connected to the oneness of God. As Hobbes shows, sovereignty is constructed by opposing the unity of the sovereign to the multiplicity of the multitude. But, a counter-sovereignty can be thought by attending to Negri's reading of *multitudo* in Spinoza, as mentioned in the introduction and will be more fully addressed in the next chapter. I understand Hobbes's thought as described above as the instantiation and paradigmatic representative of modern political sovereignty, which can and should be criticized both politically and theologically. In the next chapter, I suggest that Spinoza's idea of sovereignty, at least as read through Negri and Deleuze, provides a more potentially viable understanding of sovereignty that can inform a radical political theology.

Here I will petition Derrida's philosophy, particularly in his late work *Rogues*, to elaborate a critical reading of Hobbesian sovereignty, and then suggest that Derrida's deconstruction of sovereignty and affirmation of democracy leads into a serious critique of monotheism. The question about the limits of monotheism brings us to the contemporary relevance of Caputo and Keller, who provide resources to think theologically beyond monotheism, or to conceive God other than as sovereign power.

According to Jacques Derrida, to analyze the contemporary situation of reason and politics requires an analysis of sovereignty, "the huge, urgent, and so very difficult question, the new-old enigma, of sovereignty, most notably nation-state sovereignty—whether it be called democratic or not."[17] I will consider the discussion of sovereignty in the first essay in *Rogues*, "The Reason of the Strongest." Derrida first deploys the image of a turning wheel and claims that "the act of sovereignty . . . is an event, as silent as it is instantaneous, without any thickness of time" that institutes a sort of "rotary motion" around the self, the origin, or the self as origin.[18] This rotary motion constitutes the unity of the sovereign event, which instantiates an originary force: "sovereignty is a circularity, indeed a sphericity. Sovereignty is round; it is a rounding off."[19]

Democracy itself is not exempt from this circular sovereignty. For democracy to exist, it must be enforced, which makes it is a form of sovereignty: "Now, democracy would be precisely this, a force (kratos), a force in the form of sovereign authority."[20] This circularity also marks democracy because democracy derives its authority from the people, in whose name it exercises power. For democratic sovereignty to function, however, the multitude must be fashioned into a people with a unitary will. Derrida traces a genealogy of democratic sovereignty from an original (here, Greek) sovereign authority "of the One, of the One and Only (Unique), above and beyond the dispersion of the plural."[21] There exists "a long cycle of political theology" from ancient Greece to modern Europe and even an "unavowed political theology . . . of the sovereignty of the people, that is, of democratic sovereignty."[22] Democracy is unquestioned as the proper form of political power, but this form of sovereignty is still extremely problematic and needs to be seen as deconstructed.

Democratic sovereignty is tied to the nation-state and perhaps cannot be thought without the state: "Only a state can have a sovereign."[23] At the same time, the state's legitimacy and authority is being called into question. In this situation, democracy turns into voyoucracy. Voyoucracy is a neologism taken from the French title of the book, Voyous. If sovereignty as such is deconstructed, then states do not possess legitimate sovereign power, but rather all states are rogue states. Derrida claims that we cannot simply divide existing states into legitimate and rogue states, but rather, "as soon as there is sovereignty, there is abuse of power and a rogue state."[24] Sovereign power depends on the turning of a wheel, a sort of merry-go-round whose centrifugal force creates a form where there was previously a void and provides that form an authority to subject other forces, whether the form of a self, a people, a nation, a monarch, or a god.

Is there any alternative to sovereignty and voyoucracy? Derrida suggests that we need to think a "democracy to come" beyond or without sovereignty.

This implies another thinking of the event . . . which is marked in a "to-come" that, beyond the future . . . names the coming of who comes or of what comes to pass, namely the newly arrived whose irruption should not and cannot be limited by any conditional hospitality on the borders of a policed nation-state.[25]

A "democracy to come," then, must think "an extension of the democratic beyond nation-state sovereignty, beyond citizenship."[26] Here, Derrida raises the crucial question of radical democracy that I will consider further in chapter 5. With sovereignty, however, he considers the link between a democracy to come and a god to come in the context of Heidegger's famous interview, "Only a God Can Save Us." At the end of his provocative essay, Derrida raises the possibility of a "god without sovereignty," by reading save or *salut* as greeting, salutation as opposed to salvation. "If, god forbid," Derrida exclaims, "a god who can save us were a sovereign god, such a god would bring about, after a revolution for which we have as yet no idea, an entirely different Security Council."[27] Such a sovereign god would be another rogue.

One way to understand the death of God is as the need to think God as other than sovereign. At the same time, because of the nature of sovereign power, we may also need to think God other than as one. In an essay on "A Deconstruction of Monotheism," Jean-Luc Nancy follows Derrida in linking the unity of God to a hierarchy of power that founds and supports humanism as well as the nation-state, including the unicity of its "general form of value or sense today, that is by way of the worldwide reign of a monetary law of exchange."[28] Nancy claims that our contemporary global world, at least in the West, must be analyzed for its "fundamentally monotheist provenance (thus, to put it rapidly, the universal, law, the individual; but also, in a more subtle manner, the motif of an infinite transcendence surpassing man, and within man)."[29]

Nancy asserts a continuity between the identity of Christianity and the West, and suggests that this identity is essentially monotheistic, even if it is a self-emptying or self-deconstructive form of monotheism. At the same time, this monotheism founds the global confrontation of the War on Terror, even if we do not recognize it. For Nancy, monotheism has two sides, one that is similar to Derrida's description of the working of sovereign power: a "Unifying, Unitary, and Universal model, also Unidimensional, and finally Unilateral (which is its internal contradiction) has made possible the symmetrical and no less nihilistic mobilization of a monotheistic and no less unilateralist model," which is the second side.[30] The first model is the American version, the "national theism of the United States," while the second is the theocratic and fundamentalistic opposition to American theism as constituting an idol or false god; this second kind is the terroristic form of monotheism.

Both the nationalistic and the theocratic monotheism are two sides of the same monotheistic coin, but both also lose "the very essence of monotheism" according to Nancy, which is closer to Derrida's god, or democracy, "to come." Nancy argues that

> the "one" of the "god" is not at all Unicity qua substantial present and united
> with itself; on the contrary, the unicity and the unity of this "god" (or the
> divinity of this "one") consists precisely in that the One cannot be posited
> there, neither presented nor figured as united in itself.[31]

Although Nancy tries to rescue monotheism from the tyranny of the One, I suggest that, following Derrida's logic, the force or sovereign authority of monotheism works according the rotary motion of this lack of presence. For Nancy, monotheism is a self-emptying, which is why the essence of Christianity is also the deconstruction of Christianity. I will return to Nancy's idea of the deconstruction of Christianity in the last chapter, but here I want to trouble the motion that Nancy sees as inherent in the process of the unfolding of monotheism, which is simply the flip side of sovereign rotary motion. The one motion is centripetal, accumulating force into itself, which Derrida calls sovereignty. The other motion is more centrifugal, distributing the effects of this sovereign power, which is the enforcing of sovereign power as opposed to the instantiation of sovereign power.

The question is ultimately whether self-emptying, whose theological name is kenosis, is ultimately a distribution of a properly sovereign power, or whether it is an overcoming of that very power. One possibility, of course, is that this process of self-emptying is a ruse. Is the current theological interest in the weakness instead of the power of God a ruse, a means of appearing weak while preserving divine power, or a radical and thorough dissociation of sovereignty from the idea of divinity? As Caputo warns:

> It would be mere cunning to side with the lowly of this world in order to
> spring a trap on the unwary, who would then be visited by the mighty power
> of God Almighty, who smites his enemies. The humbling of human power in
> order to exalt the power of God is a ruse; it uses weakness in a bait-and-switch
> game, as a lure in order to spring power at the crucial moment.[32]

If weakness is a ruse, then it is part of the cunning ring of sovereignty, the appearance of weakness that preserves a sovereign core. The rotary motion of sovereignty must be turned inside out, which is a genuinely revolutionary action.

Derrida asserts that there is an "unavowed theologism" in all sovereign power that ultimately refers back to the sovereignty of God, and this trace of sovereignty haunts democracy.[33] Caputo develops the theological implications of Derrida's work and imagines a thinking of God that is weak, or nonsovereign, although he is also committed to the political significance of Derrida's reflections on democracy. Caputo understands Derrida's description of a certain "undecidability" at the heart of faith, but he wagers on a more robust and determinate religious affirmation. In an essay called "Without Sovereignty, Without Being," Caputo says that

> What Derrida has in mind by the unconditional is neither a hyperpower nor a hyperbeing, neither the form of the Good nor God the Father Almighty, but the power of powerlessness, the power of a powerless solicitation or promise or provocation.[34]

In *The Weakness of God*, Caputo argues that God's sovereign power is tied to God's being, and it is important to think the Name of God as an event dissociated from being: "By 'God,' on the other hand, I do not mean a being who is there, an entity trapped in being, even as a super-being *up there*, up above the world, who physically powers and causes it."[35] The weak power of God is the power of God's powerlessness, which is "a promise made without an army to enforce it, without the sovereign power to coerce it."[36] God's power is a radical promise, the hope of an event to come, an event absolutely unforeseen and unconditional.

Caputo remains faithful to Derrida's "to come," which means not simply an extension of the present into the future, what will happen, but rather the possibility of the impossible, the opening and noncoincidence of the present with itself, the chance that the future might be radically different than the present and the past. This futurity is the chance for democracy and is also the event that the Name of God signifies, for Caputo. The weak force of possibility is opposed to the strong force of present power, and traces of this alternative way of thinking God are read in the creation narrative of Genesis, the sayings of Jesus, the letters of Paul, and other aspects of the Christian tradition. A weakening of God disrupts the forcefulness of the tradition and allows Christians to reconnect with the hope and love promised in the Gospel texts.

Ultimately, the message of the Christian Gospel is one of forgiveness or pardon. God does not magically undo the past but remakes it anew with an impossible forgiveness that happens, which hearers are called to enact, to forgive debts and debtors radically. Such a weak power of forgiveness must "somehow be able to reach back across the temporal distance and alter the past, but do so without annihilating it."[37] Forgiveness is a form of salvation, a salve and a *salut*, welcoming and healing, which is a true resurrection rather than the magical resuscitation of corpses. Death and sin are two sides of the same coin because they represent the damning isolation of the solitary self. The self is folded in on itself and as such cannot be saved: "neither time nor salvation, neither rebirth nor resurrection, is possible in the solitary ego."[38] The ego imagines that it is sovereign and turns on itself. This unitary motion constitutes sovereignty but not salvation. Salvation consists "in the messianic coming of the Other."[39] So long as God is sovereign, God turns on God's self and cannot save or be saved but only damn. For Caputo, God is liberated from being, from being God, and is also an event to come, an "à-Dieu."

Although Caputo is critical of the formulation of the death of God, he does assert that "it is necessary to rid ourselves of God in order to witness to God."[40] And furthermore, if that good riddance is not to be a simplistic dialectical overturning and recouping of God's power after the death of God, then it has to bid adieu to God. The unitary rotary motion that constitutes and distributes sovereign power is only reinforced by a ruse, a pretense of weakness that preserves strength. If God reserves or preserves sovereignty, then this weakness is a sham. The radicality of the "to come" is without reserve and without restoration or reconstitution.

Catherine Keller is another postmodern theologian who is committed to thinking of God without or beyond hypermasculine power. She is influenced by Derrida and deconstruction, but she is also influenced by Whiteheadian process thought, eco-theology, feminism, and Deleuze. In *The Face of the Deep*, Keller develops a provocative and theo-poetic reading of creation as becoming, a continuous cocreation between God and material existence. In a subsequent book, *God and Power*, Keller opposes her theo-poetics of creation to an apocalyptic theo-politics of power.

In her reading of the first verse of Genesis, Keller fastens upon the Hebrew term *tehom*, which is usually translated as "deep": "When in the beginning, Elohim created heaven and earth, the earth was tohu va bohu, darkness was upon the face of tehom, and the ruach elohim was vibrating upon the face of the waters."[41] Keller reads tehom in the light of Derrida's reading of the Platonic conception of *khora*, a receptacle which in the *Timaeus* is described as a third thing between matter and form. Keller suggests that Derrida's "politics of khora finds an echo in the theoethics of tehom. It carves a place in which the defaced depth of the others can register as spiritual demand."[42] If tehom is khora, or khoric, then it functions as a third between creative divinity and created matter, a "deep" that can be figured more as feminine than masculine, and one that disrupts the simple sovereign of God's omnipotent power.

In her counterreading to the traditional theological account of creation ex nihilo, out of nothing, Keller develops a sophisticated reading of Genesis and Job, as well as aspects of the Christian theological tradition. She uses Derridean deconstruction and Whitehead's "differential pluralism of becoming" to articulate her position.[43] She also appeals to Deleuze's idea of the explication of a "pure implex," which is the "actualization of an implicate potency. That which is 'pure implex,' not yet explicated, is the potentiality he calls 'the virtual.'"[44] Keller brings together Derrida, Whitehead, and Deleuze around an understanding of potentiality that expresses the depth of creation theologically. Elohim becomes decentered, at best a pole or "strange attractor of creation" rather than the sole creator or creation itself.[45]

What is important in reference to divine sovereignty is that Elohim cannot be fully God in the traditional sense, but neither can tehom be God because divinity itself is distributed across different principles, and cannot simply unite. Keller says:

> In the course of this meditation, Tehom has taken on the names and aura of a certain goodness. But it has never been identified with "God," nor with the All; it "is" not *pan* or *theos*. It signifies their relation: the topos of creation, where the world surges in its virtuality, in the *complicatio*, or "folding together," the matrix of all relations. The relations, the waves of our possibility, comprise the real potentiality from which we emerge. So tehom, metonym of the divine womb, remains neither God nor not-God but the depth of "God." We do not come to *know* this infinity.[46]

Although she does not explicitly discuss monotheism (she does, however mention Nietzsche's term "monotonotheism"), Keller enacts a radical dislocation of sovereign power in *The Face of the Deep* that calls monotheism as such into question.

The political significance of Keller's reading becomes more explicit in *God and Power*. In this work, Keller critically analyzes contemporary apocalyptic themes in Christianity and American political culture, and she advocates a "'counter-apocalypse,' which finds relevance in apocalyptic narrative without acquiescing in its cruelties or its literalizations."[47] Keller opposes divine sovereignty, claiming that "the theopolitical problem is not just that a nation pretends to a godlike unilateral power, but that *unilateral power still appears as godlike at all*."[48] Keller claims that a simple antiapocalyptic perspective fails to adequately grapple with the scope and significance of apocalypticism and its appeal, especially to poor, marginalized, and dispossessed peoples.

A counterapocalyptic approach does not simply oppose divine weakness to power, but develops an alternative approach that she calls theo-poetic. Keller does "not reject the politics of theology or the theology of politics, but [wants to] move desirously toward a theopolitics of becoming."[49] This theopolitics of becoming is entwined with the theo-poetic reading of creation developed in *The Face of the Deep*. The common strand, as difficult as it is to flesh out, is love, a "physics of love" that counters the spell of greed and power. Keller concludes that a "constructive theology of becoming sustains a political theology of love," but "if God ceases to be a poetic invocation, however, and beings to control the political context, we have no longer to do with the God of love, but with the idol of omnipotence."[50]

Considering both Caputo and Keller together, we can suggest that an insistence on poetic becoming or the undermining of a hypermasculine, powerful God counters divine sovereignty, and furthermore, such weakness is not literally the opposite of strength on the register of being (although Keller does not specifically use the term "weakness" to characterize God). "Weakness" functions beyond the alternative strength/weakness for Caputo, just as "counterapocalypse" exceeds the opposition between apocalyptic and antiapocalyptic for Keller. I think that both theologians are creatively developing languages of potentiality, along the lines mentioned in the introduction, and that potentiality or virtuality in a broad sense, however distinctly specified, constitutes an attempt to reconfigure a nonsovereign sovereignty, or a power that exceeds actual power or crude force.

To escape or deconstruct sovereignty, however, one must also find a way to get around the One that accrues sovereign power. Beyond sovereignty means developing a theology beyond monotheism, as Laurel Schneider attempts in her provocative book *Beyond Monotheism*, and which Keller and Caputo both offer important resources to do. For Schneider, divine multiplicity exceeds "the logic of the One" and is incarnated in bodies that "*become* difference and so create the world."[51] Schneider draws upon Keller's theology of becoming, although she also engages with contemporary poetry and literature, and her expression is often beautifully theo-poetic. The vulnerability of God prescribes a lessening of the sovereign One, which is only possible after the death of God; that is, God can only be thought without sovereignty after the link of substantial belief in omnipotent divine power is broken. At the same time, Caputo and Keller (as well as Schneider) understand that it is not enough to banish God to overcome the problematic effects of sovereign theo-political power. The One must be carefully decentered or deconstructed, which is why Keller and Caputo are two of the most radical and creative theologians writing today, at least in American.

According to Jacques Lacan, there is such a thing as a One, formed by the knot that marks the intersection of the three registers of the imaginary, the symbolic, and the real.[52] This One is constituted by a rotary motion or a sovereign power, and monotheism names this sovereignty as God. To truly deconstruct divine and political sovereignty, we must abandon monotheism. In his thinking of the irreducible multiplicity of being, Alain Badiou seeks to formulate an alternative philosophy to the tyranny of the One and even identifies "a metaphysics of One in the work of Deleuze."[53] Democracy is a step in the direction of multiplicity, but in its classical liberal form it is entangled in a univocal sovereignty, the popular sovereignty of a general will or a united state(s) or people. I will return to the explicit question of democracy, specifically a radical democracy, in chapter 5.

What would it mean to think divinity as democracy? Even the Christian Trinity preserves at least the trace of a hierarchy (Father, Son, Holy Spirit), not to mention patriarchal masculinity. According to Caputo, "What is called for is to imagine God otherwise, to turn our thinking about God around, almost upside down or inside out," which is a revolutionary way of thinking, at once religious and political.[54] We can think God. We can think democracy. Can we think God without sovereignty? Can we conceive a radical democracy without sovereign power? Is this a potentiality, a thinking to come?

As indicated in the introduction, Giorgio Agamben has theorized potentiality and its relation to sovereignty. In the essay "On Potentiality," Agamben discusses Aristotle's distinction between potentiality and actuality in *De Anima* and *Metaphysics*. According to Agamben's reading of Aristotle, potentiality is a capacity or a faculty that touches on "*the existence of non-Being*, the presence of an absence."[55] Aristotle distinguishes two kinds of potentiality, one of which is the capacity to acquire a knowledge or ability, such as the potential to learn a foreign language. This is a generic potentiality.

But, humans have existing potentialities, that is, a person who has already learned a foreign language has the potential at any moment to read or speak it, even if not doing so at a certain moment. Agamben states that an existing potentiality, precisely insofar as it remains potential, exists as "potential to not-do, potential not to pass into actuality."[56]

Because of this capacity to not do, potentiality is related to its own privation, or non-Being. Of course, potentiality *can* pass over into actuality, but its significance here is that it does not, that it maintains itself in its potentiality and refuses to act. In an essay on Herman Melville's short story "Bartleby, the Scrivener" called "Bartleby, or On Contingency," Agamben suggests that as a scribe who has the capacity or potentiality to write but does not, or "prefers not to," Bartleby represents a "complete or perfect potentiality."[57] This potential not to be or not to do is a "fundamental passivity" that at its extreme limit can be called impotentiality. "Beings that exist in the mode of potentiality are capable of their own impotentiality," Agamben writes, "and only in this way do they become potential."[58]

Impotentiality means not only that every potentiality is related to a possible actuality, which Agamben in the essay on Bartleby calls "will," echoing Nietzsche's language, but also, more importantly, that every potentiality is related to its own impotentiality, its own capacity not to become actualized. Impotentiality is the limit of potentiality and the key to understanding human power. "Every human power is *adynamia*, impotentiality," and this is "the origin (and the abyss) of every human power, which is so violent and limitless with respect to other living beings."[59] Impotentiality is the source of limitless human power, but it is also, strangely, the abyss or ruin of this violent power. Impotentiality is related to human freedom, which is the power and freedom to accomplish radical good and radical evil based on the abyss of potentiality at the heart of humanity: "To be free is, in the sense we have seen, to be capable of one's own impotentiality, to be in relation to one's own privation."[60]

Agamben's thought is complex, but I am drawing upon it to make a distinction between the potentiality for any idea to actualize itself in a determinate way and the impotentiality of that same idea, its power not to actualize itself but to preserve its relation to privation and non-Being, which is where Agamben locates true freedom, a freedom from the necessity to actualize itself: "Here potentiality, so to speak, survives actuality, and, in this way, *gives itself to itself.*"[61] This is the gift of which Derrida speaks in *The Gift of Death*, the giving of potentiality in impotentiality, which precedes the giving that takes place in the process of the actualization of potentiality. The limit of potentiality in impotentiality is freedom, according to Agamben, even though technically speaking it does not exist in actuality. And this freedom is theological, even though it concerns not only beings but also nonbeings.

At the end of his essay on Bartleby, Agamben claims that Bartleby is a Christ figure, a new Messiah, but Bartleby "comes not, like Jesus, to redeem what was, but to save what was not."[62] Bartleby, as the ultimate figure of potentiality, indicates not creation but a second creation, a decreation, "in which God summons all his potential not to be." Decreation is the limit of creation, and salvation is the end of redemption where "the creature is finally at home, saved in being irredeemable."[63] That is, the freedom of the creature is its own decreation, its own restoration to (im)possibility, a balancing out of all that is by what is not but could be or could have been. Decreation applies to God as well, the decreation as the freedom of God to not be, which is the only way to save God now, to restore God to God's own impotentiality. A task for theology's task, in light of Agamben's work, is to think this impotentiality as the limit of potentiality.

In many ways, thinking potentiality as impotentiality counters an emphasis on sovereignty, which Agamben's work as well as Derrida's helps to challenge and to deconstruct. Sovereignty is first of all the sovereign, fully actual power of God, which is instantiated in and exercised by the political ruler. During the modern period, sovereignty becomes associated first with absolute monarchy, then, as popular sovereignty, with representative democracy, as discussed earlier in connection with Hobbes.

To think about divine power as other than sovereign and to avoid the simple opposition of power and weakness, I want to conclude this chapter by considering Judith Butler's reading of Walter Benjamin's essay "Critique of Violence." Benjamin is an important locus of many contemporary theoretical discussions, in particular his "Theses on the Philosophy of History," because he claims that historical materialism possesses a "*weak* messianic power" to "blast a specific era out of the homogeneous course of history."[64] This weak messianic power is the subject of serious philosophical and theological discussions by Derrida, Caputo, Agamben, Žižek, and Hent de Vries, among others, and Derrida's so-called religious turn occurs in his important essay "Force of Law," which partly consists of a reading of Benjamin's "Critique of Violence."[65] I will specifically consider the concept of messianism or messianicity later in the book, in chapter 9, but here I want to focus specifically on Butler's interpretation of divine power in Benjamin's essay.

In her essay "Critique, Coercion, and Sacred Life in Benjamin's 'Critique of Violence,'" Judith Butler claims that Benjamin reconfigures the biblical commandment "Thou shalt not kill."[66] Benjamin makes a distinction between a "law-instating" and a "law-preserving violence," along with another form of violence, a divine violence that Butler says is more properly messianic.[67] Benjamin contrasts divine violence with mythic violence, which crosses or overlaps the previous distinction. Butler distinguishes her reading from Derrida's, which focuses more on law-instating violence, noting that Derrida "made clear that he thought Benjamin went too far in criticizing parliamentary democracy."[68]

In what Benjamin calls mythic violence, the establishment of the law is considered fate, and this instantiation of law-making violence "petrifies the subject, arresting life in a moment of guilt."[69] Divine violence, however, is figured as destructive, as undoing the law or disestablishing the legal framework itself. Here, destruction is radically nonviolent, or excessive in relation to conventional violence. Benjamin considers divine violence along the lines of the general strike, as recommended by Georges Sorel in his *Reflections on Violence*.

Butler argues that for Benjamin, "mere life" is life subject to mythic violence and "bloody power," as opposed to a divine violence "undertaken *for the sake of the living*" that undoes the subject who is formed by the law.[70] Here, divine violence or destructive force works against the sovereign legal subject. According to Butler, divine power expiates guilt; it "constitutes an expiating moment that strikes without bloodshed."[71] Here, the problem is positive law and its mythic violence, the sovereign power to constitute a subject as subject to the law. Most monotheistic theology understands God as a divine and sovereign subject, but this is precisely what Benjamin allows us to question. Furthermore, this divine violence can be correlated with Caputo's weakness of God and Keller's theopolitics of becoming.

At the conclusion of her essay, Butler reads Benjamin's "Theologico-Political Fragment" as claiming that the rhythm of life is marked by a necessary transience, which is both a form of suffering and an experience of happiness. It is this rhythm that constitutes the messianic, a form of life that is not teleological because it is not mere life in the service of sovereign legal ends. Butler quotes Benjamin, saying that "the rhythm of this eternally transient worldly existence, transient in its totality, in its spatial but also in its temporal totality, the rhythm of Messianic nature, is happiness."[72] Following Benjamin, Butler dissociates divine violence from divine command and divine punishment. "If divine violence is not involved in the making of law but mobilizes the messianic in its powers of expiation," she writes, "then divine power would release the punished subject from guilt."[73] This release is not only a psychological mechanism but also existentially accomplishes the salving or *salut* that Derrida and Caputo both affirm. Here, the messianic event of divine violence, which is violence without violence, opposes sovereign power and its teleology. According to Butler, in a reading that accords with Eric Santner's influential interpretation of Freud and Rosenzweig, "the messianic thwarts the teleological unfolding of time" by restoring life to its transient rhythm.[74]

In conclusion, a messianic weak power of God disrupts sovereign power, including the sovereign power of divinity itself, and possesses important political implications. A strike is a model of divine (in)action because it is constitutes a refusal that creates an upheaval at the heart of political society. This model of divine violence is very close to what Agamben calls impotentiality, as discussed in the introduction, because it is the refusal to exercise a capacity to do something, not simply impotence. In our contemporary corporate-capitalist world, the most difficult and maybe the most subversive act is to choose not to do something, not to shop, not to buy, not to consume, not to work. Only a dramatic constraint of our incredible potentiality to produce, consume, and devastate natural resources can perhaps ward off social collapse and increased global warming. Such action seems incredibly urgent but virtually impossible given current political and economic arrangements. The effort required to stop or at least slow down our production, consumption, and proliferation of forms of violence is so enormous that it must be divine because "only a god can save us." But if we await such a god it will not come; only if we find a way to realize this impotentiality of divine force or weakness can we preserve our transient happiness and be saved.

3. BARUCH SPINOZA AND THE POTENTIAL FOR A RADICAL POLITICAL THEOLOGY

In the last chapter I discussed Hobbes as an exemplary founder of political sovereignty. In this chapter I shift to a different origin of modern political philosophy, Baruch Spinoza, and move from a discussion of the deconstruction of sovereignty and the weakness of God to a reconstruction of sovereignty, although this reconstruction of sovereignty along Spinozist lines does not reinstitute a traditional form of sovereignty or issue in a strong God or a strong form of political power and authority. In choosing Spinoza as an example and an inspiration for a postsecular theology, I am suggesting a reorientation of sovereignty, which has been already invoked as freedom, potentiality, and virtuality in the introduction. I am also consciously challenging the limits of the opposition of the secular and the religious, as discussed in chapter 1, and countering a more conventional theological discourse that simply declares that if our situation is postsecular, we can thereby dispense with any consideration of the secular.

I do not see my reading of Spinoza and sovereignty as oppositional to the Derridean deconstruction of sovereignty, Caputo's insistence upon the weakness of God, or Keller's idea of the theo-poetic becoming of God, but rather as complementary. The problem is the conceptual confusion of strong and weak as opposites. As any serious reading of Caputo, Keller, or Derrida makes clear, weakness or becoming is the not the opposite of power but lies beyond this simple opposition. Here I am attending to the immanent constitution of power and of theological and political thinking, which does not weakly or passively accept the terms, problems, questions, and conclusions offered up by the status quo of tradition or common sense. In the previous chapter I was concerned with the object of theological thought, God, as a concept that manifests and consolidates sovereignty; here I am interested in the process or constitution of theological thinking in an immanent way.

To think about sovereignty differently, I appeal to the conceptions of potentiality and virtuality already introduced earlier. For Deleuze, the virtual is not constrasted with the real but with the actual. For Negri, *potentia* as understood through Spinoza is a virtual or potential power that is contrasted with *potestas* or actual power. In his book on Henri Bergson, *Bergsonism*, Deleuze distinguishes the virtual from the possible, explaining that although "the virtual is not actual," it "as such possesses a reality."[1] The reality of the virtual supplies the movement of differentiation in a process of actualization. The virtual is not subordinated to the actual in a classic Aristotelian manner; rather, it exceeds the actual even as it gives rise to it. In *Bergsonism*, Deleuze contrasts the pairing "virtual-actual" with the opposition "possible-real," claiming that both virtuality and actuality possess reality. Deleuze claims, following Bergson, that "we know that the *virtual as virtual has a reality*; this reality, extended to the whole universe, consists in all the coexisting degrees of expansion and contraction."[2] All of the points that exist on every level of the universe "form the potential parts of a Whole that is itself virtual. They are *the reality of this virtual*."[3] The Whole is virtual and consists of everything in potentiality; these virtualities actualize in different and determinate ways. Deleuze states that "when the virtuality is actualized, is differentiated, is 'developed,' when it actualizes and develops its parts, it does so according to lines that are divergent, but each of which corresponds to a particular degree in the virtual totality."[4]

In *Difference and Repetition*, Deleuze maintains this duality of virtuality and actuality. He deploys a logic of virtuality to elaborate a repetition of difference, because repetition is not the realization of a prior possibility, which would be a repetition of identity, but in fact is based on difference, which makes it a virtual actualization, or an actualization of virtuality. Deleuze argues that the possible "refers to the form of identity in the concept," whereas the virtual "designates a pure multiplicity in the Idea which radically excludes the identical as a prior condition."[5] Deleuze employs the term "virtual" instead of "possible" or "potential" because he wants to exclude both identity and negativity from this concept. Both virtual and actual are real; they are two sides of the same coin.

The important distinction between differentiation and differenciation also pertains to this difference between virtual and actual. To refer to the virtual operation of difference, Deleuze uses the French mathematical term *différentier*, which the English translator Paul Patton renders as "to differentiate." The more common French word *différencier*, whose meaning is closer to the English word "differentiate," is used to refer to the process of actualization. *Différencier* is translated in English as "to differenciate" to maintain consistency with the French usage of Deleuze. This is a very technical but also a very important difference, which applies to the crucial distinction between virtual and actual in Deleuze's most important work. In the same part of text, Deleuze explains, "We call the determination of the virtual content of an Idea differentiation; we call the actualization of that virtuality into species and distinguished parts differenciation."[6]

Both virtual and actual possess equal reality; neither of these terms is essentially negative or lacking being. The virtual involves the posing of a problem and the terms in which it is presented. The actual concerns the answer, or the solution to a problem. "Whereas differentiation determines the virtual content of the Idea as problem," Deleuze writes, "differenciation expresses the actualisation of this virtual and the constitution of solutions."[7] In *Bergsonism*, Deleuze claims that there is more freedom and power in the ability to pose a problem than in answering it. Even though the virtual is real and fully determinate, it nevertheless concerns freedom. Or rather, true freedom concerns thinking of and through virtuality. According to Deleuze, "true freedom lies in a power to decide, to constitute problems themselves."[8]

Deleuze does not oppose virtual to actual in any fundamental sense; they are complementary. Negri, however, with his distinction between *potentia* and *potestas* draws out a similar distinction in terms of power, but for Negri this difference becomes more antagonistic. The difference between *potestas* and *potentia* is similar to Deleuze's between actual and virtual, except that Negri sharpens the opposition between the two terms in his reading of Spinoza in *The Savage Anomaly*. Both words can be translated as power, but *potestas* refers to actual power, while *potentia* concerns a potential power or force. In relation to God, Spinoza claims that God's *potentia* is identical with God's essence, whereas *potestas* concerns existence. Negri explains that "*potestas* is given as the capacity (or conceivability) of producing things; *potentia* is presented as the force that actually produces them."[9]

In *The Savage Anomaly*, Negri develops the link between the *Ethics* and Spinoza's unfinished *Political Treatise*, claiming that "Spinoza's true politics is his metaphysics." Spinoza sketches out a philosophy of the future, in opposition to the project of modern science and politics, "which is a mapping or plan of absolute Power (*potestas*)."[10] Spinoza consistently limits *potestas* with *potentia*, for the sake of a future, which is also freedom. In Spinoza's thought, productive imagination constitutes reality and delivers humanity from its bondage to *potestas*. According to Negri, "freedom is the infinite. Every metaphysical channel toward freedom is dissolved, making room for the constitutive decision of freedom," which is Spinoza's main goal. The State constitutes itself by denying freedom, reducing it to provide for itself a transcendent basis. This is the mystification of politics as *potestas*. Negri's reading of Spinoza, however, liberates "the social power (*potentia*) of the *multitudo*," which functions as the subject of this freedom and *potentia*.[11]

I am reading Spinoza through a postmodern lens here, using the interpretations of Gilles Deleuze and Antonio Negri to help construct a contemporary postmodern interpretation of Spinoza that directly feeds into a radical political theology, for which Spinoza would serve as a saint, if not the Christ.[12] In some ways, however, Spinoza emerges as the first quintessentially modern philosopher, which is due to his consistent identification of God and Nature. Descartes is generally granted this title for his emphasis upon the human ego, or thinking self, but Descartes also retains a medieval and Aristotelian hierarchical dualism between thought and body that Spinoza attempts to overcome with his notion of substance. In his book, *Spinoza and Other Heretics*, Yirmiyahu Yovel illustrates the complex historical and cultural background of Spinoza's family and its crossing of religious lines. Spinoza was born in Holland as a Jew, but his parents were Portuguese Marranos who fled the Portuguese version of the Spanish Inquisition when Spain and Portugal were united under the same king. Spinoza was educated in Jewish Amsterdam, but he was famously excommunicated in 1656 because he could not conform to the strictures of the Amsterdam Jewish community. Yovel explains that Spinoza's thought is the product of a complex and secret religious background that has "a Jewish framework but [is] saturated with Catholic elements and interpretations."[13] Spinoza was influenced by his Catholic tutor, Van den Ende, but he resisted many efforts by friends and colleagues to convert to Christianity.

The main point here is that a religious faith held and practiced in secret—the Judaizing Marrano—became deformed in both forms of Christian and Jewish orthodoxy and later evolved into what we think of as secularity. The secular is the product of a complex religious space, an interaction between Jewish and Christian elements that is constructed initially in secret but later becomes unhidden, manifested as nonreligious in any formal sense. According to Yovel, the religious duality at the heart of the Judaizing Marranos ultimately created "a form of faith that is neither Christian nor Jewish," and eventually "the confusion of Judaism and Christianity led in many cases to a loss of both."[14]

I am following Yovel in suggesting that Spinoza represents a singular philosophy, due in large part to his religious identity, as well as his thoughts about religion. In some ways, Spinoza's thought, as well as the Marranos' experience, provides the consistency that supplies the dash in Judeo-Christian, if there is one. Spinoza anonymously wrote both the controversial *Tractatus Theologico-Politicus*, which launched a massive critique of biblical truth, and the posthumously published *Ethics*, a dizzying geometrical treatise. Both helped to make him the "supreme philosophical bogeyman of Early Enlightenment Europe," as Jonathan Israel points out in his impressive study of the Radical Enlightenment.[15] Spinoza's thought is challenging and radical, for both contemporaries and later thinkers such as Deleuze and Negri.

I will briefly explain Spinoza's proof of the existence of God at the beginning of the *Ethics*, with particular attention to the concepts of substance, attributes, and modes. I suggest that Spinoza does not prove God so much as define God into existence. At the same time, there is a tension in Spinoza's definition between a unitary substance and a plurality or infinity of attributes. After explicating Spinoza's understanding of God, I will turn to Deleuze's and Negri's respective interpretations of Spinoza to indicate their relevance for a contemporary reconceptualization of sovereignty that is important for radical theology.

Part 1 of the *Ethics* is entitled "Concerning God." In six definitions, seven axioms, thirty-six propositions and assorted corollaries, scholia, and proofs, Spinoza defines and proves the existence and nature of God. The key terms are laid out in definitions 3, 4, and 5, where Spinoza defines substance, attribute, and mode. These terms culminate in definition 6, where he states, "By

God I mean an absolutely infinite being; that is, substance consisting of infinite attributes, each of which expresses eternal and infinite existence."[16] According to Spinoza, there can exist only one infinite substance, and substance is primary being because it alone "is in itself and can be conceived through itself." Substance is infinite and indivisible, and according to proposition 5, "in the universe there cannot be two or more substances of the same nature or attribute."[17] Attributes are defined as "that which the intellect perceives of substance as constituting its essence." By definition 6, then, substance, which is ultimately God, consists of infinite attributes. The essence of substance may be perceived and known in potentially infinite ways, even though substance is essentially one in itself, that is, the unity of all of these attributes insofar as they pertain to a substance. Spinoza distinguishes between the higher unity or oneness of substance and the plurality or infinity of attributes to affirm that substance or God is one.

The infinity of the attributes of substance, which is aspect by which we can know the essence of substance, mirrors the infinite number of modes, as explained in proposition 22: "Whatever follows by some attribute of God in so far as the attribute is modified by a modification that exists necessarily and as infinite through that same attribute, must also exist necessarily and as infinite."[18] Modes are modifications or affectations of substance and follow the attributes of God in their expression. Modes are finite determinations of substance, but there are an infinite number of modes because there are an infinite number of attributes of substance. "Particular things are nothing but affections of the attributes of God; that is, modes wherein the attributes of God find expression in a definite and determinate way."[19] The two main modifications of substance are mind and body, or the Cartesian duality of thinking things and extended things, which Spinoza ultimately wants to overcome.[20] The attributes are crucial in that they mediate between the modes and substance itself, and they are also what allow intellectual knowledge of substance and comprehension of modes. Substance is defined in such a way that it must be infinite and indivisible, and hence one. God is defined as substance, and God as substance is known by the infinity of modes possessed by God. Although "each attribute of one substance must be conceived through itself," its conception necessarily involves its relation to the one substance, which is God. Infinite attributes link the infinite modes or modifications of substance to the unity of substance in itself. Since substance necessarily exists, if in fact anything exists whatsoever, God necessarily exists insofar as God is defined as substance. Although

Spinoza seems to present proofs of God's existence, he actually defines God into existence, paradigmatically in proposition 11: "God, or substance consisting of infinite attributes, each of which expresses eternal and infinite essence, necessarily exists."[21]

I have not so much presented the progression of Spinoza's thought in part 1 of the *Ethics*, as tried to lay out how God is defined as substance in relation to attributes and modes. This discussion is highly complex, not least by the geometrical style Spinoza adopts in this book. The key, however, is the understanding of the nature of the attributes, because they allow us to pass from infinite substance to finite modes and vice versa. The status of the attributes constitutes the theological link between God and the nature, and it is through a profound reworking of the attributes that Deleuze and Negri interpret and apply Spinoza to contemporary thought.

For Deleuze substance becomes a plane of immanence and the attributes are conceived as expressions to assemble a philosophy of expression, a notion of philosophy as expression. Expression actualizes or elaborates the modes, which are affects, or becomings that take place along a plane of immanence that provides a bare minimum of unity of consistency. Later in his career, Deleuze abandons the category of expression as too intellectualistic, preferring to follow the movements of machines and of bodies in his work with Guattari on *Capitalism and Schizophrenia*, although expression may be seen as a prefiguring of his notion of the fold, as expressed in *The Fold: Leibniz and the Baroque*. Antonio Negri, by contrast, follows the development of the *Ethics* by eliminating the attributes and envisioning a direct confrontation between substance and modes. By dropping the attributes, Negri eliminates their mediating function, although the attributes return very subtly in Negri's reading of *potentia* (or potential) constituting power, in contrast with *potestas* (or actual power). Ultimately, dislocating the attributes from any understanding of mediation that precludes transcendence raises the possibility of a radical theological thinking that is Spinozistic, because it is fully immanent as constituent power and also possesses political implications that will be addressed at the conclusion of this chapter.

Deleuze wrote two books dealing with Spinoza. The first, *Expressionism in Philosophy: Spinoza*, lays out a constructive understanding of philosophy as expression rather than as a description of reality by working through complex ideas of Spinoza and Leibniz.[22] The second book, *Spinoza: Practical Philosophy*, is a brief but intense engagement mostly with the *Ethics*. In the latter book Deleuze makes a claim that was implicit in the earlier one, and which is decisive for Deleuze's own philosophy. Deleuze argues that the true significance of Spinoza is "no longer the affirmation of a single substance, but rather the laying out of a *common plane of immanence* on which all bodies, all minds, and all individuals are situated."[23] Deleuze claims that the modes of expression of substance are primary and that "a mode is a complex relation of speed and slowness, in the body but also in thought." The fundamental idea is the composition of a mode that occurs along a plane of immanence. A plane of immanence is then contrasted with a theological plan in which "organization comes from above and refers to a transcendence."[24] Here transcendence is imposed from outside, usually a dimension of height, which is what Deleuze precludes. Meaning, significance, and life are internal or immanent to the mode of composition.

We could trace Deleuze's thought forward from this key insight, to witness the elaboration of a plane of immanence in *What is Philosophy?* coauthored with Félix Guattari, and in his final essay, "Immanence: A Life." But I also want to relate Deleuze's understanding of a plane of immanence, developed in relation to Spinoza's philosophy, to Deleuze's earlier book on Spinoza, *Expressionism in Philosophy*. In this book, Deleuze uses Spinoza's thought to criticize the notion of analogy in its theological use, a critique I want to reflect on briefly before shifting to Negri's reading of Spinoza in *The Savage Anomaly*. In part 1 of the *Ethics*, as we have seen, Spinoza elaborates his three key terms: substance, modes, and attributes. He proposes that there is only one "absolutely infinite substance," which is defined as God (propositions 13 and 14). Substance manifests itself in modes, or modifications of substance. There are technically an infinite number of possible modes, but the two main ones, following Descartes, are extension and thought. I have suggested above that the main conceptual difficulty of part 1 concerns the nature of the attributes, which function to mediate between substance and modes.

Now, the challenge is to understand the attributes of substance in distinction from the traditional properties of God. Deleuze argues that theology "oscillates between an eminent conception of negation" in which negative theology goes "beyond both affirmations and negations in a shadowy eminence" and "an analogical conception of affirmation."[25] These two work together in a confusing way because they are based on a confusion of God with God's "*propria*." *Propria*, or attributes considered as properties of God based on relationships of analogy and dis-analogy, render the idea of God necessarily indeterminate. Deleuze's solution is to understand attributes as expressions of substance in continuity with modes, rather than as mediating an analogy between substance and our experience of a mode. Here is where the notion of immanence comes in, because it resists the obscurity of revelation: "revelation concerns, in truth, only certain *propria*. It in no way sets out to make known to us the divine nature and its attributes."[26] Attributes directly express the nature of substance in modes along a plane of immanence, which avoids the confusions of analogy and negative theology. Any time one posits two planes, a plane of transcendence and a plane of immanence, the problem becomes the mediation, in both ontological and epistemological terms, between the two planes. If God is simply located on a transcendent plane, then knowledge of God is impossible and religion is reduced to the problem of political obedience, as Spinoza concludes in his *Tractatus Theologico-Politicus*.[27]

The separation of the two planes does not only concern knowledge but also political power because of the need for mediation. If one plane is insufficient and is mediated by a higher plane or a higher power, then power is dissipated, or drawn away from its direct, immediate application to another level or realm from which it can then operate to impose order, harmony, and obedience. This is what Deleuze means when he criticizes, following Nietzsche, the separation of force from what it can do, which is the essence of reactive force.[28] The active force is replaced by the reactive force, which is the essence of the State as representative and mediating power, as well as God as transcendent sovereign power. The question is whether or not God and the State are equivalent in their role of mediating direct, antagonistic conflict among forces, people, and ideas, as Deleuze's and Negri's readings of Spinoza direct us to think.

The attribute is the most problematic notion in Spinoza's *Ethics* because of its mediating role between substance and mode. Deleuze tries to solve this problem with the notion of expression in order to read Spinoza's attributes as direct expressions rather than as mysterious properties of substance. In his book on Spinoza, Antonio Negri goes further than Deleuze by dispensing with the attributes altogether. Negri reads the *Ethics* more contextually, toward the development of Spinoza's unfinished *Political Treatise*, which is why Negri claims that Spinoza's metaphysics *is* his political thought. Negri explains that as the *Ethics* proceeds, the attributes drop out, the result of an antagonistic clash between substance and modes. So long as attributes occupy a middle realm between substance and modes, a medium of mediation is preserved, a back and forth shuttle between two alienated realms.

Negri takes a lesson from his reading of Marx's *Grundrisse*, which he develops in *Marx Beyond Marx*, and that lesson is one of antagonism. Negri emphasizes Marx's understanding of tendency as a method, which is functionally similar to that of attribute, and stresses that this tendency is an antagonistic tendency. That is, in the *Grundrisse* the tendency of relations of production tend to exacerbate rather than ameliorate conflicts. At the same time, Hegelian dialectics and other forms of mediation tend to subsume or reduce conflict by locating it elsewhere. "The general concept of production," Negri writes, "breaks the limits of its materialist and dialectical definition in order to exalt the subjectivity of its elements and their antagonistic relation."[29] The political problem is that the State mediates the conflicts among subjects to strip them of their power to address the increasing inequality created by capitalist conditions.

In Negri's analysis of Spinoza, after the early stage of the *Ethics*, the focus on the attributes drops away, leaving substance and mode to "crash against each other and shatter."[30] Deleuze's effort was to undo the hierarchy implied by the attributes by reading them as expressions, foldings of substances that occur in and as modes. But Negri attends to the tendency of the attributes to fade away and leave substance and mode as stark antagonists.

The question is: Why not retain mediation? Why must substance and modes fall into conflict with each other? Negri argues that it is for political reasons, and that the essence of Spinoza's metaphysics is his politics, which culminates in his unfinished *Political Treatise*, as mentioned above. As opposed to the traditional modern bourgeois theory of the state, which is fundamentally based on mediation, Spinoza's philosophy remains an anomaly because it is based solely on power: "Clearly, Spinozian philosophy is an anomaly in its century and is savage to the eyes of the dominant culture."[31] To explain the significance of power in Spinoza's thought, Negri distinguishes between two understandings of power expressed in the Latin terms *potentia* and *potestas*. *Potentia* is potential power, whereas *potestas* is actualized power. Unlike traditional Aristotelian and Thomistic philosophy and theology, however, Negri reverses the value-relationship between these two terms and suggests that *potentia* is more profound and more significant than *potestas*. These two forms of power are never separated but are importantly distinguished. That is, Spinoza grounds *potestas* in *potentia*, while bourgeois thought from Hobbes through Rousseau to Hegel separates and mystifies *potestas* as power and obscures *potentia*, which produces "the bourgeois ideology of civil society."[32] Mediation is the space of separation that allows modern political thought to separate and mystify *potestas*, actual power, while hiding its rootedness in *potentia*.

Negri suggests that Spinoza liberates *potentia* from *potestas*, or potential power from actual power, which is both a political and a metaphysical operation. For most of modern thought, following the "line of thought Hobbes-Rousseau-Kant-Hegel," *potentia* is always in the service of *potestas*, which takes the form of political and theological sovereignty. *Potentia* always requires mediation to take place as or accomplish the transition to sovereign *potestas*, and this project of sublime mediation culminates in Hegelian philosophy. This prevailing tendency of modern thought is the reason Negri works so hard to displace the conventional interpretation of the Spinozian attributes as mediating between substance and modes. Spinoza's thought is an anomaly, however, because it counters this prevailing tendency.

In Negri's reading of Spinoza, the attributes "go under," to contribute to the power of *potentia* in contrast with *potestas*. The antagonism between substance and modes created by the virtual disappearance of the attributes brings about "a dimension of the world that is not hierarchical but, rather, flat, equal: versatile and equivalent."[33] This is Deleuze's plane of immanence, and it is also the "fundamental point" where "the idea of power . . . leaps to center stage with enormous force."[34] Basically, the attributes no longer function to mediate between substance and mode in order to preserve hierarchical being, but they "have themselves been reabsorbed on a horizontal field of surfaces. They no longer represent agents of organization but are subordinated (and very nearly eliminated) in a linear horizon, in a space where only singularities emerge."[35] Essentially, the absorption of the attributes contributes to the power of *potentia*, which is then manifested as *potestas* in the constitution of reality by the productive material imagination. This process is a political process, because the *potentia* of constituting reality is the *potentia* of the *multitudo*, or the multitude. According to Negri, Spinoza's philosophy, as fulfilled in the *Political Treatise*, includes three important elements:

(1) a conception of the State that radically denies its transparency—that is, a demystification of politics; (2) a determination of Power (*potestas*) as a function subordinated to the social power (*potentia*) of the *multitudo* and, therefore, constitutionally organized; (3) a conception of constitution, in other words, of constitutional organization, which necessarily starts from the antagonism of subjects.[36]

The notion of *multitudo* that Negri finds in Spinoza is directly related to the understanding of multitude that Negri develops in "Kairos, Alma Venus, Multitudo," included as the second half of *Time for Revolution,* and that Negri and Michael Hardt express in *Multitude: War and Democracy in The Age of Empire.* At the same time, however, multitude is not explicitly related to power as *potentia* in either of these later works.

Negri's understanding of the *potentia* of the *multitudo* in Spinoza leads directly to his sweeping political works, *Empire* and *Multitude.* I want to briefly consider the conclusion of *Multitude* to see how Negri and Hardt's understanding of radical democracy fits into these theoretical notions of potentiality and virtuality. In *Multitude,* Negri and Hardt envision an understanding of democracy that would not be based on sovereignty. Sovereign power is *potestas,* and the dominant tradition of political philosophy claims that "there can be no politics without sovereignty."[37] Negri and Hardt propose the term "multitude," a translation of Spinoza's *multitudo,* which would function as a virtual multiplicity, rather than exist as the actualized sovereignty of the people. War is the expression of sovereign power, but "the multitude cannot be reduced to a unity and does not submit to the rule of one."[38] The power of the multitude is *potentia,* even though this term does not appear in *Multitude;* it is "the power to create social relationships in common."[39] Hardt and Negri appeal to Lenin and James Madison to articulate "the democracy of the multitude as [a] theoretical possibility" that is grounded upon a material and political concept of love. Although most contemporary people think of love in emotional or spiritual terms, Hardt and Negri claim that "we need to recuperate the public and political conception of love common to premodern traditions," including Christianity and Judaism.[40] Religious love in a political and material (but not in an abstract metaphysical) sense is "the constituent power of the multitude."[41]

Potentia is an immediately political term for Negri and, read along with Deleuze's work on Spinoza, helps us to think a postsecularist Spinoza beyond the opposition between religious and secular. The constitution of reality is at once political, secular, religious, imaginary, theological, and real. A plane of immanence is not necessarily a denial of transcendence, but a way to express force and meaning directly without recourse to an abstract mediation that projects the source of power elsewhere in relation to its effects. Mediation is duplicitous; it appears to resolve antagonism but in fact displaces and diffuses it, appropriating and conserving power (*potestas*) and distributing violence (invisible effects of antagonisms) throughout the social order. Our media serves the *potestas* of the State and the Corporation in this regard. The current role of the corporate media is to absorb, bleed off, and redirect any serious challenge to the social order and saturate citizens with a disorienting and numbing cascade of spectacles. Any position is immediately reduced to "liberal" or "conservative" and then plugged into a preestablished network of other associations and identified with a party (you can choose the one on the Left or the one on the Right), both of which are funded by the same corporate money. Frustrated with their impotence, people give up, tune out, and become zombies of consumption.

The power of the constitutive bodily imagination in Spinoza, however, is its direct production of a new thought, which is theological as well as political in nature, and it is radical rather than reactive in relation to current and former modes of theological, political, and philosophical thinking. The notion of a plane of immanence keeps power from running away and transmuting itself into the power of *potestas* behind our backs as it were, whether this is done by rulers, CEOs, philosophers, or God.

In theological terms, God as pure actuality, or absolute *potestas*, governs the world by total mediation. It is the separation of *potestas* and *potentia* that instantiates and preserves traditional and modern sovereignty. Some of the most potent political critiques of modern capitalism are articulated in the name of traditional religious traditions, including British Radical Orthodoxy. The political solution of Radical Orthodoxy ultimately substitutes God for the State in its role as absolute Mediator, claiming that God actually does harmonize and mediate conflict before it can break out, whereas the modern state, and its concomitant philosophies and social theories, instead exacerbates conflict and creates violence. This is the argument of John Milbank in *Theology and Social Theory*, that modern political economy is "neopagan" because it is fundamentally conflictual and agonistic.[42] Milbank acutely diagnoses and rejects the violence inherent in modern liberalism and contemporary capitalism, but his solution is to return to a premodern form of life that acknowledges the primary authority of the Church, not as an institution but as a source of harmony and community. This is a very idealized notion of medieval Christianity being petitioned as an alternative to the ravages of modern and postmodern capitalism.

I want to affirm the powerful social critique of liberal sovereignty on the part of Milbank and other representatives of Radical Orthodoxy, but at the same time I find the recommended solution of a renewed Christian orthodoxy to be utopian and incredible. Milbank dissociates the essence of Christianity from original violence, which itself is a difficult and contested move, since violence seems intrinsic to the very nature of Christianity. Christ is crucified on a cross, which is a supremely violent act, even if it is ultimately intended to overcome violence (in theory; of course the resurrection of Christ and the instantiation of Christianity do not overcome religious persecution and violence in practice). In contrast to his idealized version of Christianity, Milbank claims that modern secular society is originally and essentially violent, and he claims that any religious violence in the name of Christianity is a betrayal of Christianity. Of course, the State both creates and resolves conflictual violence, as does the capitalistic economy, where the market (as Adam Smith called it, the "Hand of God") serves to mediate and reconcile competing ends. The State is established to reconcile or mediate conflict among citizens, although it also serves to instigate conflicts with other states. Milbank strips away the mediative aspects of the modern State and capitalist economy, leaving its naked violence exposed. At the same time, its mediation is what allows both the State and the economy to function.

The problem with the State, then, is that on the religious reading it either usurps God's (or the Church's) role of mediation of conflicts among entities, or, in Milbank's more radical critique, it dispenses with this function altogether in its antagonism against Christianity. In his book on *Christ and Culture*, Graham Ward adopts a similar solution to Milbank, while focusing more on biblical and early Christianity than the modern secular world. Ward defines politics in terms of power relations that are necessarily asymmetrical and unequal. Ward argues that the revolutionary significance of Christ is not as "the leveler of hierarchies, the liberator of the subjugated." Christ is not apolitical, however, because he is concerned with "power and its authorisation. The oneness concerns the submission of all social positions . . . to Christ, and the new orders of power (and its polity) that are engendered by this submission."[43] While Ward elaborates suggestive ways to reimagine the significance of Christ for believers, his political stance is that the authority of Christ substitutes for the power and authority of the State while sublating any independent human culture.

Radical Orthodoxy substitutes an imperial Christian vision adopted from the Middle Ages for the suppression of Christianity and its relegation to the margins and private realm in the modern liberal and presumably secular state. Ward and Milbank are subtle, sharp, and important observers of contemporary theology, politics, and society, but they invoke a harmony that reinstates a more proper sovereign power rather than dismantle and reconfigure transcendent sovereignty itself, as Caputo, Keller, Derrida, Spinoza, Deleuze, and Negri offer resources to do. We cannot simply trump secular modernity with a reinvigorated Christianity.

On the secular level, the drawback of the State is that there is no higher, international authority to regulate or mediate the conflict among sovereign states, as they pursue their own heterogenous political and economic ends, and this concern leads to rationalistic and pragmatic reflection about the United Nations and international law, but the logic is similar to the theological situation. If only there were some higher power with the authority to adjudicate, to mediate and reconcile competing claims and conflicts, that would accord with what Derrida calls "the reason of the strongest" in a positive sense, the coincidence of "might" and "right."[44] But if God as the coincidence or power and benevolence does not exist, if the state is in fact a rogue state, and if there exists no international power or authority to play God in the realm of international affairs, then what can we do about the problems of political and economic inequality, the savagery of naked capitalism, and the desire for social justice, not to mention the irruptions of ethnic, religious, and terrorist violence?

I don't have the answers, but I do think that this interpretation of Spinoza assists us in thinking about political power in our contemporary world. It is a radical political act to retain *potentia* and refuse the subterfuge of transcendental mediation. If this is true, then the question is, is it possible to think a theology without transcendence, whether with or without God? If a purely immanent theological thinking is impossible, if theology is necessarily tied to transcendence, then there can be no truly radical political theology. In this case, we are left with the cleavage between a neoorthodox theology and its relationship to transcendence, however figured, and a radical political theory and action that must reject theology insofar as it is genuinely radical. But what if theology itself follows the trajectory of the attributes and folds into or under the modes of thought that constitute the productive imagination? What if the lesson of postsecularism is not that we must embrace religion but that modernity is not yet secular *or* religious enough, because these two phenomena are not exclusive? As Nietzsche explains in *Twilight of the Idols*, when we posit a separate realm of value and then question its existence we don't just lose the transcendent world, we lose this world too because we have emptied it of value: "The true world—we have abolished. What world has remained? The apparent one, perhaps? But no! *With the true world we have also abolished the apparent one.*[45] What if theology were to set for itself the task of restoring belief in this world rather than another?

In his book *Cinema 2: The Time Image*, Deleuze argues that the problem of the modern and contemporary world is a problem of belief. It was "a great turning-point of modern philosophy, from Pascal to Nietzsche, to replace the model of knowledge with belief."[46] But the fact is that "we no longer believe in this world. We do not even believe in the events which happen to us, love, death, as if they only half concerned us."[47] The project of modern cinema, according to Deleuze, as well as implicitly for modern or postmodern philosophy, and I would suggest also for theology, a radical theology, is to restore our belief in the world, this world. Of course, cinematic technologies and effects also contribute to our sense of unreality, the experience of being in a bad movie, or maybe even a good one, but ultimately just a movie. Belief cannot be addressed to another world, a different world; this is a denial of faith and a betrayal of belief. According to Deleuze, "whether we are Christians or atheists, in our universal schizophrenia, *we need reasons to believe in this world*. It is a whole transformation of belief."[48]

Following Deleuze and Negri and their respective readings of Spinoza, I suggest that we need a new Political-Theological critique as a prolegomenon for a new ethics, an anticapitalist ethics that could stitch together humanity and world, body and belief, faith and experience, democracy and power, beyond the opposition of religion and secularity. God is dead, has disappeared like the attributes, and has given way to the irreducible antagonisms between man and man, man and woman, and humanity and nature. Like the attributes, however, "God" also names the virtual *potentia* that makes it possible to restore belief. Restoring belief means transforming belief; it creates a new world, but it is not a utopia, because it is somewhere—right here and right now.

Spinoza's thought raises numerous theological-political questions, including his significance for modern liberal democracy. Negri reads Spinoza in a radical manner, and I will return to Spinoza in chapter 5 to pose the question of radical democracy. At the same time, Negri's reading of *potentia* offers a way to rethink the notion of sovereignty beyond the traditional understanding of actual power, or *potestas*, as I discussed in the introduction. Understanding *potentia* as a rethinking of sovereign attributes is not an overcoming of the deconstruction of sovereignty in the previous chapter, but an attempt to attend to the conditions of the forcefulness of conceptual and theological discourse in a supplementary or complementary way. Sovereignty, like God, does not exist. But precisely their (God's and sovereignty's) inexistence and the manner of their inexistence provides tools for the production of theological and political conceptions. According to the German jurist Carl Schmitt, political concepts cannot be fully disentangled from theological ones. In the next chapter, I will discuss Schmitt and his fellow German opponent of liberal modernity Leo Strauss to directly engage the problem of liberalism, which is both a political and a theological problem.

4. CARL SCHMITT, LEO STRAUSS, AND THE THEO-POLITICAL PROBLEM OF LIBERALISM

MODERN LIBERAL SOVEREIGNTY IS DIVIDED INTO TWO UNEQUAL forms: the political power of the people expressed by the ideology of liberal democracy and the economic power of the market as expressed by the ideology of free-market capitalism. A radical political theology refuses to divorce these two forms of sovereignty and sees liberal democracy as fundamentally corrupted and compromised by free-market ideology, where profits always take precedence over people. Representative democracy in fact is set up to protect the interests of money, property, and capital, and these always outweigh the needs of the people.

Modern liberalism is also essentially marked by the separation (at least in theory) of a secular, nonreligious space from a religious one, which functions as the free civil space for democratic processes and the free economic space for economic transactions. In this chapter I will develop an understanding of liberalism by focusing on the "theo-political" problem as distinctly understood by Leo Strauss and Carl Schmitt. According to Strauss, the problem is the distinction and separation of political philosophy from political theology, even though for Strauss this is also an ancient problem.

For Schmitt, however, the problem is the impossibility of a simple separation of political and theological concepts. I agree more with Schmitt, but Strauss's critique of Schmitt also opens up a perspective from which to understand both Schmitt and Strauss as fellow conservative opponents of liberalism.

Although Strauss takes the theo-political problem to be the fundamental difference between philosophy and theology, which many secularist and religious thinkers would agree with, I use Schmitt to show how the real theo-political problem is the problem of liberalism. Both Strauss and Schmitt oppose liberalism, although for different reasons. Here I will argue that their work is important for their criticisms of liberalism, but I will also suggest that they are wrong in the terms of their critique because they trivialize economic aspects of human existence. By way of this reading and critique of Schmitt and Strauss, I hope to show how the true theo-political problem is the problem of liberalism, but for different reasons than theirs. Liberalism is an economic, political, and moral problem, but it requires a radical, and ultimately radically democratic, rather than conservative solution.

Both Strauss and Schmitt are politically problematic because they denigrate material and economic factors of political and moral life. At the same time, Schmitt's work allows us to undermine Strauss's strict division between political philosophy and political theology, which is in fact a quintessentially modern distinction. If we cannot rigorously separate religion from public society and theology from political theory, then all cultural and intellectual situations are related in some way to the problem of political theology. In the case of both Strauss and Schmitt, this problem is liberalism, and while I disagree with their solutions, I agree with them to some extent about the problem. Toward the end of the chapter, I turn to the work of Karl Polanyi to offer a different, more radical critique of liberalism. This engagement ultimately raises the question of democracy, which will be the subject of the following chapter.

In his famous work *Political Theology*, the German jurist Carl Schmitt claims that "all significant concepts of the modern theory of the state are secularized theological concepts," and he claims that this is true both historically and structurally.[1] Historically, the standard narrative consists of an evolution from religious to secular political forms during the course of Western history. In *The King's Two Bodies*, Ernst Kantorowicz surveys the development of the notion of the sixteenth-century distinction between the king's natural body and political body as it emerges out of a theological background during the Middle Ages. Originally, "the king's duplication of persons is not founded in law or constitution, but in theology: it mirrors the duplication of natures in Christ."[2] So long as modern thought consists of the substitution of secular for religious concepts, this is a familiar story, which can alternately be celebrated or deplored.

For example, Max Weber in his influential work on *Economy and Society* understands what secularization as a process of routinization of charisma, a kind of rationalization and bureaucratization, which ultimately "dis-enchants" a religious view of the world.[3] In a more recent updating of Weber's disenchantment thesis, Marcel Gauchet also argues that Western secularization consists of a progressive disenchantment in *The Disenchantment of the World*.[4] The main difference is that while Weber remains ambivalent about the development of Western rationalism, Gauchet sees this process of disenchantment as positive and as intrinsic to the development of Western monotheism. So the early-twentieth-century view was more compatible with the Enlightenment, which posits a profound break between modern and premodern thought and society, while the late-twentieth-century viewpoint as represented by Gauchet is that there is a crucial dialectical or historical connection between premodern religious and theological attitudes and modern secular understandings. I will return to Gauchet's reading in chapter 8, by way of engaging with and criticizing Jean-Luc Nancy's notion of the deconstruction of Christianity.

But, Schmitt also affirms the idea that there is an intrinsic analogy between jurisprudence and theology based on a shared "systematic structure," not just a temporal succession.[5] Most readers understand Schmitt as indicating and deploring a historical progression of secularization. My reading of Schmitt suggests a more structural interrelationship, which accords with Talal Asad's understanding of religion in *Formations of the Secular*, as I mentioned in chapter 1 but will also discuss below.

Carl Schmitt is a singular and controversial figure, because of his striking insights into the nature of law and politics, his acute criticisms of liberal parliamentarism during the period of Weimar Germany in the 1920s, and later his decision to join the Nazi party and become a major intellectual supporter of Hitler's regime. Although his embrace of Nazism destroyed his academic career and tainted his reputation and legacy, many theorists from across the political spectrum have come to learn from the intensity of Schmitt's thought.[6] This chapter takes its point of departure from Schmitt's conception of political theology, which is not simply historical or developmental but more importantly structural. Here I explore the shape of that structure and at the same time complicate the stereotypical linear progression of religious to secular, whether valued negatively or positively.

The nature and structure of political theology concerns the status of what has come to be called the "postsecular." The postsecular rides the coattails of the postmodern and has become almost a corollary to postmodernism. That is, if modernity is defined in terms of secularity and secularism, then the transition to postmodernity entails a corresponding desecularization and a return to religion in culture and thought. One reading of political theology asserts that in a postmodern context, all of our political concepts are reverting back to their religious origin. As I stated in chapter 1, I want to resist this simplistic reading and suggest a deeper, more complicated relationship among the secular, religious, and political, one that emerges through grappling with the fundamental theo-political problem. Here it is helpful to supplement a consideration of Schmitt with another controversial political thinker, Leo Strauss.

What is the theo-political problem? The conventional answer, which is Strauss's answer, is that the question of political theology concerns the foundation of politics and philosophy. According to Heinrich Meier, who has written about both Strauss and Schmitt, "political theology is a concept that makes a distinction insofar as the determination of its intrinsic concern distinguishes political theology from political philosophy."[7] That is, political theology is absolutely incompatible with political philosophy, which is the way to distinguish Carl Schmitt from Leo Strauss. Meier shows how Strauss's review of Schmitt's book *The Concept of the Political* reveals the hidden center of faith at the heart of Schmitt's thought. Strauss's engagement with the text induces "Schmitt to give answers that make the background of faith, which is omitted by Strauss, emerge all the more clearly."[8] Despite the similarity between Strauss and Schmitt on certain levels, according to Meier their exchange shows the fundamental incompatibility between political philosophy and political theology.

As Meier explains in his book on *Leo Strauss and the Theologico-Political Problem*, "political theology and political philosophy are bound together by the critique of the self-forgetful obfuscation or of the intentional bracketing of what is most important."[9] Both political philosophy and political theology foreground the practical moral question of how best to live. This convergence on the question, however, reveals the incompatibility of their answers. Meier commends Strauss because he forces political philosophy to engage "political theology in the horizon of its strength," even though political philosophy lacks the fundamental ground possessed by political theology. Political theology grounds political life and law in revelation, or faith in divine revelation to human beings. Political philosophy finds such an appeal to divine revelation questionable, but what makes Leo Strauss so significant is that unlike so many modern political philosophers, he takes seriously the possibility of revelation.

According to Meier, "from the very beginning, political theology denies the possibility of a rational justification of one's own way of life."[10] At the same time, Strauss as representative of political philosophy also denies the possibility of a complete rational justification of the best way of life, even as he dedicates his work toward the search for that very justification. For this reason, Leora Batnitzky argues that Strauss's thought functions as a better model for philosophy and politics than that of Emmanuel Levinas, because Strauss delimits philosophy by taking seriously the philosophical possibility of revelation. Batnitzky claims that Strauss leaves open the possibility of revelation as a serious option—a position based on his understanding of medieval Jewish and Islamic thought—rather than foreclosing revelation as a nonrational philosophical option, which most Enlightenment-influenced philosophers do, even those like Levinas who want to valorize religion. Levinas can only affirm religion in a Kantian way, "within the limits of reason alone," while Strauss allows revelation to ground political theology in a way that provides a genuine alternative and opponent to his political philosophy.

Ultimately, the political philosophy of Strauss is incompatible with revealed religion, in this case Judaism, because Judaism and philosophy are "in basic opposition to one another."[11] Batnitzky appreciates Strauss's work from the standpoint of revealed religion, whereas she is more critical of Levinas and his assimilation of Judaism and philosophy. For Batnitzky, Strauss is important not because he exposes and dismisses the appeal to faith in divine revelation, but because Strauss's work represents "an acknowledgement of the fundamental *limitations of philosophy* when it comes to grounding and articulating the bases of ethical and political life."[12] Political philosophy is ungrounded, while political theology grounds itself upon divine revelation, and according to Batnitzky, Strauss acknowledges the viability of the option of political theology, even if he is committed to political philosophy. Many religious and theological thinkers, as well as many secular and philosophical ones, would affirm this fundamental incompatibility between political theology and political philosophy: they make two separate discourses, to paraphrase Dominique Janicaud.

Both Meier and Batnitzky agree with Strauss about the nature of the theo-political problem, which involves making a clear distinction between political theology (Schmitt) and political philosophy (Strauss). However, I want to trouble this confidence in the opposition and incompatibility between political theology and political philosophy from the standpoint of what Schmitt and Strauss both oppose, which is liberalism. For Schmitt, the essence of the political concerns the necessity of making clear and absolute distinctions, above all between friend and enemy, and he accuses modern liberal parliamentarism of confusing these distinctions. The basic liberal principle, according to Schmitt, is that "the truth can be found through an unrestrained clash of opinion and that competition will produce harmony."[13] Public deliberation and discussion comprises the essence of parliamentary democracy, and this deliberation avoids making absolute decisions. Here is Schmitt's famous quip that liberalism exists only "in that short interim period in which it is possible to answer the question 'Christ or Barabbas?' with a proposal to adjourn or appoint a commission of investigation."[14] If the essence of politics is unliberal, then it is also essentially theological, that is, based on the principle of making absolute decisions concerning salvation and damnation, war and peace, life and death. According to Schmitt, "liberal thought evades or ignores state and politics and moves instead in a typical always recurring polarity of two heterogeneous spheres, namely ethics and economics, intellect and trade, education and property."[15] Liberalism avoids and evades conflict, issues of state, and politics, which concern matters of ultimate seriousness insofar as they are essentially theological.

For Strauss, Christianity cannot ground the ethical life, but he is no less concerned with the issue of moral seriousness in political life, and his "Notes on *The Concept of the Political*" makes clear that "Schmitt's entire thesis is entirely dependent upon the polemic against liberalism," and furthermore this polemic is significant precisely insofar as liberalism has failed because it has negated the political, which is essential to being human.[16] Following Nietzsche, Strauss affirms "man's dangerousness," which concerns the seriousness of human life. The danger of liberalism's victory is that it threatens to establish a world without politics and therefore without seriousness. Strauss says that Schmitt "affirms the political because he sees in the threatened status of the political a threat to the seriousness of human life." For this reason, "the affirmation of the political is ultimately nothing other than the affirmation of the moral."[17] Where

Strauss parts with Schmitt is in the grounding of this moral seriousness in a Christian theological faith, such that Schmitt affirms the political provisionally to clear away the ground in order to expose the enemy, rather than affirms the political as such as an end. "Thus what ultimately matters to Schmitt is not the battle against liberalism," as Meier explains in his discussion of the exchange. The attack on liberalism is only "meant to clear the field for the battle of decision, or the theological struggle between "this-worldly and truly spiritual opponents.[18]

This is why Strauss ends his essay with the claim that Thomas Hobbes is the true founder of liberalism, because he argues that Schmitt actually views Hobbes as an enemy, not as a fellow affirmer of the political. Strauss claims that "the critique introduced by Schmitt against liberalism can therefore be completed only if one succeeds in gaining a horizon beyond liberalism." Schmitt presupposes this horizon, but he has not succeeded in showing it because he has to keep it hidden since it is in fact reactionary and dogmatic. "A radical critique of liberalism is thus possible only on the basis of an adequate understanding of Hobbes," which Strauss implies that Schmitt lacks.[19] Hobbes, discussed in chapter 3 as the founder of modern sovereignty, is an enemy for Schmitt precisely because he is not himself liberal, even though he instantiates the modern liberal paradigm.

What is liberalism, and why is it a theo-political problem, especially if one discounts the conception of Schmitt's political theology, which is polemical, reactionary, and dogmatic? Is there a critique of liberalism that is not simply reactionary or conservative? In his thought, Strauss diagnoses, following Nietzsche and Heidegger, the corrosive nihilism of historicism, and as an alternative, he appeals to the ancients in the famous quarrel between the ancients and moderns.[20] Meier claims that Strauss disparages modern life, because modern philosophy and politics envision a world in which humans "remain far beneath the potential of their nature and are capable of actualizing neither their most noble nor their most excellent qualities."[21] Both Schmitt and Strauss affirm a nostalgic and noble view of politics as means to an end, whether for theology (Schmitt) or philosophy (Strauss). Both also disparage or neglect economics and material realities, associating economics with modern liberalism. Schmitt identifies another clear political enemy in Karl Marx, who sees modern liberalism as the development of capitalism under the aegis of the bourgeois class, which then leads to class conflict, revolution, and finally the instantiation of communism. During the 1920s and 1930s, the Communist U.S.S.R. functioned as an alternative for many intellectuals to parliamentary democracy, and in some cases, such as Schmitt, the fear of communism drove him to expose the weaknesses of liberal parliamentarism and become a fascist.

Today, according to conventional wisdom liberal democracy has won its struggle against both communism and fascism, although it is now threatened by Islamic terrorism. At the same time, Strauss and Schmitt have become even more significant for their diagnoses of the problems of liberalism. If liberalism has emerged victorious, why has it been savagely attacked, not only by outsiders but within the citadels of contemporary capitalism? And is this struggle an essentially religious struggle? That is, does the resurgence of religious violence attest to a barbaric step backward, a nativistic irrational reaction against the triumph of global capitalism? Or, are Schmitt and Strauss "right" in their critiques, even if they are wrong in their solutions (and does Strauss even have a solution, other than rereading Plato and Xenophon)?

As already mentioned in chapter 1, insofar as liberalism is intrinsically connected with modern capitalism, liberalism breaks down as capitalism encounters real global limits of land, water, fossil fuels, atmospheric carbon absorption, and other finite natural resources. Capitalism demands and is dependent on indefinite if not infinite growth, but the planet is a finite resource that is being overpopulated and outstripped at exponential rates. Can capitalism exist without growth? I do not know, but I doubt it can, at least in its current form, and in fact as classical liberalism has morphed into a savage neoliberalism that is impoverishing many undeveloped countries to sustain the standard of living of wealthy nations, capitalism has become what Naomi Klein calls "disaster capitalism" or "corporatism," which is consuming the means of economic production themselves to profit from disaster, which is in fact a desperate attempt to fend off disaster itself.[22] I claim in this book that the resurgence of religion in thought and culture around the world represents a symptom of this breakdown of liberal capitalism, and for better or for worse, it augurs a significant transformation.

Constructively, I argue that to fully understand what is going on in thought and in culture, we need to recast the terms of the debate and envision a radical political theology that takes material, worldly things seriously at the same time as it realizes the profound imbrication of religion and politics. This political theology is liberal in Schmittian terms because it does not advocate a clear-cut, polemical division between religion and politics, theology and philosophy, or within religion, politics, and philosophy. At the same time, a radical political theology challenges liberalism at its most basic level, which is that of the market.

According to Karl Polanyi in his book *The Great Transformation*, liberalism in thought and deed concerns the creation of a self-regulating market. Markets have existed throughout human civilization, but they have always been subordinated to other social demands. What distinguishes the modern liberal Western world is the idea of a total market that is completely self-regulating and that treats all phenomena, including land, labor, and money, as commodities. A self-regulating market entails the interconnection of all local markets, which represent every element of economic industry, and their assimilation into "One Big Market."[23] To construct a self-regulating market, labor, land, and money must be interchangeable and treated as commodities; this is a necessary fiction because land, labor, and money are not essentially commodities, but are transformed into commodities through a utopian act of incredible violence. Polanyi details the processes throughout the eighteenth, nineteenth, and early twentieth century by which a self-regulating market is attempted under the name of "free trade." The attainment of a completely self-regulating market is an impossible goal, because "to allow the market mechanism to be sole director of the fate of human beings and their natural environment, indeed of the amount and use of purchasing power, would result in the demolition of society."[24] In fact, the single-minded effort to create a self-regulating market, led by Great Britain but followed by most of the other continental powers, led to the rise of fascism and consequently World War II. According to Polanyi, it was the collapse of the market system in the Great Depression and the abandonment of the gold standard by Great Britain and the United States that destroyed the economic order and allowed fascism to flourish as a result. "In reality," he writes, "the part played by fascism was determined by one factor: the condition of the market system."[25]

This claim may seem striking and extreme, especially since the United States was able to resurrect the gold standard in the wake of the World War II with the accords of Bretton Woods and to replace Great Britain as the leading political and economic power. But despite lip service to market capitalism and the sacrificing of various forms of social welfare from the 1970s until the present, the postwar economic and political order has survived because it has not been based on a totally self-regulating market. The idea of a self-regulating world market has been resurrected after the collapse of the Soviet Union in the notion of global capitalism, although in reality the rollback of regulations and the expansion of foreign investments have resulted from the combined crisis of a scarcity of world energy supplies and the complex financial situation of the American dollar.[26] The current economic situation in the twenty-first century bears some parallels with the 1930s, because the dollar is being challenged as the world's reserve currency. If the dollar no longer functions as the reserve currency, the result could be similar to what happened when most of the nations went off the gold standard in the 1930s, that is, protectionism, fascism, and eventually war.

Polanyi's analysis shows how economics and politics are both linked and separated in liberalism. That is, the role of the state and its policies should be separated from and subordinated to the rules of the market, but in fact this was never entirely the case. Polanyi says that "a self-regulating market demands nothing less than the institutional separation of society into an economic and political sphere."[27] Conservatives like Schmitt and Strauss protest the supplanting of politics in the grand style with technical economics, as well as the attendant confusion that results when economy and politics are separated. Marxism could be said to place politics in the service of economic liberation, which must come about through and beyond liberal capitalism.

In any case, what is clear is that even though the self-regulating market is a fiction or an impossible utopia, we are still not free of what Samir Amin calls the "liberal virus." According to Amin, in the liberal vision of society "social effectiveness is equated by liberals with economic efficiency which, in turn, is confounded with the financial profitability of capital."[28] This process is contributing to the increasing "pauperization" of the majority of people on earth, but the confounding of social good with financial profit works in such a way that most liberals cannot see or disavow the relationship between the increase of poverty and the maximization of wealth.[29] As liberation theologian and former president of Haiti Jean-Bertrand Aristide writes, "the neo-liberal strategy is to weaken the state in order to have the private sector replace the state."[30] The purpose of this privatization, which Klein documents in *The Shock Doctrine*, is the increasing accumulation and concentration of wealth for the elite and the increasing impoverishment of the majority of earth's people. In the 1980s and 1990s, most developing countries and many former communist countries embraced neoliberal policies: "they have opened their economies to the world, lowered tariffs, embraced free trade, and allowed goods and services from the industrialized world to flow in," according to Aristide.[31] And the result?

In 1960 the richest 20% of the world's population had 70% of the world's wealth, today [2000] they have 86% of the wealth. In 1960 the poorest 20% of the world's population had just 2.3% of the wealth of the world. Today this has shrunk to just barely 1%.[32]

Aristide's leadership of Haiti and avocation for the poor proved to be so threatening to the neoliberal and neoconservative elite that the United States led a second coup in 2004 to remove him, as Peter Hallward details in his book *Damming the Flood: Haiti, Aristide, and the Politics of Containment.*[33] Faced with "the unruly threat of 'popular democracy,'" the United States countered with liberal democracy, whose values "have for some time been indistinguishable from those of the transnational elite, and are perfectly compatible with the preservation if not intensification of global inequalities."[34]

For Leo Strauss, the protest against liberalism and *homo economicus* is meant to insist on the moral nature of the human being, and traditional political philosophy assists in that endeavor. For Carl Schmitt, politics must decisively oppose economics to expose the enemy in its most naked sense, the denigration of spiritual humanity to material stuff and the obscuring of the theological war between good and evil. Both, however, fail to grapple explicitly or sufficiently enough with the evils of the self-regulating market, the construction of satanic mills that grind commodified social humanity into dust.[35] Markets in themselves are not evil but become forces of evil when they and corporations trump any and all human interests. The fantasy of modern capitalism is that the free market encapsulates the entire social and political sphere; this fantasy is both impossible to completely enact and detrimental in its effects. Markets of course can and need to function within circumscribed limits.

What is the status of religion in the context of the liberal market? As we can see in John Locke's *Letter Concerning Toleration*, the establishment of liberalism relegates religion to a solely private status, an affair of the heart. Locke writes that "I esteem it above all things necessary to distinguish exactly the business of civil government from that of religion, and to settle the just bounds that lie between the one and the other."[36] Religion should be tolerated so long as it does not impinge upon the actual workings of the state and the market. Politics involves publicity, and what is publicly relevant concerns the establishment, maintenance, and enforcement of markets with the impossible goal of constituting a completely self-regulating market.

This ideal of a self-regulating market functions as a utopian, or religious, ideal, but religious activities should not affect the functioning of the market as such. Religion in a liberal context is private and nonpolitical, at least directly. Here is the separation between modern political philosophy and what passes for political theology: for the former, explicit religious concerns and commitments are banished from political and economic consideration. The political element is foregrounded in early modern political philosophy as the concept and reality of the nation-state takes form, while the more explicitly economic aspects of liberalism are theorized later, beginning with Adam Smith and continuing through the nineteenth century. As Polanyi explains, the political and economic are both conjoined, that is, they both function and work together, and disjoined, or thought as distinguished into two separate realms, especially in the nineteenth century. Although secularism is generally viewed as the absence of religion or religious commitments, what is generally called "the secular" is constituted by the liberal public sphere.

As discussed in chapter 1, Talal Asad's work in *Formations of the Secular* is important for an understanding of the development of modern secularism, even though he fails to specifically address market capitalism in his account. Asad counters Schmitt's historical reading, which sees theological ideas and practices being replaced with secular ones. Asad's genealogy of secularism as an ideology that regulates both the secular and the sacred in political terms complicates a linear straightforward account where secular society simply replaces religious society, for better or for worse. He explains that secularism does not simply entail the negation of religion, but it implies and is based upon a certain "*kind* of religion that enlightened intellectuals . . . see as compatible with modernity." In this case, "only religions that have accepted the assumptions of liberal discourse are being commended, in which tolerance is sought on the basis of a distinctive relation between law and morality."[37] The religious is not replaced by the secular, but secularism as an ideology of the modern liberal nation-state regulates religion, mostly in terms of public and private.

Although many religious and nonreligious people would view the secular as the complete opposite of religion, Asad's genealogy of the secular and of secularism shows their interdependence. He says, "I am arguing that 'the secular' should not be thought of as the space in which *real* human life gradually emancipates itself from the controlling power of 'religion' and thus achieves the latter's freedom."[38] Rather, secularization is also seen as generating *true* religion. Asad details the role that secularization and religion play in the construction of modern nationalism and the rise of capitalist nation-states, and his study shows that the secular is a complex religious form. The secular originates as a term of theological discourse that then paradoxically comes to mean an emancipation from theology as a form of false consciousness, a release that helps to achieve human freedom, which is ultimately a freedom of the market.[39]

As a possible counterargument to my reading of Asad, however, one could return to Leo Strauss and appeal to his idea of persecution. Strauss argues that what we call secular is not new but has always been hidden, requiring that the fundamental struggle between political philosophy and political theology be carried out at least partly in secret. During a time when direct and honest expressions of atheism or secularism would subject the author to the threat of persecution, including even death, he or she had to resort to esoteric means of expression. "Persecution, then," Strauss writes, "gives rise to a peculiar literature of writing, and therewith to a peculiar type of literature, in which the truth about all crucial things is presented exclusively between the lines."[40] In his book *Persecution and the Art of Writing*, Strauss examines Maimonides, Farabi, and Spinoza carefully and esoterically, alert to the distinction between contradictory statements made by these authors. Strauss claims that to our modern eyes, these writers seem to contradict themselves, but this is an effect of their writing under the threat of persecution. He says that as a rule, if an author makes a vulgar or common statement, agreeing with the masses, and then elsewhere makes a statement contradicting this vulgar statement, "the statement contradicting the vulgar view has to be considered his serious view."[41]

If Strauss is correct, then perhaps we can reinstate the absolute opposition between reason and revelation that was discussed above and carefully read the history of Western philosophy as the esoteric struggle of political philosophy over against the predominant political theology, at least until modern times. Strauss argues that political philosophy is sharpened and strengthened from the battle because there is so much at stake, while with the victory of modern liberalism, philosophy's task becomes too easy because it does not have to take political theology seriously as an opponent. I want to appreciate Strauss's insight into persecution, but I want to radicalize it with the psychoanalytic idea of the unconscious. Strauss bases his work and his philosophy on the attempt to discern the intentional and conscious meanings of the philosophers he studies, but the notion of the unconscious ruins this attempt in any complete way. Strauss may reject or resist the idea of the unconscious, but if we take it seriously, then we have to learn to read symptomatically as well. That is, an author may suffer internal rather than simply external persecution, and this may affect and distort the text in various ways. Furthermore, as I suggest below, the idea of the unconscious is important for a radical political theology because it undermines the simple-minded notion of a conscious allegiance to a faith, as if we can always choose *to* believe, what to believe, and how to enact such belief.[42]

The idea of the secular retains an important place in the conception of a radical political theology, as affirmed in chapter 1. A radical political theology refuses the false choice between embracing a determinate historical religion and endorsing a simple-minded secular atheism. Every secular form is residually religious, just as every religious form is inherently secular and at least potentially heretical. We need to think beyond this modern opposition, and the notion of the unconscious helps us do this. Too often the question of religion is put in terms of conscious allegiance based on a Protestant notion of freedom that now seems incredible. Do you believe in this religion, that religion, or no religion at all? Even if the notion of belief is supplemented or replaced by that of practice, this fails to grapple with the radicality of the idea of the unconscious, which means that one's identity, beliefs, and intentional practices may not be determined or fully determinate on the conscious level. (How) do I know what I believe? Am I a Christian? An atheist? A Buddhist? What if I don't know, or am in principle unable to decide the truth? I will return to the political implications of the unconscious in chapter 6, by way of a discussion of the contemporary crisis of law and Deleuze's notion of the event.

Many liberals believe that the main reason to oppose political theology is the problem of religious violence, which has become more visible in our world as liberalism struggles to maintain itself. Why not resolve the theologico-political problem by delinking religion from politics? In response to the contemporary political power of Christian fundamentalism and the Religious Right, intellectuals such as Sam Harris and Christopher Hitchens advocate a resecularization, or a severing of the link between religion and politics.[43] In an essay addressing the religio-political situation in Algeria, Derrida also affirms this separation. Derrida states: "We take a stand for the effective dissociation of the political and the theological."[44] This is a natural and liberal response, but if Asad is right then it cannot work. The secular functions no less than religion as a form of political power. Again, Asad concludes that the categories of "politics" and "religion" turn out to implicate each other more profoundly than we thought, a discovery that has accompanied our growing understanding of the modern nation-state. The concept of the secular cannot do without the idea of religion.[45]

Religion cannot be completely separated from politics, and the idea that it can is a liberal illusion, the fantasy of secularism as an ideology. At the same time, the secular cannot be severed from religion; it is a complex religious form. If Asad is correct that the concept of the secular cannot do without the idea of religion, then this is a postliberal, postmodern, and postsecularist insight. To appreciate Asad's analysis we do not have to choose to affirm or practice a traditional form of religion, but we must recognize the implication of the secular in the religious and, furthermore, the essence of liberal secularism in the concept of the market, which Asad does not explicitly develop.

Can religion do without the notion of the secular? Or without reference to some form of secularization or disenchantment? I would argue that we cannot think religion apart from or without the notion of secular, and that this is the meaning of the term "postsecular," if it has any meaning, although I prefer the term "postsecularism." "Religion" and "secular" are modern terms, and they are interdependent; we cannot think one without the other. The secular cannot be abolished to "save" religion, or a particular institutional or practical form of religiosity. I am complicating the historical evolutionary story where religion disappears and is replaced by the secular. According to Asad's analysis, this is not historically accurate, no matter which side one chooses to affirm. I am acknowledging the *structural* claim of Carl Schmitt in his articulation of a political theology, even if this is not a simple structure, because the religious and the secular cannot simply be disentangled or pulled apart.

As indicated in chapter 1, a radical political theology thinks the theological notion of the *saeculum*, as affirmed by the Death of God theologian Gabriel Vahanian, in terms of what Gilles Deleuze calls a plane of immanence.[46] A secular plane of immanence does not exclude the theological or settle questions of transcendence, but it argues that all discussions of transcendence must at least be referenced on the plane of immanence, which is the minimum consistency necessary to constitute a shared world of intersubjective experience.

We cannot eliminate religion from society or completely separate religion from politics. A secular or postsecularist political theology retains critical resources, however. Radical political theology thinks the embeddedness of the religious in the political and offers insights to help prevent the escalation of violence that threatens when particular religio-political formations, including that of fascism, become predominant. This is not simply the restoration of liberal tolerance, because there exists no neutral, nonreligious public space in which to arbitrate among disputes.

In conclusion, the opposition between secular and religious grounds the distinction between political philosophy and political theology, as seen by Strauss and Schmitt. If the fundamental incompatibility between philosophical rationality and faith in a revealed divine law is quintessentially modern and liberal, then the distinction between political theology and political philosophy begins to crumble. What is the theologico-political problem to which both Schmitt and Strauss point in controversial and insufficient ways? It is the breakdown of liberalism and the crisis of concomitant concepts such as secularity, modernity, and democracy. Political theology in its widest and most radical form concerns the political constitution of society and humanity, and it is residually secular because it attempts to think political theology without a determinate political theology, or what Jacques Derrida calls a "religion without religion." At the same time, it calls its own liberal status into question, not for the sake of a traditional religious or philosophical form nostalgically imagined, nor for the cynical manipulation of those who are duped and controlled by religion in a Machiavellian fashion.

Radical political theology attempts to think a future beyond liberalism, a future that is humane, or failing that, at least human. The question is whether opposing the devastating capitalist market of modern liberalism necessitates opposing democracy. That is, is liberal democracy the only form of democracy or can there be democracy without liberalism? Most opponents of liberalism also oppose democracy, although much of the significance of Hardt and Negri's collaborative project in *Empire* and *Multitude* involves the elaboration of a radical conception of democracy. In the next chapter, I will sketch out some concepts to help us think more deeply about radical democracy.

5. ELEMENTS FOR RADICAL DEMOCRACY

PLASTICITY, EQUALITY, GOVERNMENTALITY

THE PROBLEM OF CONTEMPORARY DEMOCRACY DIRECTLY CONCERNS the crisis of liberalism. On the one hand, liberalism is under attack, both politically and theologically. Liberalism as an ideology is exhausted. On the other hand, a neoliberalism continues to function economically under the surface of a faltering American global empire. Part of the confusion about liberalism is caused by the question of whether it is an economic or a political form. In the modern world dominated by Europe, liberalism has functioned to support both economic capitalism and political democracy. If liberalism ceases to function, then capitalism and democracy must change or become extinct.[1]

Today, we live in a political and theological climate in which liberalism is on the defensive ideologically, although economically neoliberalism has embraced an extremely savage form of capitalism. Democracy is still invoked as the justification for the operation of neoliberal capitalism and contemporary practices of American imperialism, but many people have become more cynical about the present status of democracy in the United States and elsewhere. Two strategies become apparent: one can either abandon democracy in abandoning liberalism and embrace a Machiavellian neocon-servatism where (American) might makes right, or one can try to recuper-ate or restore a vital tradition of democracy. The latter may entail restor-ing liberalism, but it usually entails reforming the most savage aspects of American and global capitalism.

A good example of someone who tries to do the latter is Jeffrey Stout, who attempts to reform and revitalize liberal democracy. In his book *Democracy and Tradition*, Stout defends modern democracy as a tradition against the nostalgic traditionalism of Stanley Hauerwas and Alasdair McIntyre, as well as against what he considers a radical apocalyptic postmodernism.[2] Stout provides a thoughtful and ethical discussion of ways to renew and enrich modern democracy, and he recognizes the fact of plural value-commitments of contemporary Americans as well as the fact that one cannot draw a hard and fast line between religious and secular spheres. Stout affirms that "the social practices that matter most directly to democracy . . . are the discursive practices of ethical deliberation and political debate."[3] But he ends up reduc-ing democracy essentially to social and ethical practices and fails to grapple with its implications in the most unjust effects of contemporary capitalism.

Unfortunately, I do not think it is possible to restore liberal democracy, precisely because liberalism has morphed into a disastrous neoliberalism that provides only a thin veneer of moral justification (free markets) for the unfettered triumph of money and global capitalism, as Naomi Klein analyzes in *The Shock Doctrine*. According to Klein, as discussed in the introduction, acolytes of Milton Friedman at the University of Chicago developed a recipe of economic and political shock therapy that instigates or appropriates a crisis to privatize essential functions of society. The shock doctrine was first applied in Latin American countries in the 1970s then expanded to other areas of the globe in the 1980s and 1990s.

This process culminated in the second Bush administration, whose "shock and awe" reduced Iraq to rubble partially to create a blank slate for corporate capitalism. At the same time in the United States, the administra-tion pushed to sell off the core functions "intrinsic to the practice of govern-ing" to private corporations: "the military, police, fire departments, prisons, border control, covert intelligence, disease control, the public school system, and the administering of government bureaucracies."[4] Corporate capital-ism thrives off of disasters, and the pace has increased over the last three decades. The neoconservative movement is only the culmination of this process in which it is impossible to separate the "military project—endless war abroad, and a security state at home—from the interests of the disaster capitalism complex, which has built a multi-billion dollar industry based on these very assumptions."[5] Democracy is still professed, but the corporatist state is not democratic at the level of human beings. Liberal democracy is dead, something we can only mourn.

If we seek to overcome neoliberalism and to oppose contemporary capitalism, then must we also reject democracy? Is it possible to think or envision a radical democracy beyond liberal or neoliberal capitalism? If we cannot restore democracy, then perhaps we can free ourselves from this specific inheritance of it. In his book *The Politics of Post-Secular Religion*, Ananda Abeysekara claims that the only viable postcolonial future for democracy lies in "un-inheriting," which is "a pathway of thinking about the (aporetic) heritage of our democratic modernity and all its (deferred) promises of the future that we cannot receive or reject."[6] Following Derrida, Abeysekara argues that the democratic promise is always deferred, which renders democracy spectral in a certain sense. We cannot simply inherit or recover it, and the process of un-inheriting democracy necessarily involves mourning.

We can mourn the failure of democracy and its future, if it has one. The opening of un-inheriting also provides an opportunity for conceptualizing a radical democracy. Radical democracy is not the same liberal democracy but a refashioning of democracy anew, an attempt to think democracy beyond liberalism and colonialism, even beyond capitalism. As Aristide claims, "our concept and practice of democracy must make a giant leap forward. We must democratize democracy."[7] Democracy is integrally related to the modern conception of political theology, even if during most of the modern, liberal period democracy was seen as providing an alternative to political theology, a nonreligious, secular space that divorced church and state. As we have seen in the last chapter, however, modern liberalism is not simply divorced from issues of political theology, a fact most visible at the origin of the modern democratic tradition, represented by Spinoza, and at its end, represented by Schmitt, considered separately in chapters 3 and 4. Rivisiting their thoughts about the history of political theology, however, is useful for considering how best to intervene in order to force an opening for thinking about radical democracy.

To fashion concepts to help us think about a radical or democratized democracy, I want to briefly reflect on this modern history of political theology, taking note of its bookends in Spinoza and Schmitt. Spinoza's *Theological-Political Treatise* from 1670 inaugurates an immanent political theology that corresponds to a burgeoning democratic age, whereas Schmitt's *Political Theology*, first published in 1922 and later revised and republished in 1934, arrives at that crisis point when there is the unmistakable realization for many of the breakdown of the modern, liberal democratic order. With Spinoza we encounter a case of political theology that is almost the exact opposite of Schmitt. Whereas Spinoza hearkens the beginning of the modern, liberal, democratic order, Schmitt exposes or perhaps even hastens its end. Whereas Spinoza's theology functions as a political propaedeutic, Schmitt begins with modern political philosophy and lays bare its theological root: "All significant concepts of the modern theory of the state are secularized theological concepts."[8] And finally, Spinoza was almost the prototypical iconoclast, an "outcast twice removed"—to the Jewish community a heretic who was rightly excommunicated at age twenty-four, and to the Christians an "atheist Jew" regarded by his contemporaries as "the most impious and most dangerous man of the century." Schmitt followed his powerful critiques of the foundations of the Weimar Republic by becoming a supporter of Adolf Hitler and a member of the Nazi party (at the invitation of Martin Heidegger).[9]

By taking Spinoza and Schmitt as our models, we might conclude that the exploration and articulation of this modern political theology is the mark of a transitory phase within society and political culture. In addition, bringing them together might help assess what the current theoretical interest in political theology reveals about the world we now inhabit, specifically regarding the nature of the political and the theological. And finally, we might suggest new concepts or images of thought with which we might unite or cut across the specific interests in the materialist, immanent, and postculturalist turns of contemporary thought, interests that converge upon a radical political theology and perhaps culminate in radical democracy, which will be characterized in terms of plasticity and equality in the latter part of the chapter.

First, let us return to the work of Spinoza and Schmitt who together not only represent historical bookends but also opposite ends of the politico-theological spectrum. Spinoza's book was regarded by his contemporaries as "subversive," "blasphemous," and "diabolical," but since has been called "pioneering" and a "neglected masterpiece." It is credited not only with beginning the tradition of higher criticism of the Bible but also with laying out the frame for the modern secular state. While the bulk of the *Tractatus* is more concerned with religious interpretation than political analysis, its primary intent, as Spinoza makes clear in the preface, is both an expression and a defense of the liberal freedoms a modern democratic society affords its citizens as persons of free conscience:

> Now since we have the rare good fortune to live in a commonwealth where freedom of judgment is fully granted to the individual citizen and he may worship God as he pleases, and where nothing is esteemed dearer and more precious than freedom, I think I am undertaking no ungrateful or unprofitable task in demonstrating that not only can this freedom be granted without endangering piety and the peace of the commonwealth, but also the peace of the commonwealth and piety depend on this freedom.[10]

For Spinoza, superstition is incompatible with a free society. Therefore, the task of his religious analysis, which in many ways was antitheological or at least secular in its theological orientation, is to deliver humankind from its ill-founded superstitions and to expose the mystery of despotism to the light of reason. In this way, he divests the sovereign of divine authorization and makes the case for a popular sovereignty wherein authority "is vested in all the citizens, and laws are sanctioned by common consent."[11] As Matthew Stewart puts it, "[Spinoza's] fundamental aim is to replace the reigning theocratic conception of the state with one founded on secular principles."[12]

While the welfare of the people is now raised as the highest and final good—an immanent value befitting a democratic age—this has profound implications for the status of religious authority and the proper place of religion in society. As Spinoza writes, "the welfare of the people is the highest law, to which all other laws, both human and divine, must be made to conform."[13] In the words of Kant, this would be a "religion within the limits of reason alone" but also a religion circumscribed by the will of the people as the right of the state. From here, we cannot help but wonder, once the force of religion is acquired solely from the right of the state, what is to prevent it from becoming yet another tool in the state's apparatus of power? With Spinoza's delimitation of religion, what begins as the defense of freedom— specifically, the freedom of conscience for the citizen and the freedom of the state from religious control—has the stated effect of consolidating the state's power. In so doing the irony emerges that religion has been destroyed as an autonomous intermediary, thereby weakening one of the most potent checks on the state's potential abuse of power.

Spinoza articulates a justification of virtue as power, and he links democratic republicanism with the modern state specifically as it emerged in Holland, albeit only temporarily. The de Witt brothers were murdered in 1672 near the end of his life, and Holland took a more autocratic turn with the consolidation of power by the Stadtholder William of Orange.[14] In his unfinished *Political Treatise*, Spinoza defines sovereignty as the communal "right, which is defined by the power of the people . . . and is possessed absolutely by whoever has charge of affairs of state."[15] If this power "belongs to a council composed of the people in general, then the state is called a democracy."[16] Spinoza provided an understanding of sovereignty as the power of the people that became identified with the form of the modern state in a representative democracy, but there remained some aspect of Spinoza's thought that was anomalous, unassimilable, or "savage" to the modern liberal state, as Negri argues in *The Savage Anomaly*, because for Spinoza this power operates more directly via the *potentia* of the multitude than indirectly through parliamentary councils. As Rocco Gangle suggests in an essay on "Sovereignty and State-Form," Spinoza provides resources to think about sovereignty and democracy beyond the modern nation-state. The immanent power of democratic form may be unlinked from the specific form of the modern state. Gangle claims that "we must find a way to distinguish democracy as a generic form of practice from democracy as a species of the nation-state."[17]

According to Pierre Manent, who fails to consider Spinoza in his intellectual genealogy of modern liberalism, the "democratic project" is essentially paradoxical and duplicitous; it posits a separation between human nature and sovereignty that it then struggles unsuccessfully to overcome. Every "effort to escape division and overcome it only seems to deepen it."[18] Democracy was perhaps a naïve and impossible project from the beginning, and it is interesting to compare Claude Lefort's subtle analysis and critique of communist ideology and utopianism with Manent's critique of liberal democracy. Indeed, at the end of his book *Complications*, Lefort acknowledges the complicity of socialist utopianism in the utopianism of economic liberalism, "the generator of practices that, if they had evolved freely, would have been devastating."[19] In fact, these practices have been devastating, as discussed in chapter 4 in reference to Karl Polanyi.

Returning now to Schmitt, we saw in the previous chapter that he identifies the paradox of liberal democracy primarily to eliminate it. For him, political theology is primarily concerned with the concept of sovereignty, not as democratically conceived by Spinoza but rather as delineated in the state of exception. Political theology is a response to the perceived crisis of political neutralization and is fundamentally undemocratic in the sense that its analysis sees modern democracy naturally and inevitably giving way to the purely administrative economic state. Indeed, an indication of this antidemocratic thrust is given in the famous opening line of the book: "The sovereign is he who decides on the exception."[20] By defining sovereignty by the state of exception and by his equation of theology to politics, Schmitt shows his penchant for a more traditional theology and an authoritarian form of politics where, just as a transcendent and omnipotent God operates outside the bounds of natural law, the sovereign is authorized to disregard every social norm and rule. The state of exception as described by Schmitt is an order without law wherein the state has "the monopoly to decide." As Schmitt writes, "what characterizes an exception is principally unlimited authority, which means the suspension of the entire existing order. In such a situation it is clear that the state remains, whereas law recedes. Because the exception is different from anarchy and chaos, order in the juristic sense still prevails even if it is not of the ordinary kind."[21]

Schmitt's rendering of sovereignty as the state's monopoly to decide is a far cry from the democratic ambitions of Spinoza. It also reveals a different employment of theology. Whereas Spinoza is read as the prototypical secular theologian whose immanent critique of religion, like Marx centuries later, was the beginning of a much broader political program and democratic revolution, Schmitt draws on a classical theological image of a transcendent God as an analogue to, and rationale for, his critique of the contradictions and emptiness of the liberal democratic order. For Schmitt, sovereign power is essentially theo-political, and I tried to suggest in chapter 4 how the more conventional, diachronic reading of Schmitt, where secular concepts simply replace theological ones, is more conservative and less intrinsically significant than his structural argument about the implication of political and theological conceptions.

This concept of sovereignty from Schmitt has recently come under discussion by a number of political theorists, most prominently Giorgio Agamben, who demonstrates the endemic dangers when the state of exception becomes the contemporary norm or working paradigm in so-called liberal democracies. I will return to Agamben's reading of Schmitt in his book *State of Exception* in the discussion of the crisis of modern law in chapter 6. Other philosophers, such as Jacques Derrida, have argued, most notably in his book *Rogues*, that the political concept of sovereignty has been rendered virtually obsolete. For Derrida, as we saw in chapter 2, not only has the notion of sovereignty been rendered obsolete by global capital, but the very notion itself contributes to the abuse of the law and is thus in contradiction to democracy itself, particularly a democracy "to-come" that is essentially related to justice. Likewise, as suggested in the introduction and in chapter 3, Michael Hardt and Antonio Negri have suggested what might be termed a "postnational" or "transnational" form of political sovereignty. This critical intervention on the part of Hardt and Negri is conducted to create a more radical practice and form of democracy after classical modern liberalism's demise. In his book *The Savage Anomaly*, Negri has also attempted to frame this radical democracy using Spinoza as read through Marx and Deleuze, as we saw in chapter 3. Here the *potentia* of the multitude, which is composed of a constitutional organization based on the antagonism of subjects, is affirmed and contrasted with the determinate *potestas* of the state in its actual sovereign Power.[22]

In light of these fundamental critiques of the concept of sovereignty, we must ask what a political theology might look like that is not predicated on this notion, or at least not oriented around this concept of sovereignty. Specifically, what concepts or forms of thought might help us to reconceptualize democracy in a radical or revolutionary way? While Hardt and Negri speak of the multitude as an already existing subject that is the engine of social production, they simultaneously acknowledge that it still "needs a political project to bring it into existence." Yet, their political project remains explicitly bereft of the religious or the theological. That is to say, though mindful of Schmitt and critical of the basic assumptions operative in modern liberal political philosophy, they still assume a wall of separation between religion and politics and still remain within a secularist orientation. Therefore, what is still needed is an alternative political theology that provides a theological supplement to this conceptual revolution in the basis of democracy itself. The remainder of this chapter will offer tools to help conceptualize a radical democratic thinking that contributes to a radical political theology in a postsecularist context.

Most forms of political theology are conservative or reactionary insofar as they oppose modern liberalism and seek to restore a more traditional state of affairs by grounding political practice in religious doctrines. I seek the reverse: to open up a new radically democratic space for political theory and practice with a different understanding of religion. That is, in a postsecularist context, it is no longer possible to simply oppose the religious and the secular, which means that religion cannot be divorced from politics. But most contemporary versions of political theology seek to restore a conservative or nonmodern version of religious authority and practice, whereas my project offers a radical political theology that affirms a conception of democracy beyond liberal capitalism.

The passage from Spinoza to Schmitt forms a trajectory of modern politico-theological thinking. To break this circuit open for a more radical political theology, I want to insert three concepts associated with three important thinkers of our contemporary social condition: plasticity as theorized by Catherine Malabou; equality as understood by Jacques Rancière; and finally, governmentality as analyzed by Michel Foucault. These three conceptions provide useful tools for political analysis, and the first two particularly offer potential interventions to help create a radically democratic thinking and practice.

To begin with governmentality is to acknowledge the continuing importance of Michel Foucault's work. In his 1977–1978 lectures at the Collège de France, published as *Security, Territory, Population*, he provides a genealogy of the apparatuses of the modern state to describe new forms of governmentality. Although Foucault does not mention Spinoza and barely references Schmitt in these lectures, his discussion covers much of the same territory. The concept of governmentality, which means the art of governing a people or managing a state, "correspond[s] to a society controlled by apparatuses of security."[23] Modern governmentality is composed out of distinct forms:

> [first] from the archaic model of the Christian pastorate, and second, by drawing support from a diplomatic-military model, or rather technique, and finally, third, how it could only acquire its present dimensions thanks to a set of very specific instruments, the formation of which is exactly contemporaneous with the art of government, and which is called, in the old, seventeenth and eighteenth century sense of the word, police.[24]

According to Foucault, the art of governing is most directly derived from a pastoral, Christian function, that of caring for human souls. The modern state is born when "governmentality became a calculated and reflected practice."[25] The modern European state replaces the medieval empire and achieves a perspective of "indefinite governmentality" in which states become viewed as permanent entities without any external telos.[26] Here the pastoral function is internalized into state form, which state adopts the techniques and mechanisms of disciplinary power. Ultimately, this pastoral art of governmentality and these disciplinary techniques are wedded to an idea and institution of police that emerges in the seventeenth and eighteenth centuries. The concept of the police was originally much broader than it is now and concerned the entire population, including the numbers, health, activity, and circulation of people. Foucault says that "what police has to govern, its fundamental object, is all the forms of, let's say, men's coexistence with each other."[27] This fundamental object is life and concerns what Foucault famously calls "bio-power." The ultimate exercise of governmentality, its sovereign form, is bio-power. The police are the primary instrument of this bio-power, which regulates life in its totality, including particular religions. Ultimately, concepts such as "society, economy, population, security, and freedom are the elements of the new governmentality whose forms we can still recognize in its contemporary modifications."[28]

But at the end of his lectures, Foucault sketches the significance of "counter-conducts" against the state and its governmentality, which take the form of a revolutionary eschatology in which the "indefinite governmentality of the state will be brought to an end and halted."[29] Just as a pastoral form of religion infused modern governmentality, a religious eschatology has fueled these counter-conducts. There are two main forms of counter-conduct. The first is "the affirmation of an eschatology in which civil society will prevail over the state," and the second is an anarchic breaking with all bonds of obedience. This latter version of eschatology takes "the form of the absolute right to revolt, to insurrection, and to breaking all the bonds of obedience."[30] According to Foucault, there is not a direct link between the religious movements in early modern Europe and this revolutionary eschatology, but there is a filiation. Furthermore, these counter-conducts work both with and against the governmentality of the state in complex ways.

Following Foucault, we can oppose the indefinite governmentality and bio-power of the state with an indefinite, or infinite, eschatology. This eschatology is a permanent counter-conduct or counter-governmentality that serves radical democratic action and takes a religious or quasireligious form, whether or not it has a determinate religious content. The second concept involves thinking and enacting a radical equality, taken primarily from the work of Jacques Rancière. Equality can function as an eschatological counter-conduct, in Foucault's terms, because it works against existent forms of governmentality. In books such as *The Philosopher and His Poor*,

Disagreement, and *The Ignorant Schoolmaster,* Rancière demonstrates how philosophy in its ancient, aristocratic forms and its modern, progressive ones is based on a fundamental commitment to upholding inequality and denying or suppressing revolutionary ideas and people who reject social and intellectual inequality.

In a more recent book, *The Hatred of Democracy,* Rancière shows the link between equality and democracy, and exposes the antipathy that democracy generates even in people who profess faith in democracy. He isolates and critiques a new form of "antidemocratic discourse" that associates the terrors of totalitarianism with "the very essence of the democratic revolution."[31] This fear of radical democracy is not new; it is prefigured in Plato, for whom democratic law is "nothing but people's pleasure for its own sake, the expression of the liberty of individuals whose sole law is that of varying mood and pleasure, without any regard for collective order."[32] The problem with democracy lies deeper than simple concern with pleasure, however, because democracy itself is responsible for the ultimate political crime, which is the crime against kinship. According to Rancière, politics proper begins when the power of birth is undermined. Democracy "signifies a rupture with the order of kinship," which attempts to organize "the human community without any relation to God-the-father."[33]

Democracy founds politics, but every determinate political organization desires to banish democracy and reestablish an oligarchy based on birth or wealth. Politics itself, which is essentially democratic, is the "foundation of a power to govern in the absence of [natural] foundation."[34] The power of the people to govern is not the sovereign power of the majority or the population, but simply the power of anyone at all, "the equality of capabilities to occupy the positions of governors and of the governed."[35] Rancière traces some of the transformations of governmentality and politics in the modern period, similarly to Foucault's more detailed analyses in his lectures. The idea of equality is revolutionary despite the attempts to contain, deny, and destroy it. Society exists because of inequality, and we must renounce any faith in a utopian society that will equalize the unequal. "Unequal society does not carry an equal society in its womb," claims Rancière. "Rather, egalitarian society is only ever the set of egalitarian relations that are traced here and now through singular and precarious acts."[36] Democracy provokes fear and hatred among those constrained to defend privileges of wealth and kinship, but it liberates anyone strong enough to "know how to share with anybody and everybody the equal power of intelligence, it can . . . inspire courage, and hence joy."[37] This joy is not completely separated from Spinozist joy, as Negri's work helps us to understand. Democracy is intrinsically egalitarian and works against sovereign power and privilege, including the conducts of governmental bio-power. According to Rancière, equality is not a given state or situation, and it is also not a utopian achievement. We will never create a society that is equal in fact. Equality, however, is an eschatological presupposition, a religious right of indefinite revolt against inequality in the name of God, or justice, or freedom, or whatever other name is invoked.

In an essay discussing the concept of democracy, Alain Badiou follows the trajectory of Rancière's work, although he distrusts the normative consensus that has accrued to the word: "In fact, the word 'democracy' concerns what I shall call *authoritarian opinion*," because "it is forbidden, as it were, not to be a democrat."[38] On the one hand, democracy is a state-form, a figure of sovereignty or power, in which case it cannot properly be a philosophical concept. On the other hand, "democracy" may still be relevant "*as long as democracy is grasped in a sense other than a form of the state*," as we also saw in Gangle's essay on Spinoza.[39]

Insofar as democracy can be severed from its state-form, which would be necessarily be a radical democracy, it "presents equality" in the sense that it strives for "the impossibility, in the situation, of every non-egalitarian statement concerning this situation."[40] Following Rancière, Badiou sharpens the opposition between democracy and the state, because equality is intrinsic to a philosophical concept of democracy, and because a state is naturally non-egalitarian when the essential function is "the non-egalitarian inventory of human beings."[41] The modern nation-state is the locus of representative liberal democracy; to think democracy radically, we must think and practice democracy beyond or without the state as its precondition. This does not mean that states do not or will not continue to exist, but democracy cannot be shackled to the state. The restriction of democracy to the state in modern representative democracy constrains the power of the people to favor the free markets of liberal capitalism, where profits always count more than people.

We cannot simply construct an equal society, at least in a state, but we can employ the eschatological potentiality inherent in human being in revolutionary ways. A radical political theology is not the reinstantiation of a properly sovereign divine power but rather the disarticulation of power as such. There is no absolute Other outside of the plane of immanence in which we think and live, but this plane is not a well-rounded sphere. Plasticity configures and disfigures our plane, even as it configures and disfigures our thought.

Plasticity is a Hegelian concept from the *Phenomenology of Spirit*, articulated powerfully by the philosopher Catherine Malabou. In her book *Plasticity at the Dusk of Writing*, Malabou explains, building on the work of Hegel, Heidegger, and Derrida, that for her plasticity involves "the capacity to receive form . . . and the capacity to give form," as well as the explosive "power of annihilation of form."[42] Plasticity is not passive flexibility or malleability; it refers to the shaping, folding, and even explosiveness of form, our forms of thought, our situations, and even our brains. Plasticity suggests that we need new configurations of philosophy of religion and political theology to adequately think contemporary figurations of culture and life. Our concepts and our bodies are marked by this fundamental but complex and polyvalent plasticity, and we possess opportunities for experimental modes of thinking and living democratically.

Malabou opposes the plasticity of form, which exceeds simple presence, to the Levinasian or Derridean trace, which refers more directly to the absence of form.[43] Plasticity is immanent, whereas the trace evokes a distant transcendence. She articulates a vision where plasticity functions as the motor-schema of philosophy, which replaces modern, Western, linear history with a more complex "ultra-historical configuration of the world."[44] This ultra-historical configuration is based on a neuronal or neuroplastic understanding that Malabou develops in her book *What Should We Do with Our Brain?* Neuroplasticity characterizes the nature of our brains, which work to give form, make connections, receive forms, and possess the ability to repair broken connections and forge new ones.

Recent discoveries in the neurosciences are among the most important and provocative developments for human knowledge and self-understanding, but Malabou argues that we have not yet developed a complex enough theoretical understanding to fully incorporate the radical implications of these events.[45] The plasticity of our brains makes us free, allowing us to create our history in political terms. According to Malabou, plasticity allows us to make our history by "seizing the link between the genetically non-determined aspect at work in the constitution of our brains and the possibility of a social and political non-determinism, in a word a new liberty, a new signification of history."[46] That is, plasticity names the connection between our brains and our politics and names it in a radically decentralized and democratic way.

Contemporary neoliberal global capitalism offers an ideological account of the brain, one that hierarchizes its functions and turns it into a command and control center that imposes order upon flexible workers. By contrast, Malabou's account of plasticity offers ways to think not simply the brain, but the organization of our thoughts and our lives in a material and egalitarian way. This democratic plasticity resonates with the equality asserted by Rancière, and it works against the modern and postmodern forms of governmentality analyzed by Foucault. The activity of plasticity in its passive, productive, and explosive forms generates another possible world, what Malabou calls an "*altermondialisme biologique.*"[47]

In Malabou's explanation of the concept of plasticity, the active shaping and the passive reception of form work together, one could say dialectically. Malabou's signature notion of plasticity combines these functions with an understanding of form itself as explosive or destructive. This destructive element of plasticity is not the whole of plasticity, but it is what makes plasticity such an important concept today. The explosion of form, which is indicated in the phrase "plastic explosives," refers to the charge that immanently animates our brains, our lives, and our thought. Destructive plasticity is painful and destructive,[48] but it is also the charge that blasts open the continuum of historical order that coalesces in governmentality. According to Walter Benjamin, a historical-materialist approach to history seizes a "revolutionary chance" to "blast a specific era out of the homogeneous course of history."[49] This chance is not simply antireligious but constitutes what Benjamin calls a weak (or nonsovereign) messianic power. Malabou assimilates this weak, explosive charge to form itself, which provides a way to think the forceful generation of equality and democracy in a religious, alter-worldly counter-conduct.

Plasticity is at work in the brain, but Malabou does not simply describe a state of affairs. Following the nature of this plasticity, she develops and deploys it in important social, philosophical, and political ways. Human society is plastic not *because* human brains are neuroplastic, but human plasticity is our social brain, our ability to think and act. To create and shape another world, to think and live differently, is extremely difficult but also absolutely necessary because of material inequality, scarcity of natural resources, and global climate change. The struggle for diminishing resources may transmute liberal capitalism into something more akin to fascism, which is why we need to work for a radical democracy that is committed to ideal and material equality and willing to experiment with new forms of governmentality. Religion is not extrinsic to this process but a vital part of it, though less obviously so than in the noisy violence of the fundamentalists, many of whom wittingly or unwittingly reinforce global capitalism. Here religion is not restricted to or understood solely to be intentional belief, as in most versions of Protestant Christianity and liberal modernity.

For many people, religion is narrowly viewed as the theoretical commitment to this or that prepositional truth-claim. For me, as evidenced by the studies of many historians of religion, religion extends beyond belief to incorporate a wide range of orientations, activities, and social practices. As suggested at the end of the previous chapter, the significance of incorporating psychoanalytic theory into religious studies is the recognition that belief resides at a conscious level of a subject, while important questions remain about unconscious personal and social processes. Religion is not just a commitment to supporting a social order; religion is not completely convertible with the social as Emile Durkheim suggests. Sociologically, the only way to resist particular social and political forms is to appeal to another social and political order, usually an ancient order that is nostalgically invoked in comparison to the present order. This perspective, however, is fundamentally conservative, and I oppose a conservative understanding of religion not as wrong but as limited and incomplete. Here, in the context of radical theology, religion is the eschatological commitment to democracy and to the need to revolt in order to create and recreate democracy anew, at every moment.

The religious supplement to the project of radical democracy is not merely a supplement, but rather an inherent aspect of the force of such an attempt. Explosive plasticity is inherently religious not in its invocation of an external transcendence, but in its deployment of an immanent, nonsovereign power directly to life and thought. Plasticity and equality become pragmatic forms of counter-conduct opposing the predominant neoliberal and neoconservative forms of governmentality that capture and constrain life for the service of bio-power. Offered here are elements to configure political theology differently due to the extraordinary confla(gra)tion of politics and religion today. Plasticity and equality can be seen as contemporary theoretical forms of potentiality beyond liberalism; that is, they constitute forms of potentiality rather than forms of present actuality, as discussed earlier in this book in reference to Derrida, Negri, Agamben, and Deleuze. I will return to the idea of plasticity in the last chapter, where it will be contrasted with messianicity as an immanent form of freedom.

6. LAW BEYOND LAW

AGAMBEN, DELEUZE, AND THE UNCONSCIOUS EVENT

THIS CHAPTER ENGAGES A KEY ASPECT OF DEMOCRACY AND contemporary political theory, which is also a central theological notion, that of law. Representative democracy is based on procedural laws that express the will of the majority and also protect minorities from injustice. Representative democracy also prevents the concentration of tyrannical power, at least in theory, with an institutional separation of powers. Unfortunately, for many people today laws are seen as not only arbitrary and ineffectual but also, more importantly, as structurally unjust rules that benefit the financial elite. As this trust in the lawful forms of representative democracy breaks down, the main alternative to cynicism and the embrace of a might-makes-right approach is the increasing attraction of a literalist or scripturalist divine law that limits and authorizes human law. As an alternative to either of these options, in this chapter I develop the idea of a law beyond law that is more compatible with my vision of radical democracy. This law beyond law is the result of a productive but in some respects unconscious event, and I appeal to Gilles Deleuze in my understanding of the event. Before turning to Deleuze, however, I want to utilize Giorgio Agamben's theorization of bio-politics to generalize Carl Schmitt's state of exception in order to set up the problem of law.

A major aspect of the crisis of contemporary democracy today concerns the notion of law, which can be witnessed in fiercely contested disputes concerning, on the one hand, the nature and present status of the United States Constitution, the Bill of Rights, and presidential signing statements in domestic laws and policies and, on the other, the status of International Law, including the applicability of the nuclear Non-Proliferation Treaty and the Geneva Conventions to contemporary and potential conflicts in Afghanistan, Iraq, Palestine, Iran, and North Korea. For many observers, the rule of law appears to be in serious danger, if not already completely compromised by what Jacques Derrida calls "the reason of the strongest" in *Rogues*.[1] The most important question, which cuts right to the heart of democracy, is the relationship between law and reason, on the one hand, and law and force, on the other. Democracy is usually predicated on the idea of the expression, representation, and actualization of the strongest reason, at least in a majority of subjects. That is, the strongest or best reason should decide the case. But, a rogue state enforces its own reason, its own interests, and therefore institutes the reason of the strongest. If we do not believe that any state acts from any other reason than its national interests, then every state is a rogue, including and especially the most powerful, the United States.

This problem may appear new, but it was theorized in the early twentieth century by Carl Schmitt in works such as *Political Theology* and *The Concept of the Political*. In chapter 4, I analyzed Schmitt's general understanding of sovereignty and its relation to political theology and modern liberalism and in this chapter I want to focus

ing about law, largely in cc

in *State of Exception*. Acc

and political legitimacy li

coincides with the legality

istration's practice of utiliz

Military Commissions Act

As the famous opening

eign is he who decides on th

the "exception" refers to un

without charge or trial ind

Schmitt argues that the tru

suspend valid law."[4] Furthe

[Handwritten annotation: Kahn disputes this reading of Schmitt — as exception is problematic outside + inside norm]

exception founds politics as such for Schmitt, because only a political entity has the capacity to be "the decisive entity for the friend-or-enemy grouping; and in this . . . it is sovereign," as Schmitt writes in *The Concept of the Political*.[5] That is, politics is based on the distinction between friend and enemy, and the sovereign decision is the ability to decide who is a friend and who is an enemy ("You're either with us or with the terrorists").

For classical Enlightenment political thinkers such as John Locke or Jean-Jacques Rousseau, sovereignty is more essentially identified with the legislative power, which is the law-making power of the general or popular will.[6] As I have already discussed, modern democracy is based on the idea of popular sovereignty, the sovereignty of the people, which replaces that of a monarch. This popular sovereignty is then expressed in elected representatives. According to Rousseau, sovereignty is indivisible and infallible because it expresses the general (rather than the individual) will, which is why "no exemption from law will ever be granted, on any ground whatsoever, in a well-regulated government."[7] We may argue that law has always been a façade created by the strongest to veil their interests from the weak, cloaking those interests in the guise of universal law. And in part this process hides and justifies modern capitalism, as I discussed in chapter 4.

Even if this is the case, however, we still need to carefully analyze and understand how sovereignty and political power has been gradually dislocated from law during the twentieth century. Schmitt discerned the disjunction of sovereignty from law, and he tried to avoid the "worst" alternative of dictatorship by grounding the sovereign decision in judicial power, according to Giorgio Agamben's reading in *State of Exception*.[8] Unfortunately, however, without a strict separation of judicial and executive powers, the state of exception becomes the rule. Agamben argues that in this situation, which characterizes the contemporary United States, "the juridico-political system transforms itself into a killing machine."[9] Today, the executive sphere of government has set itself up above the judicial and (in particular) the legislative branches of the U.S. government, thwarting the traditional checks-and-balances framework set up by the Founders of the nation in the Constitution. Congress becomes continually more irrelevant to a strong executive bent on usurping its law-making powers. This situation has not substantially changed even after a change in administration with the presidential election of 2008.

According to Agamben, the crisis of law today is that it has no power to enforce itself because sovereignty, the living force of law, has been stripped out of it. This crisis in Western legitimacy generated by the dissociation of sovereignty from law characterizes what Agamben calls bio-politics, following Michel Foucault. Bio-politics is the direct application of political force to life, what Agamben calls "bare life," without any mediation or amelioration by law or social category. Formal law is divorced from bare life, which leads to the contemporary crisis of law and its exacerbation by exceptional and cynical acts of political force.

One response to the current situation of bio-politics is the effort to reconstruct society on the basis of religious law, most visibly monotheistic Biblical or Qur'anic Law. For example, as mentioned in the introduction, Christian Reconstructionism as elaborated by R. J. Rushdoony in *The Institutes of Biblical Law* sees the reinstitution of Mosaic Law as the antidote to "the increasing breakdown of law and order" in contemporary society.[10] For Reconstructionists, the Christian understanding of the Mosaic Law as encapsulated in the Ten Commandments forms the basis for social organization. According to Gary North, "Christians need to abandon all traces of natural law theory" and establish "righteous civil government [as] a legitimate means of evangelism" based solely on revealed biblical law.[11]

While Christian Fundamentalism emerged in the 1890s to articulate a place of refuge in a godless world, this new fundamentalism favors remaking society, first in the United States and then the world, on the basis of God's fundamental laws. For Christian Reconstruction, biblical law involves "building a new world by means of . . . God's permanent moral and institutional blueprints." In this context, a reconstructed United States becomes the means by which "whole nations are disciplined by Christ."[12] Christian Reconstructionism is a form of Christian Dominionism, an effort to assert Christian principles and power in contemporary life. According to Chris Hedges, "Dominionism is a theocratic sect with its roots in a radical Calvinism. It looks to the theocracy John Calvin implanted in Geneva, Switzerland, in the 1500s as its political model."[13] Dominionism uses the opportunities afforded by democratic society, but its goal is a Christian theocracy. Some believers see this contemporary Calvinist theocratic neofundamentalism as the only genuine alternative to the skepticism of a social and legal relativism that takes refuge in moral feelings or the cynical manipulation of law by power.

Fundamentalist recourse to divine law is not restricted to Christianity, of course, but also applies to conservative and puritanical forms of Islam, particularly Wahhabism and Salafism and their influence on popular twentieth-century groups such as the Muslim Brotherhood and Jamaat-I Islami.[14] Wahhabism and other forms of neotraditionalist or Salafi Islam seek to restore original Islam, but their restoration of *sharia* is more extensive and strict than it was in Muhammad's time.[15] As Tamara Sonn points out, Islamism serves to rigorously separate everything that is foreign from Islam, which is "the solution."[16] The problem to which Islam is the solution is the basic unfairness of Western models of law and justice, but the situation of Islamic fundamentalism also points to the breakdown of traditional Islamic law. The alternative, after the disappointments of twentieth-century movements embracing socialism, Marxism, and Arab nationalism, is a return to Islamic law, which parallels the emergence of Christian Reconstruction. For example, the primary work of Abu A'la Mawdudi, the founder of Jamaat-I Islami, is entitled *Islamic Law and Constitution*, and Islamic law is presented as the resolution of all current problems.[17] This understanding of Islamic law is simplistic, utopian, and incoherent, according to Muslim legal scholars like Khaled Abou El Fadl. Puritans such as 'Abd al-Wahhab, Mawdudi, and Sayyid Qutb "imagined Islamic law to be a cure-all," but this was a response to a situation in which the authority of Muslim jurists has been undermined and their functions appropriated by technocratic nonexperts.[18] According to Abou El Fadl, "with the explosion in self-declared experts in Islamic law, and the absence of credible institutions that can discredit or vouch for the qualifications of fatwa issuers, there is complete chaos in the world of Islamic law."[19]

Sonn also argues that the development of recent expressions of political Islam is marked by "utopian visions and a defensive outlook," which distinguishes it from the more optimistic and aggressive tones of some recent Christian fundamentalist expressions.[20] In the United States by contrast, conservative religion is commonly used to promote the spread of global capitalism. Christian and Islamic neofundamentalisms, then, are distinguished mainly by whether they aggressively promote themselves through a strategic alliance with capitalism (Christianity) or defensively resist the destabilizing economic and military effects of Western-capitalist expansion (Islam). But they share a similar approach to law. In his analysis of *Globalized Islam*, Olivier Roy shows how most of the concepts Muslim neofundamentalists use are borrowed from the West. For example, "debates on sharia, women and legal punishments are regularly expressed in terms that fit modern Western concerns or even pretend to show how Western concepts are better implemented in Islam."[21]

According to my reading, the significance of religious law today in Islam, Christianity, and other religions is related to the destabilizing expansion of global capitalism and is a reaction to the contemporary crisis of law. This reaction takes the form of a "return of the repressed," where the law that has been abandoned by cynical neo-Realism is reactivated in broad, simplistic, and literalistic ways. This embrace of a divine law that takes textual and scriptural form becomes a panacea for all social, economic, and moral problems, and in its intensity is expressed in powerful and dangerous ways, which may also be channeled to serve the interests of both the weakest and the strongest.

If this analysis is correct, then one way to understand the current "clash of civilizations" between Islam and the West, which is sometimes explicitly identified as Christian and other times secularized as "free," "liberal," or "democratic," is to see this conflict at least in part as an ideological superstructure that masks deeper military and economic forces—including issues of finance and energy—at work in shaping our biopolitical world. The fundamental symptom of these political and economic forces then seems to be the noncoincidence of law and power, a crisis in the status, applicability, and enforceability of law itself.

In response to these forms of reconstructionist fundamentalism posing as traditionalism, Western liberals often take a defensive posture and nostalgically attempt to recover forms of Enlightenment faith in law and reason. Unfortunately, these attempts are unsuccessful because they do not acknowledge the depth of the crisis of law that Carl Schmitt was one of the first to expose. Other intellectuals abandon liberalism out of intellectual honesty and become (neo)conservatives, but this is a desperate and cynical move, one that is ultimately nihilistic. Law is upheld as legal force by neoconservatives only insofar as it conserves the social order and promotes and protects the established powers, which wittingly or unwittingly serves the bio-political machine. Many intellectuals and politicians influenced by Leo Strauss fall into this category.[22]

To provide a constructive alternative to this contemporary crisis of law, I will briefly discuss Agamben's understanding of the relationship between law and life. Agamben poses the problem of contemporary bio-politics, and he hints toward a solution but does not develop it in detail. To sketch out a potential solution, after my reading of Agamben I will turn to Gilles Deleuze to sketch a thinking of law as the result of what Deleuze calls an event. The event is compatible with the psychoanalytic idea of the unconscious, and

Deleuze is also read from the standpoint of the work of Jacques Lacan, Alain Badiou, and Slavoj Žižek. A post-Lacanian reading of Deleuze, as well as Deleuze and Guattari, provides resources to think law productively beyond determinate and conscious law; that is, beyond the nostalgia for the recovery of liberal, Enlightenment forms of law. At the same time this reconstruction of law as unconscious event avoids both the literalistic reading of conservative religious law and the nihilistic reading of cynical neorealism.

In *State of Exception*, the follow-up to his important book *Homo Sacer*, Agamben analyzes the corruption of law using its linkage with a state of bare life and the violence that is authorized under the name of a state of exception which ultimately becomes the rule. According to Agamben, reading Derrida's famous essay "Force of Law" with Schmitt's political philosophy generates a conception of the force of law without law, which Agamben writes as "force-of-law." He claims that "the state of exception is an anomic space in which what is at stake is a force of law without law (which should therefore be written: force-of-law)."[23] This is a logical paradox, a suspension of law that paradoxically founds law, and Agamben analyzes this situation in the context of Roman Law. The sovereign (Caesar) is both inside and outside the law, but his ultimate authority resides in this anomic space, in being a state of exception to the law. The suspension of law in the case of martial law or a state of emergency brings law beyond itself, delivers it up to another law, that of force, the force-of-law. Any acts committed during the suspension of law belong to a nether realm, a quasimythical or mystical space beyond the sphere of law. The state of exception enacted in a state of emergency or martial law is not exactly a dictatorship, Agamben claims, but rather a state of necessity that constitutes a judicial void, "a space devoid of law, a zone of anomie in which all legal determinations—and above all the very distinction between public and private—are deactivated."[24] Here, the judicial and executive powers by their nature devise and enact a space beyond law, a space that renders the legislature power irrelevant.

Agamben uses the thought of Walter Benjamin to radicalize Schmitt's thought in a way that applies very clearly to contemporary American politics: the state of exception, the emergency state of a war on terror, becomes the rule, the norm, the ever-present reality which will never come to an end, just as former Vice President Cheney claimed that the War on Terror "will not end in our lifetime." Benjamin reads the crisis of fascism over against Schmitt's infamous support of the Nazi regime in a radical way, and Agamben shows how this situation characterizes contemporary American law as well:

Now that any possibility of a fictitious state of exception—in which exception and normal conditions are temporally and locally distinct—has collapsed, the state of exception "in which we live" is Real and absolutely cannot be distinguished from the rule. Every fiction of a nexus between violence and law disappears here: there is nothing but a zone of anomie, in which a violence without any juridical form acts.[25]

The state of exception in which we live contains at its center as "the 'ark' of [its] power . . . essentially an empty space, in which a human action with no relation to law stands before a norm with no relation to life."[26]

At the conclusion of his book, Agamben explains that the bio-political machine works by suspending law and life, even as it keeps them together in that very suspension or state of exception. We live in a worldwide state of exception, in which "the normative aspect of law can thus be obliterated and contradicted with impunity by a governmental violence that—while ignoring international law externally and producing a permanent state of exception internally—nevertheless still claims to be applying the law."[27] Now, Agamben forecloses any possibility of return to a classical state of law, and he cautions against nostalgia for the liberal Enlightenment. He argues, following Benjamin, that we must break apart the relationship between life and law to disable the bio-political machine. This is "the only true political action . . . that which severs the nexus between violence and law."[28] He poses the question of a "pure law" that "is the question of a possible use of law after the deactivation of the device that, in the state of exception, tied it to life."[29]

Agamben thus appeals to Benjamin at the conclusion of *State of Exception* for the notion of a "pure law," freed from bio-politics and disentangled from life. According to Agamben, the "zone of indiscernability" of law established by the state of exception, while negative in its present effects, could potentially represent an opportunity to radically construct a "pure law" that is messianic but also immanent, because it would be a law that is not grounded in life, morality, scripture, or institutions. What form would such a "pure law" take? Agamben leaves this idea undeveloped, but I want to reflect further on the idea of a pure law, which would consist of a "law beyond law."

In his essay "Force of Law," which serves as a key resource for Agamben's reflections, Derrida names such a law beyond law "justice." He claims: "I want to insist at once to reserve the possibility of a justice, indeed of a law [*loi*] that not only exceeds or contradicts law but also, perhaps, has no relation to law."[30] Justice exceeds law; while every particular or determinate law is deconstructible, justice itself is not deconstructible. Justice is that in the name of which every law is instituted. Here is the striking claim that launched the career of the "later" Derrida: "deconstruction is justice."[31] Justice is the incalculable with and for which one calculates the law.

The space between justice and law is exposed by attending to the "performative power" that lies "at the origin of every institution." Derrida calls this power "the mystical" and claims that the foundation of every authority rests on a kind of faith or credit.[32] This is the mystical foundation of authority, which is also an aporetic foundation, because it is not a solid or substantial ground in any determinate theoretical or legal sense. Law cannot exist without justice, and justice is unthinkable with law; but, justice represents a space beyond law, or a law beyond law by which law functions. For Derrida, justice is not the suspension of the law as an exception, as in Agamben's description of Schmitt, that is, an exception that serves to sustain and further the bio-political machine. No, justice in Derrida is essentially what Agamben calls "pure law" in *State of Exception*.

In his book on *Saint Paul*, Badiou provides theoretical tools to reflect further on the relationship between law and life, particularly in reference to Paul. I will say more about Paul in the next chapter, but here I want to focus on Badiou's discussion of law and sin in Paul. Badiou reflects on Paul's dense discussion of the law in Romans 7, where the existence of the law, he says, brings about consciousness of sin. According to Badiou, "the law is what gives life to desire," which is considered to be sinful insofar as it is intrinsically connected to death.[33] Autonomous, unconscious desire opened up by the law is "the path of death"; "sin is the life of desire as autonomy, as autonomism."[34] Animals naturally desire, but this is desire is innocent, on the side of life, and prior to the law. Once the law appears, sin is associated with death because the subject is cut off from the object of desire.

The "subjective unconscious" that Badiou locates in Paul's thought refers to the gap that separates the subject from the object of desire. Since desire is incorrigible, so is sin, whether or not the law's prohibition is transgressed. Therefore, the prohibition instituted by the law ("Thou shalt not . . . ") means that subjects can only realize themselves through the desired object, which is irrevocably cut off. The law sets subjects on the path of death, because they value themselves negatively in relation to the desired object, which is seen on the side of life. The relation between the subject and the object is sin because sin takes the form of an "involuntary automation," or death.[35] Paul's theology accomplishes a decentering of the subject, because grace functions as a "pure act" that closes the gap, or reverses the poles of life and death.[36] This is the resurrection's essential meaning, according to Badiou, which is similar to Caputo's understanding of resurrection in *The Weakness of God* as discussed in chapter 2.

Resurrection restores the subject to life, to a universal truth beyond the law. According to Badiou,

> Resurrection summons the subject to identify himself as such according to the name of faith (*pistis*). . . . In the guise of the event, the subject *is* subjectivation. The word *pistis* (faith, or conviction) designates precisely this point: the absence of any gap between subject and subjectivation.[37]

The closing of the gap between subject and subjectivation means that there is no separation between the subject and the objectified desire. Paul restores the subject to the side of life by restoring "the living unity of thinking and doing." This reconnection of subject and life beyond the law can be viewed in at least two ways: on the one hand, cynically as originating a bio-politics insofar as life serves exceptionally to preserve a law without law, or what Agamben calls force-of-law; on the other hand, we could also read Badiou's Paul as contributing to a thinking of law beyond law: "Law returns as life's articulation for everyone, path of faith, law beyond law. This is what Paul calls love."[38] Law beyond law would here coincide with a kind of life beyond life, at least for simple bio-political control.

One way to signify such a law beyond law, following Badiou, Derrida, and Agamben, would be to understand it as the law of the unconscious; not the negative unconscious automatism of sin that Badiou articulates via Paul, but a more productive unconscious that I will associate more closely with Deleuze. The unconscious should be understood not dualistically as an entity below or behind consciousness but structurally alongside conscious thought and practice, in a properly Lacanian manner. For Lacan, the unconscious is structured like a language, which gives it an apparently static character. However, "it" speaks and thus dynamically brings the subject into being.[39] From the perspective of Deleuze in *The Logic of Sense* and Deleuze and Guattari in *Anti-Oedipus*, the unconscious is less explicitly linguistic than in Lacan's work and more explicitly productive. In the context of Deleuze (and Guattari), an unconscious event could be a name for a pure law beyond law. Although *Anti-Oedipus* is often read over against Lacan, I suggest that Deleuze and Guattari elaborate a productive unconscious that inscribes a new law into being, and they provide resources for a more dynamic, poststructural Lacanianism.

I have set up the bio-political problem with Agamben, who is one of our most acute contemporary political thinkers. But, at the end of *State of Exception*, while Agamben does hint at a solution through Benjamin, he fails to develop it further. Of course, it may be naïve to offer solutions, especially complicated ones, when the most urgent task now is to work to disable the bio-political machine. The problem Agamben poses, however, is how to conceive a law beyond law rather than a law without law, or force-of-law. Furthermore, the only way to fully think of a "pure law" or a law beyond law is from the context of psychoanalysis, which points to the central cultural and theoretical significance of Freud's work. The post-Freudian unconscious is not simply an individual desire, but after Lacan the unconscious is primarily social and even political.[40] The idea of the unconscious, if understood *politically*, offers resources to think this pure law apart from bio-politics.

Contemporary philosophers such as Alain Badiou and Slavoj Žižek have developed the political implications of Lacan's thought.[41] My solution, however, which is not a solution to the urgent practical problem of how to disable to bio-political machine, but a theoretical contribution of how to begin to think about a law beyond law, consists of a reading of Deleuze (and Guattari), which allows one to think the unconscious productively as event. To get from Agamben to Deleuze, then, I must proceed through Lacan. To read Lacan into Agamben and Deleuze in a contemporary theoretical and political context, however, I am also reading Agamben and Deleuze, at least implicitly, in the context of Žižek and Badiou. Both thinkers provide key insights into the nature of what I am calling the "unconscious event." I am also presupposing rather than directly discussing their work, excepting the brief consideration of Badiou's discussion of law in Paul above. In a broad sense, Badiou and Žižek provide a speculative, even metaphysical understanding of Lacan, and they provide resources to think both being and event in a sophisticated philosophical, psychoanalytic, and political manner. They also do not emphasize the productive nature of the event as Deleuze does, although Deleuze plays down the notion of the unconscious because of his polemics against Lacan and Freudian psychoanalysis.

Like most other French structuralists and poststructuralists, Deleuze was greatly influenced by Lacan. Lacan reads Freud's idea of the unconscious along with the linguistics of Ferdinand de Saussure, where linguistics structures the unconscious in a social and symbolic sense, which is why Lacan claims that the unconscious is "structured like a language."[42] Lacan deploys his own threefold typology by distinguishing between the imaginary, the symbolic, and the real, but he understands the unconscious mostly as symbolic. Furthermore, Lacan's social and linguistic unconscious is shared intersubjectively, rather than being the property of an individual, as it is in Freud's work. Deleuze engages positively with Lacan and the unconscious in his book *Difference and Repetition*, and Félix Guattari, Deleuze's collaborator, was a Lacanian psychoanalyst. In the 1970s, however, Deleuze and Guattari became more and more critical of the Lacanian unconscious, especially its assimilation to the symbolic. In *Anti-Oedipus*, Deleuze and Guattari view the unconscious as productive rather than symbolic, and they associate the unconscious with the real. But, despite their antipathy to the family triangle of mommy-daddy-baby that they see privileged in Freud and Lacan, Deleuze and Gauttari do follow Lacan in seeing the unconscious as social and political in its effects, and their engagement with the real as a more significant category occurs around the same time that Lacan shifts toward a more explicit discussion of the real.[43]

Deleuze understands what Lacan calls the "real" to be the result of a process of material production, rather than a speculative subtraction or a voiding of ontology, as Badiou would formulate it. The production of the real is the becoming of an event, and Deleuze articulates the concept of an event in *The Logic of Sense*. In a complex appropriation of Lewis Carroll's *Alice in Wonderland*, Deleuze elaborates two series, a series of sense and language that Carroll's work opens up and a series of bodies that cannot be connected to sense directly. (This idea of body is more properly associated with the work of Antonin Artaud.) Sense occurs along a surface, whereas bodies have depth. Here we have an opposition between sense and body, and what occurs between them is an event. In an important way, *The Logic of Sense* is a book about the event. The event is not a third thing and does not simply mediate between sense and body, because the event is inextricably tied to sense. The conception of an event is caught up in the superficial and paradoxical logic of sense: "the event is sense itself."[44] Events are surface effects of sense and language, which means that they are symbolic rather than real, in Lacanian terms. *The Logic of Sense* is more structuralist than *Anti-Oedipus* because events are associated completely with sense and language. But in *The Logic of Sense*, Deleuze is already striving to understand how the event extends beyond sense.

In a strange way, events are effects of sense, but they extend beyond sense, or they extend sense beyond itself. According to Deleuze, "events are like crystals, they become and grow only out of the edges, or on the edge."[45] The edge of sense is where events occur, with a profound extension or double articulation of sense. This expansion of sense can also be seen as a fractal, in addition to a crystal, where the fractalization or repetition of a self-differential and differentiating process produces an event. In a way, since the event occurs along the outside of sense, the event is unconscious. Sense concerns meaning and language, whereas depth concerns bodies in their passion. These two series do not connect to each other, but the impossible passage from sense to body occurs in and through the event. Deleuze is straining toward an understanding of the event that connects language to the other series of bodies.

Even though technically an event must always be associated with sense, it possesses a special relationship to body that allows it to reach beyond sense. In writing about the author Joe Bousquet, Deleuze claims that Bousquet "apprehends the wound that he bears deep within his body in its eternal truth as a pure event."[46] A pure event is a kind of wound, as Deleuze affirms; every event is "a kind of plague, war, wound, or death," because it occurs in relation to body.[47] The event creates or produces sense because it is capable of connecting to body and transfiguring body into sense. Once it is expressed, "the splendor and the magnificence of the event is sense."[48] But this is the result—the result of a univocalization of being that the event communicates to language in its becoming, that is, in its being an event.

In *Anti-Oedipus*, Deleuze and Guattari emphasize the productive nature of desiring machines, which directly produce the real. Desire is not inherently imaginary, based on the fantasy of what the subject who desires lacks; rather, "desire does not lack anything." According to Deleuze and Guattari, "the real is the end product, the result of the passive syntheses of desire as autoproduction of the unconscious."[49] In naming the production of the real by desiring machines an event, I am stressing the continuity between *The Logic of Sense* and *Anti-Oedipus*, and also showing how Deleuze, with the aid of Guattari, moves away from the symbolic, structuralist reading of events as pure expressions of sense, toward an explicitly productive understanding of an event in relation to bodies. Here is Deleuze's turn toward the real, which mirrors Lacan's in the early 1970s.

Desire produces the real, which is a social and political rather than solely an individual production: "social production is purely and simply desiring production itself under determinate conditions"[50] Deleuze and Guattari criticize Lacan's separation of desire from the real and desire's relegation to a purely symbolic order. Schizophrenic language provides a way to radically question the bourgeois model of symbolic reality based on forms of neurotic disavowal. And the method of schizo-analysis developed by Deleuze and Guattari pushes capitalism to and perhaps even beyond its limits, at least in theory.

They ask:

> Wouldn't it be better to schizophrenize—to schizophrenize the domain of the unconscious as well as the sociohistorical domain, so as to shatter the iron collar of Oedipus and rediscover everywhere the force of desiring-production; to renew, on the level of the real, the tie between analytic machine, desire and production?[51]

The unconscious is not imaginary or symbolic, but "it is the real in itself." The productive unconscious is "anti-Oedipus" because Oedipus serves as the name for that which organizes and controls—represses—the productivity of the desiring-machines. Oedipus becomes the name under which Deleuze and Guattari criticize psychoanalysis.

How do these desiring-machines work? Deleuze and Guattari claim that "every object presupposes the continuity of a flow" which the machine interrupts to produce an object.[52] They write that "every machine, in the first place, is related to a continual material flow (hylè) that it cuts into."[53] If the material flow is the real, then symbolic reality subtracts from the real to produce an object. But, the real is the process, not the material flow that is posited beyond the productive workings of the machines. Every machine is a machine of a machine, which means that every machine both interrupts and reestablishes a flow or continuity of material processes: "In a word, every machine functions as a break in the flow in relation to the machine to which it is connected, but at the same time is also a flow itself, or the production of a flow, in relation to the machine connected to it. This is the law of the production of production."[54]

The production of the real is the production of an event, even though Deleuze does not continue to privilege this term in *Anti-Oedipus*. The event is strictly speaking unconscious. An unconscious event is the product of a strange sort of law, because it is the law of the unconscious, or rather, the law itself is partially indeterminate and incalculable as an expression of the event.

Although for Lacan the law of the unconscious is the "Law of the Father," the paternal law of the symbolic, for Deleuze the law functions beyond any determinate law or measure, out of the father's grasp. Law beyond law is (the) unconscious, which is another way of indicating the conditions of possibility for an event, which Derrida has demonstrated are just as much the conditions of *im*possibility for an event, just as Badiou has radically severed the event from being or ontology. Law becomes tied to the unconscious and related to the event, which is inherently unconscious. Again, from a Deleuzian perspective, an event is produced rather than simply encountered. The unconscious is thus both productive and political.

Law is not unconscious in the sense that it is a mysterious unknown, but it directly concerns the social unconscious; this is the point of Lacan's reading of Freud. An event is also the result of the productive unconscious; that is, the dynamic unconscious produces events, which is the lesson of Deleuze (and Guattari). Pure law concerns not conscious belief, the allegiance or affiliation to this or that principle, party, position, or God, but rather the unconscious Other, who mediates an event. The event itself is unconscious and bears the law within itself as law-giving power or instituting potentiality— it is an irruption of the subject but not the conscious subject or ego. Conscious or determinate laws are the effects of events inscribed on the surface of sense. Bio-politics then exploits these determinate laws to regulate bodies in a violent manner, forgetting the true nature of law as event.

I am reading *The Logic of Sense* and *Anti-Oedipus* as complementary works concerning the event. *The Logic of Sense* surveys and expresses the event from above, from the standpoint of sense and the spreading of sense into event. *Anti-Oedipus* generates the event from below, from the basement as it were, in its material, bodily, and machinic production. The event is a singularity, a specific occasion that occurs, stitching together both body and sense. According to my interpretation of Deleuze, the political is constituted by the plane of immanence, which he describes in one of his last essays as "a life."[55] Just as in *What is Philosophy?* where the plane of immanence is prephilosophical, here the plane of immanence is more precisely prepolitical, but it gives rise to political events and provides the consistency for their political significance.

Law concerns the specific conditions of an event, which is a productive and constructive effort. Even though an event in itself cannot be completely predicted or predetermined, events occur. My constructive interpretation of law in Deleuzian terms understands it as the political counterpart to the philosophical task of the creation of concepts in *What is Philosophy?* A thinking of law beyond law concerns the creation of a new political event, which is both a practical and a theoretical project. This more explicitly political reading of Deleuze results partly from the problematic that Agamben sets up with his analysis of contemporary bio-politics, and partly from the pressure of contemporary Lacanian political thought (Žižek and Badiou). By linking Deleuze (and Guattari) with Agamben through Žižek and Badiou, an understanding of law beyond law emerges that fleshes out the situation that Agamben indicates at the end of *State of Exception* in his appeal to Benjamin.

My reading is thus opposed to Peter Hallward's reading of Deleuze's work as profoundly and problematically nonpolitical. In *Out of This World*, Hallward reads Deleuze dualistically as opposing creative becoming to created being. He claims that since for Deleuze "being is creativity, it can only fully become so through the tendential evacuation of all actual or creaturely mediation."[56] Hallward's quasi-gnostic interpretation of Deleuze evacuates Deleuze's thought of any notion of relation. Although Deleuze was critical of standard notions of relation, including the relations of representation and mediation, it goes too far to claim that Deleuze's thought possesses no relation between creativity and created being. The creature is a fold of creativity that participates in a continuing creativity based on its creativity and createdness. Because Hallward reads Deleuze's binary distinctions as oppositional, he mistakes distinction for opposition and loses the tension provided by the plane of immanence. Deleuze criticizes the withdrawal of the appeal of transcendence, or the removal of sense and value from life to another realm. Hallward's reading simply repeats the standard Western opposition of immanence to transcendence, this time by identifying Deleuze's celebration of immanence as a surreptitious transcendence because Deleuze affirms the virtual creativity inherent in immanence. According to Hallward, "the political aspects of Deleuze's philosophy amounts to little more than utopian distraction," because Hallward does not realize the political implications of Deleuze's thought.[57] The constructive nature of Deleuze's thought directly concerns the political, contrary to such contemporary readings. In *Cinema 2*, "the people are missing"; they must be filmed, invented, constructed, and this creation is a political act an event for which no determinate law can be given.[58] To take the people as they are and then apply the force of laws to control them produces bio-politics. To express the law that establishes an event is a revolutionary political act.

If we unfold the truth of this insight into the essence of pure law as unconscious event, we can situate law beyond bio-politics, which is a hypocritical and cynical strategy that manipulates law as a façade which controls bodies as a way to perpetuate greed and power. We can also understand our contemporary fundamentalists' affirmation of a divine, hyperconscious law as a return of the repressed, a desperate response to the contemporary crisis of law. The notion of a pure law toward which Agamben gestures at the end of *State of Exception* can be formulated, through Žižek and Badiou, for a specific, post-Lacanian reading of Deleuze, one that affirms Deleuze as a thinker of the event. The event is generated by a radical law, a law of the unconscious, a law or *nomos* that must necessarily be unconscious. In *A Thousand Plateaus*, Deleuze and Guattari contrast striated and smooth space, a law based on *logos* with a nomadic, *nomos*-law.[59] *Nomos* is a smooth, unconscious law that contributes to deterritorialization, an absolute deterritorialization that at its limit "can be called the creator of a new earth."[60]

Nomos-law is productive of a law beyond law, or at least a form of law that exceeds bio-political control. This nomos-law is unconscious in the sense of being before and beyond simple consciousness. Of course, the unconscious event must become conscious in some respects for us to become aware of it, but it emerges from the unconscious or originally as unconscious. To think the event as both productive and as unconscious, and to see it as productive of a kind of law, is extremely complex and somewhat abstract, not to mention incredibly difficult to imagine put into institutional form, but it provides a theoretical alternative to both modern liberal law based on the general will of the people as represented in liberal-capitalist institutions and the reactionary assertion of a literalist and scripturalist divine law that intervenes in and trumps human institutions and laws. This scripturalist law is a kind of return of the repressed, because it emerges as the liberal legal tradition is breaking down and appears to offer an alternative to both cynical despair and the ambiguities of postmodern relativism and pluralism.

The concept of the event has become an extremely significant notion in contemporary intellectual discourse, and it possesses important political and theological implications. What is an event, and how does it break with contemporary forms of intolerable oppression, injustice, or even simply vacuity and trivial banality? I am arguing that Deleuze's conception of the (productive and unconscious) event is rich and resourceful, especially when thought in the context of the bio-political situation articulated so acutely by Agamben. In the following chapter, I will continue to develop a Deleuzian understanding of the event by reading Deleuze into the contemporary theoretical discussions about St. Paul.

7. RADICAL THEOLOGY AND THE EVENT

ST. PAUL WITH DELEUZE

THIS CHAPTER CONTINUES TO ELABORATE ON SOME OF THE theological implications of Deleuze's notion of the event, which was discussed in the previous chapter in relation to law and the unconscious. The event is an unconscious rather than simply a conscious or intentional event, and it is productive of a different kind of law, a law beyond law that exceeds bio-political control. The law of the unconscious event is also much different from either the nostalgic restoration of modern liberal law in a cynical era or the scripturalist restoration of divine law to solve the problems of human fallibility. The unconscious event is potential or virtual rather than simply actual, in terms of the discussion in the introduction. Here I further develop my understanding of the Deleuzian event by reading him with some of the current theoretical discourse about St. Paul.

The apostle Paul has been the focus of many recent philosophical and theological discussions of law and event, especially in the context of Continental philosophy. But, Deleuze's philosophy has not been considered as a contemporary referent for most discussions of Paul, mainly because of Deleuze's antipathy toward Paul, following that of Nietzsche.[1] Paul is important theologically because he is the first and most influential Christian theologian. Paul is also significant politically, as he is seen more and more radically as a powerful critic of the first-century Roman Empire. The United States considers itself a democratic republic, but its actions and status appear more imperial in the early twenty-first century, and the analogy holds even if the American Empire is declining financially and economically much faster than the Roman Empire did.

The contemporary theoretical engagement with St. Paul has been touched off largely by Alain Badiou's book *St. Paul: The Foundation of Universalism.* Badiou reads Paul as a "poet-thinker of the event," as well as a militant figure in his uncompromising fidelity to the event.[2] Badiou reads Paul as an atheist; that is, Badiou discounts the truth of Paul's event, which is the resurrection of Jesus Christ.[3] Badiou desires to capture the militant fidelity of Paul's example for contemporary politics, although he brackets the particular truth of Paul's revelation.

In the United States, this encounter has largely been an encounter between Continental philosophy and historical New Testament scholarship.[4] Into this exchange, I want to insert theology as a "vanishing mediator." Slavoj Žižek, who has done much to bring the significance of Badiou's work to an English-speaking public, borrows the term "vanishing mediator" from Frederic Jameson to relate German Idealism, particularly Schelling, to Lacanian psychoanalysis in *The Indivisible Remainder.*[5] A vanishing mediator is a third that brings together two alternatives or oppositions, but in doing so hides itself in such a way that it seems to vanish, and most readers remain stuck within an alternative or oppositional logic. Ironically, theology becomes a vanishing mediator in contemporary discussions of Paul that oppose interpretive-philosophical and historical-exegetical strategies.

Theology, however, is not simple or self-identical in its nature. Rather, it is divided at its origin into a traditional theology and a radical theology. This division is structurally similar to Derrida's distinction between two essential sources of religion, "the experience of belief" and "the experience of the unscathed, of sacredness or of holiness," in his essay "Faith and Knowledge."[6] Traditional or orthodox theology is more concerned with restoring Paul to his originary stature as the primary apostle and theologian of the resurrection event and reclaiming or reestablishing fidelity to the truth of this event, however that is interpreted or understood, literally or metaphorically. But radical theology is willing to follow Badiou and set the "event" free from the resurrection and read St. Paul under the pressure of the death of God.

Radical theology is here the penumbral shadow of the more properly atheistic philosophy of Badiou and Žižek, but it retains the form of theology as a discourse in its willingness to think philosophical formulations in their ultimacy and pressure their meaning and value. According to Gilles Deleuze's reading of Pierre Klossowski in an appendix to *The Logic of Sense*,

> it is our epoch that has discovered theology. One no longer had to believe in God. We seek rather the "structure," that is, the form which may be filled with beliefs, but the structure has no need to be filled in order to be called "theological." Theology is now the science of nonexisting entities, the manner in which these entities—divine or anti-divine, Christ or Antichrist—animate language and make for it this glorious body which is divided into disjunctions.

After Deleuze, after the death of God, theology is no longer restricted to apologetics in the service of dogmatics. The traditional image of theology persists throughout the twentieth century, and is what is at stake in many of the contemporary debates between phenomenology and theology,[7] but it is not necessarily the only form of theology.[8]

In this chapter, I will reflect from the viewpoint of radical theology about the event of Paul's thought as it affects contemporary theory, which is ultimately a thinking of the event. Deleuze's understanding of the becoming of the event implicitly contrasts with and pressures Badiou's Platonic reading concerning the possibility of an event that coheres into an ontology and Žižek's dialectical and Hegelian reading of the event as an incredible contradictory tension. That is, I do not directly engage Žižek and Badiou, but their interpretations of the event provide a context for my reading of Deleuze.

To investigate the temporality of the event, I will demonstrate that, despite superficial appearances to the contrary, there is a resemblance between Heidegger's temporality, which in its early version is inspired by Paul, and Deleuze's exposition of the syntheses of time in *Difference and Repetition*. The temporality of repetition in *Difference and Repetition* rebounds in *The Logic of Sense* into a thinking of the event. These Deleuzian theses all pertain to what I claim is ultimately a theological question, that is, "What is an event?" By naming Deleuze as the contemporary thinker of the event, I am associating Deleuze with St. Paul, despite Deleuze's declared opposition to Paul, following Nietzsche. Although Deleuze follows Nietzsche too closely in his antipathy toward St. Paul on the topic of judgment, by following the thread of the event we can assemble a Paul-effect for Deleuze. This project also involves folding Deleuze's other saint, Spinoza, back toward St. Paul. Finally, at the end of the chapter I will consider some of the contemporary political stakes of this reading of Paul and the event.

Paul is the original Christian theologian, the closest interpretive account we can get of the event of Christ. Nietzsche calls Paul the first Christian, which is a derogatory charge, and says that Paul mistakes or distorts the essence of Jesus's quietist asceticism and creates a persecution-machine, a priestly form of religion that encapsulates Platonism for the masses, whose main function is to root out and destroy profound and powerful desires.[9] A century later, however, Jacob Taubes makes a similar claim without the negative connotations. "My thesis implies," Taubes writes, "that Christianity has its origin not properly in Jesus but in Paul."[10] In fact, Taubes argues that Paul reduces Jesus's dual commandment to love God and to love the neighbor, condensing it into one commandment, to love one's neighbor: "No dual commandment, but rather *one* commandment. I regard this as an absolutely revolutionary act."[11] This is Paul as precursor to Emmanuel Levinas.

Now, I am not reconstructing Paul's understanding of time in a historical sense, but rather showing how a certain interpretation of Paul provides the impetus for an altered approach to temporality that marks twentieth-century philosophy. Heidegger's thought of being is indebted to his study of Aristotle in the 1920s, but his understanding of temporality can be traced to his phenomenological studies of early Christianity. In *The Phenomenology of Religious Life*, Heidegger grapples with Paul in his attempt to develop a phenomenological method that is adequate to lived experience.

Heidegger explains his notion of formal indication early in The *Phenomenology of Religious Life*, in the context of an encounter with early Christianity. The formal indication is a more subtle, supple, and concrete way of thinking historical relationship and continuity than the general notions on which philosophy usually relies. The formal indication communicates, above all, a situation, or what is decisive in "factical life experience itself."[12] Furthermore, this situation is paradigmatically related to Paul's existential situation, that is, Paul's historical enactment of proclamation. Heidegger, like Badiou, brackets the specific content of the object of proclamation (Jesus as Messiah) but stresses that "Christian religiosity lives temporality." This is a formalization, but not an abstract, empty formalization, because what is essential about early, Pauline Christian experience is its distinctive relationship with historical existence. Heidegger writes, "Christian factical life experience is historically determined by its emergence with the proclamation that hits the people in a moment, and this is unceasingly also alive in the enactment of life."[13] The temporal structure of proclamation, in the concrete situation in which Paul proclaims it, provides Heidegger with a key—a formal indication—to the nature of temporality itself: "Christian religiosity lives temporality as such."[14]

This primordial insight into temporality that Heidegger finds in Paul lies at the heart of the fuller expression of temporality as historical existence in *Being and Time*. Heidegger opposes his phenomenological and existential description of time to a linear conception of time understood as a progressive sequence of moments or now-points. In *Being and Time*, Heidegger produces an existential analytic of the experience of being-in-the-world on the part of the being that can ask the question of being, or Dasein. Being is understood as care, or concerned existence, and Dasein is concerned about its existence because it exists temporally. Attention to concerned existence uncovers a more authentic understanding of time, and prescribes a more authentic existential being-in-the-world. In *Being and Time*, an authentic experience of time replaces the specifically Christian and Pauline notion of the proclamation of the event.

Heidegger explains the co-implication of past, present and future as follows:

> Only in so far as Dasein *is* as an "I-*am*-as-having-been," can Dasein come towards itself futurally in such a way that it comes *back*. As authentically futural, Dasein, *is* authentically as "*having been*."[15]

According to Heidegger, the essence of being is time. Time is not linear, however; it is projected towards the future as it faces and grasps the past in the present moment. Dasein experiences being historically, as temporality. This temporality is lived historically because only in its relation to its past does Dasein extend into the future. The present is an effect of this attempt to take account of existence as Dasein undergoes the experience of being thrown into the world. Future, past, and present are folded together into the existence of the human being in a complicated way that is actualized in existence as a repetition. Because Dasein is oriented toward the past, it experiences temporality as a kind of repetition into the future.

In some ways, chapter 2 of *Difference and Repetition* can be read as a commentary on this sentence of Heidegger in *Being and Time*, in which Deleuze attempts to radicalize Heidegger even further toward difference and the future. In his later work, Heidegger attempts to retain the force of this insight into temporality while abandoning the subjective and humanistic connotations of thinking being from the standpoint of Dasein, and in particular Heidegger abandons any attempt to grasp temporality existentially and turns toward an understanding of how the event (*Ereignis*) of being in its temporal occurring appropriates us within it.

Although Deleuze is more explicitly influenced by Bergson, a careful reading of *Difference and Repetition* shows that Heidegger's thought is present, most explicitly in the "Note on Heidegger's Philosophy of Difference" that is appended onto the end of chapter 1. Deleuze explains that difference in Heidegger does not primarily concern negation: "the not expresses not the negative but the difference between Being and being," which is ontological difference. Furthermore, "this difference is not 'between' in the ordinary sense of the word. It is the Fold, *Zwiefalt*. It is constitutive of Being and of the manner in which Being constitutes being, in the double movement of 'clearing' and 'veiling.'"[16] Deleuze develops a more elaborate thinking of the Fold in a metaphysical sense in *The Fold: Leibniz and the Baroque*, but already in *Difference and Repetition* the three syntheses of time in chapter 2, "Repetition for Itself," take the form of a fold or a folding. Just as Heidegger elaborates an ontological thinking of time in opposition to modern conceptions of subjectivity in *Being and Time*, in *Difference and Repetition* Deleuze enacts an ecstatic temporality in a threefold process dislocated from any substantial subjectivity.

An event takes place; it occurs in and as time. Deleuze does not use the language of event in *Difference and Repetition*, but in many ways his thought here concerns the same topic as *The Logic of Sense*, which explicitly grapples with the logic of the event, and in *Difference and Repetition* the authentic repetition of difference should be understood as constituting an event. In *Difference and Repetition*, Deleuze constructs a notion of repetition that is based on difference rather than identity. Repetition occurs temporally, with three syntheses of time divided into past, present, and future. Temporal synthesis or repetition constructs the subject, rather than a self-identical subject undergoing or performing a repetition. The self is constructed by temporal syntheses as, for Heidegger, Dasein *is* temporal existence. The difference is that for Heidegger, Dasein is essentially historical and oriented toward the past, while for Deleuze repetition based on difference is ultimately futural.

The first form of repetition, which Deleuze calls a "passive synthesis," takes place under the sign of the present. The passive synthesis of imagination from Hume to Bergson constitutes the most basic form of experience, which is habit. A habit is a contraction that draws difference from repetition, and "these thousands of habits of which we are composed . . . thus form the basic domain of passive syntheses." Finally, "the world of passive syntheses constitutes the system of the self," but is a multiple and "dissolved self."[17] The first synthesis of time "constitutes time as a present, but a present which passes."[18] The first synthesis can only take place within the framework of a second synthesis, that of memory.

Memory is an active synthesis; it constitutes time "as the embedding of presents themselves." Deleuze appeals to Bergson's *Matter and Memory* and Proust's *In Search of Lost Time* to explain how time as memory forms a representation that grounds the time of the first synthesis. Memory is an active synthesis because it provides context and continuity for experiences, as well as an orientation. This orientation is also always toward the past, because the second form of time synthesizes what has passed. The pure past in itself is reconstructed or resurrected out of contemporary experience to envelope it: "the present exists, but the past alone insists and provides the element in which the present passes and successive elements are telescoped."[19]

Now, the problem becomes the difference between the active and passive syntheses, which leads to the third synthesis of time, the futural. Deleuze introduces the third form of time by way of Kant's transcendental philosophy, which takes "the form of a transcendental Difference between the Determination as such and what it determines."[20] Kant determines existence with the "I think," which takes place as a determination of time. Kant thereby uncovers "a paradox of inner sense," because the temporal determination of identity also undermines it, dividing it in two. The Kantian self is split between the active transcendental apperception that performs the syntheses of knowledge and the empirical ego that appears under the transcendental conditions of representation.

According to Deleuze, Kant incorporates time into the subject, an event that fractures the subject: "It is as though the I were fractured from one end to the other; fractured by the pure and empty form of time."[21] This pure and empty form of time is the third form of time, which both conjoins and disjoins the previous two. Deleuze claims that "time itself unfolds (that is, apparently ceases to be a circle) instead of things unfolding in it (following the overly simple circular figure)."[22] Time ceases to take the form of a circle and unravels or unfolds. Time takes the form of a caesura, a development that both fractures the I and signals the death of God. "If the greatest initiative of transcendental philosophy was to introduce the form of time into thought as such," Deleuze writes, "this pure and empty form in turn signifies indissolubly the death of God, the fractured I and the passive self."[23] Furthermore, Deleuze asserts that it is Hölderlin who draws out the consequences of Kantian thought here and is the true successor to Kant: "it is Hölderlin, who discovers the emptiness of pure time and, in this emptiness, simultaneously the continued diversion of the divine, the prolonged fracture of the I and the constitutive passive of the self."[24] Hölderlin, of course, is for Heidegger the poet-thinker par excellence, and this discussion of time in *Difference and Repetition* can be read as broadly Heideggerian.

Repetition is the production of something new rather than the repetition of something previously existing, and the third synthesis, the pure form of time, indicates this aspect of repetition. The third repetition is "the repetition of the future as eternal return."[25] By associating Nietzsche's thinking of the eternal return with the pure and empty form of time, Deleuze provides an alternative reading of Nietzsche, based on his earlier book *Nietzsche and Philosophy*, where the eternal return is not circular or substantial because only what is different returns, or what returns is always different.

The third synthesis is the "final synthesis of time," in which "the present and past are in turn no more than dimensions of the future."[26] The three forms of time are modes of repetition, but Deleuze arranges all of them under the sign of the future. Repetition is essentially futural rather than recollective or passively constitutive. Deleuze mentions Kierkegaard and Charles Péguy as important thinkers of repetition, but he criticizes them "because they were not ready to pay the necessary price. The entrusted this supreme repetition, repetition as a category of the future, to faith."[27] Faith is problematic for Deleuze because it restores or resurrects God and the self beyond all authentic repetition. Faith is inescapable for belief; but when it becomes hypostasized as a vague but determined future, it becomes comic. In reference to Kierkegaard and Péguy, Deleuze claims that "there is an adventure of faith, according to which one is the clown of one's own faith, the comedian of one's ideal."[28]

Deleuze names the pure form of time "death." Death is the disjunction of life, the fracture or split within the living being, that cannot be reduced to negation or limitation. Paul's proclamation is a work against death, but death (the death of Christ) is what makes Paul's proclamation possible, makes it an event. Death is the death of identity in the process of eternal recurrence. This death splits time into past (active synthesis, memory) and present (passive synthesis, habit), and it is what gives a future, Deleuze proclaims, following Nietzsche, Paul's antipode. Resurrection is not resurrection of any prior identity; it does not preserve the substance of self, Christ or God. To have faith is to roll the dice, not to have the certainty of true belief. Living is being-towards-death, but death is not simply the terminus or telos of life; it is that which makes living possible, that from which life proceeds.

Identity is an effect of difference. Differences are primary and constitute identities, which are not identical, but similar. At the secondary level, differences differentiate, that is, "they relate the first-degree differences to one another."[29] Deleuze explains this process in relation to Heidegger:

> In accordance with Heidegger's ontological intuition, difference must be articulation and connection in itself; it must relate different to different without any mediation whatsoever by the identical, the similar, the analogous or the opposed. There must be a differenciation of difference, an in-itself which is like a differentiator, a *Sich-unterscheidende*, by virtue of which the different is gathered all at once rather than represented on condition of a prior resemblance, identity, analogy or opposition.[30]

The differentiation of differences is accomplished by an internal self-relation, but it is not a relation of identity. Differences relate according to a temporal process of differentiation, which Deleuze describes as a dark precursor.

The dark precursor is "a force which ensures communication," because although "thunderbolts explode between their different intensities . . . they are preceded in their path by an invisible, imperceptible dark precursor, which determines their path in advance but in reverse, as though intaglioed."[31] The dark precursor names the productive aspect of the empty form of time. The thunderbolt is the event, but it is presaged by the dark precursor, which Deleuze in the *Logic of Sense* calls the "void." The dark precursor generates sense. The dark precursor is the Heideggerian Not, *das Nicht*, or as Deleuze suggests earlier in chapter 1, the *Zweifalt* that relates Being and being. Deleuze also says that Heidegger does not goes far enough in his attempt to think "original difference" because Heidegger cannot conceive being as "truly disengaged from any subordination in relation to the identity of representation."[32] Deleuze radicalizes Heidegger's philosophy of difference and does so primarily through his reading of Nietzsche's eternal return against Heidegger's critique of Nietzsche as the last metaphysician. Nietzsche provides an interpretation of the third form of time that is productive because repetition is solely and completely related to difference.

I am suggesting that a careful reading of *Difference and Repetition* betrays Heideggerian themes, most importantly concerning Deleuze's discussion of time. That is, the temporality that mediates difference and repetition is inspired to a great extent by Heidegger's meditations on time from *Being and Time* onward, even though Deleuze prefers to cite authors such as Bergson and Nietzsche to push beyond Heidegger. Furthermore, Heidegger's intuition of a new thinking of temporality is generated out of an engagement with early Christianity, in particular Paul. Heidegger's insight into Pauline temporality eventually passes into Deleuze's thought, though this is a somewhat speculative genealogy.

Deleuze's thinking about time in *Difference and Repetition* becomes even more Pauline when read from the perspective of Giorgio Agamben's *The Time That Remains*. Agamben provides a magisterial commentary on the first ten words of Paul's Letter to the Romans, and he theorizes the basic structure of Paul's messianic time. According to Agamben, messianic time is the time that time takes to end, which cannot be adequately represented, although it is always lived. Messianic time is the straining of time toward its end before it actually comes to an end. To understand messianic time, Agamben refers to the French linguist Gustave Guillaume and his concept of "operational time." The very representation of time takes time, and Guillaume attempts to conceptualize this time that time takes to form a representation as "a time-image." Agamben says that "Guillaume defines 'operational time' as the time the mind takes to realize a time-image."[33] Agamben then defines messianic time as "the time that time takes to come to an end, or, more precisely, the time we take to bring to an end, to achieve our representation of time."[34] The term "time-image," although not used in *Difference and Repetition*, later becomes a central concept for Deleuze, especially in his *Cinema* books. At the same time, the idea that later acquires the name "time-image" is expressed in *Difference and Repetition*, that is, the third synthesis, the pure and empty form of time. If Agamben is correct about Paul, then Deleuzian time is profoundly Pauline, even though Agamben does not refer to Deleuze in *The Time That Remains*. Deleuze's time is not explicitly Pauline, and in many importantly ways it is Freudian and Nietzschean; but, it is significantly Heideggerian as well as Pauline in Agamben's terms. To draw out the messianic significance of Deleuze's philosophy, I turn to his thinking of the event in *The Logic of Sense*.

An event is an affair of language, a production of sense, rather than simply the interaction of bodies. The event is already associated with sense, that is, with meaning or signification. In *The Logic of Sense*, Deleuze uses the occasion of Lewis Carroll's work to articulate two series, one of sense, language, or surface and one of bodies, affect, or depth. In a proper sense, the event is associated with sense in the former series. Deleuze says, "we will not ask therefore what is the sense of the event: the event is sense itself."[35] An event concerns the passage from body to language, but it is a surface effect, it takes place across a surface: "It is by following the border, by skirting the surface, that one passes from bodies to the incorporeal."[36] Events take place along an edge and spread like crystals. Sense is generated by the becoming of the event as it spreads across a body, as we saw in chapter 6.

Between these two series runs a cut. In addition to Lewis Carroll's writings, Deleuze privileges the Stoics in *The Logic of Sense*. He quotes Émile Bréhier, who says that the Stoics distinguished two planes of being, corporeal and incorporeal being. Bréhier writes, "when the scalpel cuts through the flesh, the first body produces upon the second not a new property but a new attribute, that of being cut."[37] The attribute is an incorporeal quality that determines the corporeal being differently. The cut, or the distinction between body and attribute, explains the difference between body and sense. Sense concerns the attribution or orientation of corporeal being, which is a superficial determination that creates and communicates meaning. The cut is an example, that is, the difference between body and sense is not necessarily or literally a cut, but it is an invisible and imperceptible distinction.

Deleuze later associates the wound with a pure event. He ponders, "why is every event a kind of plague, war, wound or death?"[38] The wound of thinking that an event constitutes is related to death as the name for the pure and empty form of time that is the third synthesis in *Difference and Repetition*. The reason "event" is a more significant term than sense in *The Logic of Sense* is because even though Deleuze associates event completely with sense, it has the uncanny ability to connect to a body, to pass from the corporeal to the incorporeal plane by means of a spreading along an edge. And this passage directly concerns the third form of time, because the event in its relation to the pure and empty form of time generates sense and meaning on the surface plane of language. In a sense, the event is the dark precursor of sense, even though it can only be described as sense.

Sense is generated out of nothing, a void, or nonsense. Nothingness is not substantial or nihilistic, because it is directly productive, as discussed in the previous chapter in relation to law. According to Deleuze, "nonsense functions as the zero-point of thought, the aleatory point of desexualized energy or the punctual Instinct of death," and the termination of sense in nonsense explains why sense is essentially paradoxical.[39] The paradox of the absurd at the limit of sense concerns an "extra-being" added to signification that relates it to being.[40] The becoming of this extra-being is an event that produces sense.

So what sense do we make of Paul? Not Paul in his time, but Paul's significance for us now? Philosophically, Paul is important because he is the first philosopher of the Christ-event. At least, he is the first theologian, that is, thinker or theorist of the event. Paul's letters take place along the surface of language and concern the production of sense. This is the production of the sense of Christianity, which is also the provision of a law, a new law of love.[41] Paul argues that law institutes a reign of sin as consciousness of law-breaking: "Law intruded into this process to multiply law-breaking" (Romans 5:20). "But where sin was thus multiplied," by our becoming consciousness of it, "grace immediately exceeded it" by Christ's victory of life over sin and law as death (Romans 5:21). Paul's interpretation of Christ is not simply a second-order reflection, but according to a Deleuzian logic, it is already inherently an event. We cannot get behind sense or the surface play of language to descend into the depths of pure body. Jesus as Christ is pure body as incarnation being, and the passion of Jesus is the passion of body as body. The event of Jesus's passion does not make sense, and attempts to represent the sense of the passion directly produce grotesque and tragicomic effects, as the movie *The Passion of the Christ* shows.

As we shift from Jesus to Paul, we see a concomitant search for the historical Paul, an effort at the retrieval of the radical Paul from the clutches of orthodoxy, patriarchy, or worse.[42] Paul now represents the sense of the passion of Christ, which cannot be located in Jesus. This is why Paul's thought is an event. We cannot pass through Paul to get to Jesus; we can only access Jesus by his significance through Paul.

Now, the question for Paul, which determines the sense of Christianity as a whole, is how many events are there? One or two? Are crucifixion and resurrection one event or two distinct but sequential events? We can think of this situation in at least three different ways, if we consider St. Paul's situation from the perspective of Deleuze. On the one hand, we could take the traditional view that they are one event, that is, two aspects of the same process. In this case, resurrection is an incredible reversal of crucifixion. One dies and is put to death as a criminal by the Empire, and this is natural and normal. But what is stunning is the claim that this person is raised from the dead, even though this claim is less unique in the ancient world. Two distinct moments of one event occur on the same plane of (supra) history and form the core of a salvation narrative that is then generalized or extended to all humans and all of history.

The problem with this scenario, as its implications unfold over time, is the time inserted between the crucifixion and the resurrection, which takes the form of a pure Sabbath, a dead Saturday. This pure and empty form of time in the Deleuzian sense, at the heart of the Christ event, dislocates the reverse repetition of the resurrection and renders it inoperable. In more Derridean language, *différance* lies at the center of Christianity, and the temporalization of the passion means that resurrection is already delayed or deferred because the passion takes time and takes place.[43] Once the resurrection is cut off from the crucifixion, the crucifixion takes the form of historical reality, and the resurrection is relegated to the realm of the fantastic imaginary. This interpretive process occurs during modernity, which is encapsulated synecdochically by higher biblical criticism, with its liberal and psychological conclusions about Christianity and religion in general. How, asks David Friedrich Strauss and many others, could this one man be raised from the dead and no others? What psychological effect must he have had upon his disciples for them to refuse to accept his death? Or else, what moment of mass psychosis must have struck to compel his followers, already stricken with grief, to convince themselves that their master has returned? One of the difficulties with this psychological reading, however, is its extension to Paul, whose dramatic experience comes much later and takes a very different form.

I want to suggest that the traditional reading is incredible, despite its appeal to many contemporary readers. We cannot pass back into the immediate situation of Paul, unmediated by two thousand years of history and thought. We cannot sustain the same belief in a literal resurrection; however, we modify its nature and significance to make sense according to our liberal and postliberal sensibilities. At the same time, however, the second reading is not Deleuzian enough. The pure and empty form of time that lies between the crucifixion and the resurrection does not concern *chronos*, a chronological order, but is a drop of time in its pure sense, what Deleuze in his *Cinema* books calls a "time-image."[44] The time-image is a cut that relates crucifixion and resurrection not as a before and an after, but as the duality of *The Logic of Sense*. Deleuze argues that the event should not be "confused with its spatio-temporal realization in a state of affairs."[45] Rather, the crucifixion concerns the body, the pure body and its absolute passion and its depths, while the resurrection is an event of sense because it refers to the signification of Christ's body, its transfiguration along a surface. This is a paradox, but Deleuze has shown how the logic of sense is paradoxical because it is multidirectional: "good sense affirms that in all things there is a determinable sense or direction; but paradox is the affirmation of both senses or directions at the same time."[46] Furthermore, the history of Christianity is nothing if not a series of paradoxes, and thus it could be said to demonstrate a logic of sense.

But specifically, in what way is the Christ-event a paradox? That is, how can death signify life? Recall that every event bears "a kind of plague, war, wound or death."[47] Death is the kernel of every event, the death or passion of bodies in their becomings. According to Deleuze, willing the event is not resignation to the wounding of body, but "willing the event is, primarily, to release its eternal truth," which means that ultimately "this will would reach the point at which war is waged against war, the wound would be the living trace and the scar of all wounds, and death turned on itself would be willed against all deaths."[48] Deleuze appeals to Nietzsche's formulation of *Amor fati*, to will and love what happens, which means not resignation to fate, but a transvaluation of it. "We are faced with a volitional intuition and a transmutation," Deleuze writes. This transmutation involves affirming the event in a particular way to provide it a particular direction or orientation, which is the production of sense. Willing the event involves "a change of will," which is "a sort of leaping in place (*saut sur place*) of the whole body which exchanges its organic will for a spiritual will."[49] The spiritual will "wills now not exactly what occurs, but something in that which occurs, something yet to come which would be consistent with what occurs, in accordance with the laws of an obscure, humorous conformity: the Event."[50] We can read this striking passage from *The Logic of Sense* as a commentary on the Christ-event and thereby read Deleuze as a contemporary St. Paul.

The passage from body as body that is expressed in the crucifixion to the sense or significance of the resurrection is the transmutation and the event. The proclamation of the resurrection is the result of an enormous spiritual will that transvalues the grotesque torture and death of a Jesus-body, hanging from a cross, to the good news that Christ is alive. The event makes sense in this paradoxical way. The resurrection is not a separate event, and it does not occur in "reality," but it is the sense of the Christ-event. The term "event" here is crucial, and in some ways exceeds sense, because it over-hangs sense and reaches down to the passion of bodies to incorporate the wound or death into sense. But, the event is never detached from signification. Using religious language, Deleuze calls the transmutation of what happens into an event an "immaculate conception": "the event is not what occurs (an accident), it is rather inside what occurs, the purely expressed. It signals and awaits us."[51] Using Deleuze's logic of sense, which is more profoundly a logic of the event, we can read the significance of the Christ-event in contemporary theoretical terms. The event occurs along the cut between the crucifixion of the resurrection that forms the pure and empty form of time. Furthermore, this reading is the result of a truly radical theology that is willing to take responsibility for the event and to risk the generation of sense, rather than accepting it ready-made from previous events of thinking.

From the standpoint of Agamben's reading of Paul, the Christ-event is one event, and messianic time is the time that remains for the resurrection to be fully accomplished. Similarly, the dead Saturday expresses the operational time of the crucifixion, the representation of the time it takes for the crucifixion to take place, to come to an end. Of course, Paul expected the resurrection to come to an end much more quickly than two millennia, and Agamben is not that far from Badiou (although Badiou is much more critical and skeptical of language than Agamben) in his attempt to formalize a messianic structure of language out of Paul's writings without wishing to adhere to Paul's precise interpretation of a specific salvific-historical event. The difference between Agamben and Deleuze is that Agamben's thought is more teleological, because messianic time is always defined by its end toward which it is straining to reach. For Deleuze, time is futural but not teleological in this way, which may mean that it is not strictly speaking messianic, at least as Agamben understands it. Agamben says that Derrida's philosophy is not messianic, because for Derrida, "the trace is a suspended *Aufhebung*, that will never come to know its own *plērōma*. Deconstruction is a thwarted messianism, a suspension of the messianic."[52] On the one hand, we could say that Derrida's thought is fully and overwhelmingly messianic precisely because it never reaches its end. On the other hand, this critique of Derrida would not simply apply to Deleuze, who does not use the term "trace" because of its negative connotations, and because he understands sense and event as purely productive processes. For Deleuze, the time-image is less directional, less chronological, and therefore less operational than it is for Agamben. If it is the straining toward an end that determines the messianic, then Deleuze's philosophy is not messianic; but if one detaches the time-image from chronological movement and sees how it is productive of sense with an event, then one can understand Deleuze's relation to Paul without the explicitly messianic relation, or to put it in Agamben's terms, to understand the messianic in Deleuze as not messianic.[53] I will return to this discussion of messianicity in the next chapter to contrast messianicity with Catherine Malabou's conception of plasticity.

In this context, we can also consider Paul as a saint for Deleuze, because he expresses the sense of the Christ-event, here elaborated in Deleuzian terms. Deleuze can be said to have three saints, Spinoza, Nietzsche, and Bergson, although he also terms Spinoza the "Christ of the philosophers."[54] Following Edith Wyschogrod's lead in *Saints and Postmodernism*, we can read Paul as a postmodern saint, in this case a Deleuzian saint, even if we have to read against the grain of Deleuze's intentions regarding St. Paul.[55] This reading would roll Paul's thinking of the event forward into Spinoza's ontological substance, and vice versa, folding Spinoza's substance (*Deus sive natura*) back into Paul's proclamation of the essential temporality of the event.

Of course, Deleuze does not consider Paul a saint, and he closely follows Nietzsche in his antipathy toward Paul, most explicitly in his essay "Nietzsche and Saint Paul, Lawrence and John of Patmos." In this essay Deleuze accuses Paul of "inventing a new type of priest even more terrible than its predecessors," because Paul relies on the doctrine of immortality to intensify guilt and sin to create "the doctrine of judgment."[56] Deleuze opposes Paul to Nietzsche by implicitly affirming Nietzsche's reading of Jesus as a Dostoyevskian idiot, a simple and innocent being who inadvertently lends himself to the creation of the most terrible persecution machine the world has ever seen. Paul would be the inventor of this machine, and his opposition to the Roman Empire combined with the image of the Apocalypse, the imminent return of Christ whose return is indefinitely deferred, "invents a completely new image of power: the system of Judgment."[57] The Last Judgment is a program created to enslave the world in its image of vengeful power, to get back at the powers that be for their power, and it is the result of an enormous *ressentiment*.

Nietzsche's interpretation of Christianity is a powerful critique. I would not argue that it is wrong; certainly Christianity has all of these elements, and it is and has been a brutal persecution machine, even if that aspect does not exhaust Christianity. I am suggesting, however, that Deleuze follows Nietzsche too faithfully in his interpretation of "the black Saint Paul."[58] Contemporary historical and biblical scholarship has emphasized the radicality of St. Paul and his revolutionary significance that precedes the establishment of a Christian orthodoxy. The line, if there is one, between revolutionary and reactionary Christianity does not lie between Jesus and Paul, but falls after them. In addition, as Jacob Taubes suggests, we can better see Nietzsche as a rival to St. Paul in his attempt to offer European thought a new system of values, a viewpoint that corrects Deleuze's oppositional reading. Taubes writes:

> Who has determined the values of the Occident, in Nietzsche's own sense, more deeply then Paul? So he must be an important man. Because what did Nietzsche want? The transvaluation of values. Well, so there we have someone who pulled it off! And on this point, Nietzsche is very envious too. So he has to say: this guy pulled it off because the poison of resentment holds sway within him.[59]

Taubes argues that there is an incredible proximity between Nietzsche and Paul because both were engaged in a similar struggle. Taubes also claims that Nietzsche interprets his experience of the eternal return as a great ecstatic experience in light of Paul's Damascus experience. The eternal return is "the metaphysical key to understanding everything . . . just as the Damascus experience is the metaphysical key for Paul."[60]

Nietzsche makes a strategic choice for atheism, and Deleuze follows his lead because he humanely opposes "the cruelty of the pang of conscience," that "Christianity hypostasizes sacrifice rather than abolishing it, and thus perpetuates it."[61] We may or may not make the same choice, or we may not know exactly what it means to choose theism or atheism, Christ or Antichrist.[62] But, we can read St. Paul in a way that avoids a forced choice and appreciates his profound importance because he generates the sense of what becomes Christianity for the event. Radical theology attends to the sense of the event without being caught within the either-or alternative expressed by the opposition of Paul and Nietzsche, whose contemporary form is expressed as Christianity or nihilism: *tertium non datur*.[63] Deleuze supplies a more supple, more paradoxical, and at its limits even a more theological thinking in *The Logic of Sense* and other books.

In our contemporary political situation, we have no simple positive alternative with which to oppose our contemporary capitalist empire. Historical understanding of early Christianity provides resources for contemporary radical political thought, because it sharpens the opposition between Christ's kingdom and the Roman Empire that crucified him. The problem is that the Christ-event has largely run its course. Its sense has oriented Western and world history for two millennia, but we cannot simply cling to it nostalgically. To proclaim an old-fashioned, worn-out event in a desperate attempt to short-circuit global capitalism is what Deleuze would call a bad repetition, because it is based on a presumed identity. In fact, I will suggest in the next chapter, in relation to the work of Jean-Luc Nancy, that part of the contemporary significance of Christianity is to maintain the coherence and identity of the West.

We are in search of a new event to proclaim; we are fumbling around, trying to make sense of an event to-come. This event may or may not occur in the future; it is not simply a question of what will happen, but a futural possibility in the present, which is also the possibility of having a future. So long as we preserve this openness to the future, we have the possibility of an event. This approach is a Derridean variation on Heidegger's *Gelassenheit*. *Gelassenheit* means letting-go or letting-be, and one option is to stop grasping or trying, to let go and await the event, which may or may not come. According to Derrida, the event is "unconditioned" and "unforeseeable," and therefore always "to-come."[64] According to Heidegger, "Only a god can save us," which means that we cannot save ourselves. The best we can do is adopt an appropriately faithful attitude toward being. Even though Badiou attempts to formalize being in quasimathematical terms, he ends up close to Heidegger and Derrida in some ways, because he spells out the conditions for the possibility of an event based on his understanding of being, then prescribes a militant fidelity to the revolutionary event when and if it occurs.[65]

What if an event does not occur? Are we completely passive in anticipation of its existence? The choices seem to be to proclaim an ancient and possibly irrelevant event, prophesy the hope for a future event, or proclaim the nothing, which is the nihilistic option. These alternatives presume that we no longer have faith in history or the inevitable progress of humanity and life. Hegelian and Marxist teleologies seem incredible or impossible.

If the Deleuzian alternative is credible, then we are forced back on sense and body. As Spinoza famously remarked, we still do not know what a body can do. According to Deleuze in *Cinema 2*, the current situation involves a crisis of belief in the world: "whether we are Christians or atheists, in our universal schizophrenia, *we need reasons to believe in this world*."[66] The fabric that ties sense to body has become frayed and torn and needs to be reconstituted. As I suggested in chapter 3, our challenge is to stitch sense to body in order to create a new ethics that is anticapitalist in the wake of a theopolitical critique. The link between sense and body is an event; even though the event takes place from the side of sense, it reaches body to transfigure and express it. Paul functions as an example, an exemplary figure, and an inspiration, but at the same time merely an example and not a model to be repeated. America is not ancient Rome. For us, this is both better and worse.

Who has the vision to proclaim the event that is occurring at this moment, in its horrific brutality and its awesome opening to the infinite? This event can be named as the end of global capitalism, because capitalism is reaching real earthly limits of resources that make indefinite growth impossible. This event can be understood in material, physical, ecological, social, political, philosophical, and also theological terms. The task of radical theology is to think the event, which demands the theological vision of a new St. Paul. My contention is that Deleuze provides important theoretical resources to think the event, and therefore he is a contemporary successor to Paul. In the next chapter, I will suggest that a plastic understanding of the event is more useful than a messianic interpretation of the event.

8. PLASTICITY AND THE FUTURE
OF THEOLOGY

MESSIANICITY AND THE DECONSTRUCTION OF CHRISTIANITY

WHAT IS AN EVENT? MUCH OF THE THEOLOGICAL AND POLITICAL stakes of contemporary thinking lies within this question, which I tried to address by way of Deleuze in the previous chapter. The event refers to the possibility of something new, something radically unforeseen, a break with the present and the potentiality of a future. Part of this question of the event, as it manifests itself in the work of Deleuze, Derrida, Badiou, and others, concerns to what extent we await or produce it, to what extent any newness or freedom is possible, and to what extent an event can or may shake the present political order and its discontents. The event is one of the names, along with God, freedom, potentiality, and others, that indicate a stirring beyond the immediate register of bodies and significations. An event is revolutionary because it radically transforms the political conditions of living and thinking together.

In this final chapter, I turn to the question of the future, which is not only a future to-come but also a plastic future, to elaborate the significance of the philosopher Catherine Malabou's work for thinking about political theology. Plasticity is a kind of freedom, though not one opposed to material constraint. To appreciate Malabou's conception of plasticity, already introduced in chapter 5, I will contrast plasticity with messianicity. Messianicity concerns the religious and theological appropriation of deconstruction, including what Jean-Luc Nancy calls the "deconstruction of Christianity." A messianic reading of the deconstruction of Christianity is politically and theologically problematic, I suggest, and I will contrast this reading with a more plastic understanding deconstruction, including the deconstruction of Christianity.

One way to read some of the last writings of Jacques Derrida as well as some of the most recent works of Jean-Luc Nancy, including *Dis-Enclosure* and *Noli Me Tangere*, is to understand the end of deconstruction as the deconstruction of Christianity. That is, after deconstructing Western metaphysics and onto-theology, one sees that the most pervasive, profound, and problematic spirit of what we call the West is named Christianity, and the need for its deconstruction coincides with what has been called "the return of religion" in contemporary society and thought.

An effect of what has been called postmodernism has been to undermine the singularity of the Enlightenment, or the decisive break between European modernity and every other form of human culture. If the uniqueness of modernity is called into question, then there may exist as many continuities as discontinuities between European modernity and what preceded it. Theorists such as Marcel Gauchet have articulated a trajectory that began in ancient Greece and ancient Israel, and it is this trajectory, rather than the specific Enlightenment articulation of it, that is unique.[1] This trajectory can be understood in a more conventionally modern form as progressive, in a more philosophically sophisticated way as dialectical, or sometimes in a more authentically postmodern version, following Walter Benjamin, as messianic.

In *Specters of Marx*, Derrida argues for a messianic spirit of Marxism. According to Derrida, the "formal structure of promise . . . remains irreducible to any deconstruction."[2] Any emancipatory promise carries with it a kind of messianic eschatology. This messianic is formal or structural and constitutes a "messianic without messianism" that is at work in the idea of justice or the idea of democracy.[3] On the one hand, there are the historical, determinate messianisms, the so-called Abrahamic religions, and on the other, there is this indeterminate promise that also characterizes Marxism as well as any thinking of promise, of hope, of democracy, or of justice. "The messianic appeal belongs properly to a universal structure" that exceeds even the horizon of the biblical religions themselves.[4] For Derrida, this "messianic without messianism" opens up the religions of the Book beyond themselves and any conceivable recovery. However, this universal messianic structure can be read as providing a sense of the West, an opening beyond the closure of onto-theology and metaphysics. Although Derrida provides tools to deconstruct the opposition between West and non-West, his practical focus upon Western, European thought consolidates a certain structural integrity for this tradition.

Although Derridean reflection on messianicity has opened up the study of religion in important and progressive ways, and although the concept of the messianic remains important and vital, I cannot help worrying about it and want to elaborate a critical perspective. But this critique of messianism and the exploration of a plastic alternative should not give ammunition to the shortsighted and sometimes painfully ignorant dismissals of Derrida's thought. My worry is that this move toward messianicity reflects at least in part a strategy to defend Eurocentrism and Western culture by linking it temporally with its history and cutting off any spatial diffusion or contamination of separate cultures. For example, while Mark C. Taylor criticizes any simple faith in providential or progressive history, he asserts the Protestant Christian identity of modern Western culture. "The distinctive institutions of the modern world," he writes, "are inseparable from Protestantism and its history."[5] At its limit, the spirit of Christianity is identified with the spirit of the West, and even if some of its forms are criticized as dangerous, superstitious, fundamentalist, or malevolent, this spirit remains accessible to "us" in the form of time, or can be reactualized at this moment.

For Gianni Vattimo, messianicity takes the form of weakness, the weakening of the Christian tradition in particular. This weakening is a process of secularization. Vattimo celebrates this process as the destiny and fulfillment of Christianity itself rather than as a falling away from a primary origin. In *The Future of Religion*, Vattimo claims that "the Christian revelation has cogency insofar as we recognize that without it our historical existence would not make sense."[6] Christianity is intrinsic to our cultural and historical existence to such an extent that our existence would be incomprehensible without it. The essence of the Christian revelation is its own fulfillment in nihilism, that is, the weakening of its strong truth into hermeneutics, the liquidating of its own and every other foundationalism. Vattimo claims:

Should it recognize that the redemptive meaning of the Christian message makes its impact precisely by dissolving the claims of objectivity, the Church might also finally heal the tension between truth and charity that has, so to speak, tormented it throughout its history.[7]

This weakness is messianic in terms similar to Derrida, except that Derrida's messianicity is more structural and Vattimo's is more historical. But Derrida's work also raises the aporia as to whether it is simply possible to separate the formal and structural from the historical, even if he leans toward one pole. Derrida emphasizes a structural "messianic without messianism" while Vattimo's more historical reading proposes that "postmodern nihilism (the end of metanarratives) is the truth of Christianity."[8] As we will see, Nancy's deconstruction of Christianity can be read both as Vattimo's historical revelation and as Derrida's messianic promise.

The West has been constructed again and again, in manifold ways, over against its Others. In many ways its main foil has been Islam, as Tomoko Masuzawa points out in *The Invention of World Religions*. As the discipline of world religions was constructed in the late nineteenth century, Islam was linguistically and culturally identified as Semitic, along with Judaism, in contrast to an Aryan European Greek and Asian Sanskrit.[9] For much of Christian history, Judaism functioned as an internal Other to complement Islam's status as external Other, and modern antisemitism was an attempt to exclude Judaism from the identity of the European, Christian West. This attempt failed, though not before culminating in a horrific Holocaust, and Masuzawa also describes how in response to surging fascism and antisemitism, "certain liberal Protestants, Jews, and some Catholics in tow attempted to form a united spiritual front of 'Judeo-Christian' tradition.[10]

With the Allied victory, Judaism was successfully integrated into European and Western modernity, leaving Islam as the singular exception. The Eastern religions, of course, functioned to sustain the opposition, and they could serve as objects of romanticized fascination and as exoticization. The Cold War, of course, provided a screen that masked this interreligious conflict, casting it as an alliance between the religious and democratic West against a Godless communism. With the collapse of the U.S.S.R., Islam has emerged once again as the fundamental "enemy" of the West in many religio-political contexts. Mohammed Arkoun, similarly to Masuzawa, critiques this political identity of the West and suggests that a conception of "Mediterranean space" (following Fernand Braudel) could help deconstruct the "fundamental polarity of a substantialised Islam on one hand, and on the other (depending on the side of the divide), an 'enlightened' or Satanized West."[11]

While the European Enlightenment came to represent a break with a religious past, it also served as a cloak for Protestant Christianity to set itself apart from Judaism and Roman Catholicism. In a postsecular context, the primary separation shifts from a temporal break between religious and secular to a more spatial break between cultures. Temporality, which in a post-Heideggerian sense is the essence of being, composes the identity of cultures in a historical sense, with Western culture privileged as always, but now the boundary between its religious and its nonreligious identity is blurred.

In Giorgio Agamben's commentary on Paul's Letter to the Romans, "messianic time is the time that it takes time to come to an end, or, more precisely, the time we take to bring to an end, to achieve our representation of time."[12] As we saw in chapter 7, Agamben sees Paul expressing the paradigmatic form of messianic time, which in Paul's case is the time between the happening of the Resurrection and its completion in the return of the Messiah. In a more general sense, messianic time is operational time, or "the time that the mind takes to realize a time-image."[13] As messianic or quasimessianic time, Christianity would remain operative even as it disables, deconstructs, or renders inoperable all determinate forms of time.

In messianic terms, Christianity as such is a *pharmakon*, both poison and cure. As a cure, in its originary form as expressed by St. Paul, Christianity provides the opportunity for an opening, a universality or a "*déclosion*," beyond the enclosure that traps Western metaphysics in its snare. According to Jean-Luc Nancy, the heart of the Western tradition is a Christian heart, and "the only thing that can be actual is an atheism that contemplates the reality of its Christian origins."[14] If Christianity is coextensive with the West, and here Nancy agrees with the reading of Marcel Gauchet, then Christianity as such "is in a state of being surpassed," that is, a state of self-surpassing Christianity.[15] The deconstruction of Christianity, then, would be to bring that self-overcoming of Christianity to an end. But would this be the end of Christianity, and if so, would it also be the triumph of Christianity? Nancy reads the essence of Christianity with Heidegger's notion of the Open, as "an absolute transcendental of opening" that would admit of no closure or closing.[16]

Is Christianity as such an opening, or does it provide one? Can Christianity be deconstructed, or is it deconstruction itself—and as such undeconstructible? In *On Touching—Jean-Luc Nancy*, Derrida grapples with the enormity of the task of deconstructing Christianity, and cautions Nancy about its possibility:

> What Nancy announces today under the title "the Deconstruction of Christianity" will no doubt be the test of a dechristianizing of the world—no doubt as necessary and fatal as it is impossible. Almost by definition, one can only acknowledge this. Only Christianity can do this work, that is, undo it while doing it. Heidegger, too—Heidegger already—has only succeeded in failing at this. Dechristianization will be a Christian victory.[17]

That is, self-deconstruction would be an essential part of the nature of Christianity from the beginning, and therefore the deconstruction of Christianity would be in a way the fulfillment of Christianity, and in this sense the triumph of Christianity.

Along with the engagement with religious topics and themes in Derrida's later work, we can ask seriously whether or not deconstruction has always been essentially a religious movement? The deconstruction of Christianity is important partly because it concerns the possibility of deconstruction itself. Deconstruction is Derrida's translation of Heidegger's term *Destruktion* into French. Heidegger used a Lutheran term, *destructio*, that in its original meaning carried an evangelical connotation—to destroy the outer shell in order to liberate the living kernel within.[18] Furthermore, Heidegger's early work in the 1920s on the *Phenomenology of Religious Life*, which prefigured *Being and Time*, was based on a new understanding of Christian temporality, mainly in St. Paul, as discussed in the previous chapter.[19] In this context, Alain Badiou's reading of Paul in *Saint Paul: The Foundation of Universalism* must be read as structurally similar to deconstruction, even though Badiou insists on his atheism more unambiguously. For Badiou, Paul's discourse is paradigmatic because it represents "a pure fidelity to the possibility opened by the event."[20] The Resurrection of Christ is "pure event, opening of an epoch." Even though Badiou does not believe in the Resurrection event, he affirms the structure of Paul's thought as a form of fidelity to an event that is in a way very close to deconstruction, shorn of Badiou's set-theoretical mathematical ontology.

I contend that the notion of plasticity, taken from the work of Catherine Malabou, provides important resources with which to think the deconstruction of Christianity. Plasticity concerns form, but it stretches our ordinary understanding of what form is and means. According to Malabou, plasticity has at least three functions: 1) the capacity to receive form in a passive sense; 2) the ability to give form more actively; and 3) the power to annihilate form.[21] As distinguished from ancient Greek plasticity, which related more specifically to the arts, modern plasticity concerns more precisely the form of human subjectivity.

In his *Critique of Pure Reason*, Kant struggled to articulate how human mental capacities could both give and receive form, and he ended up positing a duality between passive sensory intuitions and an active transcendental apperception. The latter, however, appeared secondary to the material form of human representations, so Kant conceptualized the transcendental imagination as a form-giving power that could re-present sense intuitions under the form of categories of understanding. Heidegger's book on *Kant and the Problem of Metaphysics* demonstrates the complex but fundamental status of the transcendental imagination in the first *Critique*. Heidegger argues that Kant shrinks back from his insight into the significance of the transcendental imagination in the *Critique of Pure Reason*, which is why he has to rewrite it and relegate the transcendental imagination to an inferior position in the second edition of the first *Critique*.[22]

It is Hegel, however, who fully and successfully formulates the modern nature of human subjectivity, and he does this by modeling it on divine subjectivity, as Malabou shows in her book *The Future of Hegel*. For Hegel, the process of representation (*Vorstellung*) "seals into one the divine *kenosis* and the *kenosis* of the transcendental subject."[23] What does this mean? Representation for Hegel functions in a way similar to the transcendental imagination in Kant, and it refers to a schematism, the providing of a schema, which is not an image in a literal sense. Whereas the transcendental imagination troubled Kant because it threatened to mix up the empirical and the transcendental, for Hegel the process of representation is more straightforwardly and productively a process of temporalization, a temporal formation.

The key insight is that Hegel helps to fashion an understanding of modern subjectivity by reading human subjectivity as he reads divine subjectivity, as kenotic and self-othering. Hegel reads the Christian Trinity in an unorthodox way, according to which each persona consists of a progressive alienation that is not the manifestation of a lack, but "the appearance of a new ontological guise of time."[24] As Malabou, explains, divine alienation is a manifestation of temporalization, a linear becoming of an event, the Incarnation, in which "God envisages himself as a moment," a necessary moment, but also one that must pass.[25] Hegel's speculative reading of Christianity writes plasticity into the heart of the human subject: his kenotic alienation is the same as God's, he sees himself as a moment of time in which he is a part, a manifestation of temporalization that achieves the fulfillment of his essence in history, even as it ends.

Returning to the three significations of plasticity articulated by Malabou, the active giving of form and the passive receiving of form both apply to the process of representation, *Vorstellung*, which is a dialectic of self (active shaping or forming, assimilating, consuming) and other (passively being shaped or formed, giving oneself up to another). The annihilation of form, however, pertains to the *Aufhebung* itself, and this is Malabou's key insight, which also complements Slavoj Žižek's reading of the Hegelian dialectic as a negative rather than a positive, accumulatory process. The alienation of human self-expression, for instance as labor, creates and projects a future, a linear "time in which the subject 'sees itself as a passing moment.'"[26] Sublation cancels and preserves, but it only preserves or constitutes a future by canceling or destroying the present, a present moment it generates by giving itself a sense of a linear succession.

Modern subjectivity is derived from Christian theology, here seen in Hegel. Is the deconstruction of modern subjectivity in some way a releasing or restoring of this original Christian essence? How could it be recouped? In or with what? And would we want to embrace it or bid it *á-dieu*? If plasticity can be seen to come in the wake of deconstruction, is this a dialectical movement, a shift in the strategy to save the modern Western (white, male) subject? Or as an explosion in thinking, a subversion of what even deconstruction saves (justice, the Name of God)?

To think the deconstruction of Christianity in a radical instead of conservative or reactionary way, we need to emphasize the essential difference between deconstruction and all forms of Heideggerian and Lutheran *Destruktion*. As Derrida avers, "a 'deconstruction of Christianity,' if it is ever possible, should therefore begin by untying itself from a Christian tradition of *destructio*."[27] If this untying or delinking is possible, then the difference between the Derridean and the Lutheran and Heideggerian forms of deconstruction have to do with time. *Destruktion* is linked to the form of linear time paradigmatically elaborated by Hegel. Deconstruction for Derrida, however, is spacing, or a time conceived as spacing, that articulates "the becoming-time of space and the becoming-space of time."[28] To think time as spacing, or the spacing of time, which is not simply a reduction of time to space, is to see where deconstruction separates itself from *Destruktion* and ultimately becomes plasticity.

The spacing of time, which in the work of Gilles Deleuze becomes a time-image, involves the multiplication or proliferation of forms of temporalization in noncoincident moments. This proliferation, this branching, this plasticity of time understood as spacing, stretches beyond the horizon of Christianity and modern philosophy, offering new possibilities for configuring God and humanity, male and female, animality and machine. The spacing of temporality is becoming a brain, and *a brain is the incarnation of time in a body.*

Here we could sketch three forms of time:

1) The first is circular time, time as eternal return. Every circle presupposes a center, around which everything rotates. The absolute center is the unmoved mover, God as that around which everything turns. In a more particular sense, the form that time takes is its receptacle, *khōra*, which is a relatively more passive configuration of form.

2) The second form of time is the line, as discussed above. Linear time is active because it seizes itself in consciousness as a moment, but it can be grasped only in its passing. Linear time is paradigmatically Christian and given its modern expression by Hegel, as Malabou's important reading shows.[29]

3) Finally, time is plasticity itself, absolute plasticity. Here is time in its explosive capacity, understood as spacing (Derrida) or as time-image (Deleuze). The form of plastic time is bifurcation, which leads to a fractalizing of temporalization, an unfathomable involution. Here the proliferation of multiple forms of temporality exceeds the ability of a subject to seize them as moment and construct a linear sequentiality. The ability to function as a brain depends on the ability to set up parallel networks, loosely connected inference systems that do not run through a central processor or programmer. There is no ghost or god in the machine; the machine is not just a machine, however, but an adaptive system of such incredible complexity that it generates new forms of complexity, or additional layers of plasticity.

From her reading of plasticity in Hegel, a term she takes from the *Phenomenology of Spirit*, Malabou has pivoted to engage and expand theoretically on the concept of plasticity in the neurosciences. In her book *What Should We Do with Our Brain?* she claims, "Our brain is plastic and we don't know it."[30] According to Malabou, we are neuronal humans but we have no idea how to negotiate the gap that separates the neuronal network within the brain from the mental one seemingly outside of it. Some of the most vital contemporary research is taking place in the neurosciences, and even when we are made aware of its findings, we do not yet possess the theoretical tools to incorporate them, which are what Malabou is helping to provide. We remain trapped within insipid frameworks and presuppositions that ask questions like whether or not there exists a "god gene," or if not, how our religious beliefs evolved.[31]

The plasticity of the brain is so radical that we create our brains, which is not simply a mechanical or even organic process. We think that our brains make us, forgetting that we also make our brains, never glimpsing the possibility of becoming-brain, that is, a pure time-image, a "little bit of time in its pure state," as Deleuze says.[32] Malabou writes, "The plasticity of time is inscribed in the brain."[33] Brain cells are both differential and transdifferential. Stem cells possess both the capacity to differentiate themselves into additional cells of the same kind of tissue and the ability to develop into cells of other types of tissue. Specifically, plasticity within the brain names the ability of stem cells—neurons or glial cells—to shift or modulate between one and the other, between self-differentiation and transdifferentiation.[34] Plasticity refers to the incredible resilience of form of adult brain cells, not only infant or fetus stem cells. Furthermore, this plasticity of modulation extends beyond our solely physiological account of the brain into the initial representation of the self, or "proto-Self," which is unconscious, and into the conscious self. Plasticity indicates the productive giving of cellular and mental forms, the reception of form in and on the body and mind, and ultimately the annihilation of form, the dying of neurons that is required to generate a self, or the forgetting of experiences that is necessary to continue having an identity.

The incredible difficulty is that we can think the absolute or pure form of time as messianicity (Benjamin, Agamben, Badiou, Derrida) and as plasticity (Deleuze, Derrida, Malabou). Here is the confrontation, the payoff, the stakes of the confrontation over the deconstruction of Christianity. So long as time is understood as literally formless, it inevitably takes the form of the messianic, which is a pure force, even if it is thought as a weak force rather than a strong force, a messianism. Plasticity allows the necessary form to be thought as the giving, taking, and destruction of form, in a branching that is creative rather than simply responsive or passive. This creativity is a new form of freedom, although it is more virtual and potential than actual in a determinate sense.

Where should we locate Nancy's deconstruction of Christianity in this alternative? In *Dis-Enclosure* he provides resources to think the deconstruction of Christianity both as messianic destruction, which never comes to an end so long as the West continues, and as spacing, which can be read as plasticity. Nancy says that the *éclosion* or eclosure (burgeoning or expansion) of the world gives way to a *déclosion*, dis-enclosure (opening up, un-closing). Eclosure is the expansion but also the enclosing of space, and he associates this fundamental expansion with Columbus and European modernity. The discovery of America represents "a world in the process of eclosing in the world, and even more, in the process, if I may say so, of eclosing the world within it and around it."[35] We could think about this situation of eclosion with Deleuze and Guattari's language of deterritorialization and reterritorialization. Eclosure is the deterritorialization that allows for reterritorialization, or enclosure of space. But *déclosion* or dis-enclosure is an absolute deterritorialization that cannot be reterritorialized.

Déclosion is an absolute opening because it concerns "the process of spatialization itself."[36] *Déclosion* thought as absolute opening and absolute spacing can be read differently than a simple messianic temporality. The distinction seems to depend on an understanding of time. So long as time is thought as end, or ending, the status of temporality stretched between an event and its end is messianic, at least in a Christian sense.

Alain Badiou claims that his reading of Paul is nonmessianic, because for Paul the event has taken place. But I would suggest, following Agamben, that it is messianic precisely because the event has happened, even though it is also still occurring, fulfilling itself, coming to an end. He writes, "with Paul, for example, we have a notion that is not contained in the idea of messianism, since at issue is the process of the coming of God himself, such as *it has taken place*."[37] This is precisely the definition of Christian messianism—the event has taken place, but it has not yet been brought to an end because one can still be faithful to it.

Badiou theorizes this situation less as time and more as fidelity to an event that has taken place, but I am arguing that the event cannot be contained within or restricted to the literal moment of the resurrection, which does not take place in time, but explodes time itself in powerful, productive, and destructive ways. This is both Pauline and structurally messianic, as Agamben has shown in *The Time That Remains*, and for Benjamin the messianic has the same structure. So long as one thinks time in relation to its end—the end of metaphysics, the end of the West, the end of Christianity, the end of time itself—it is thoroughly messianic and inherently Christian. And furthermore, deconstruction has shown that this end never arrives; it is infinitely and indefinitely deferred, and we live off of the messianic power that forever takes time to its end.

But, if time is thought as spacing, and as birthing or hatching, this is a plastic understanding of time that is, I suggest, nonmessianic. It brings nothing to an end. Messianism is fundamentally about ending, and in a sense the entire structure of Christian and Western thought is obsessed with death. For Derrida, as for any thinker responsible to the enormity of the Western tradition, whether one is trying to reform, transform, or renew it, the world wears and weighs upon a thinker. This is an enormous and extraordinary burden, and Derrida experiences the death in and of the West as mourning. I do not want to trivialize this mourning or this responsibility. It is internal to and constitutive of European responsibility, but it is not the entire story. To quote from a novel by Margaret Atwood: "they think I should be filled with death, I should be in mourning. But nothing has died, everything is alive, everything is waiting to become alive."[38]

What is happening now, according to Nancy, is that "another life, another respiration, another weight, and another humanity is in the process of emerging."[39] To think the stakes of such a transformation, we have think the eclosure or opening up of the world more radically: "no longer an eclosure against the background of a given world, or even against that of a given creator, but the eclosure of eclosure itself and the spacing of space itself."[40] A general dis-enclosure of opening/closure opens up in a way that approaches or becomes plasticity as Malabou theorizes it. Nancy touches on the destructive capacity of dis-enclosure in a way that accords with Malabou's emphasis on the explosive character of plasticity. He writes, "dis-enclosure confers upon eclosure a character that is close to explosion, and spacing confines it to a conflagration."[41] Plasticity or dis-enclosure concerns this explosive opening that ends Christianity and the West differently than does messianicity.

Plastic time concerns the synaptic gap that is not an absolute break but rather a threshold. In all plastic generation of form, Malabou claims that there is an energetic explosion, because transformation requires "a rupture, the violence of a gap that interrupts all continuity."[42] The synaptic gap is the opening or passage that enables transformation, and plasticity works with and across this gap. According to Leonard Lawlor, Derrida and Foucault, as well as Deleuze, provide a way "to move along the path from the deconstruction of Christianity to life; it provides the only way to move beyond Heidegger."[43] Lawlor reads Foucault and Derrida in detail and suggests that Derridean spacing is a gap (*écart*) that can be read in conformity with Foucault's analysis of "man and his doubles." Foucault claims that these doubles or doublets are produced by what Lawlor explains is "a hiatus, miniscule and yet invincible."[44] The minute but impassible gap is both a limit and a passage to life, to a new concept of life that Lawlor calls a "neovitalism." I would hesitate to embrace this term "neovitalism" and suggest that what Deleuze calls "a life" in his last essay, "Immanence: A Life," extends far more broadly than what we usually think of as life in a biological sense. Life thought as "conflict," "battleground," and "place of the dead" at the end of Lawlor's book refers to a certain powerlessness and finitude that remains in continuity with major themes in Western metaphysics.[45] Plasticity affirms life in a material and spiritual sense at one and the same time, nondualistically. Plasticity is a kind of creative freedom, but not the freedom of spirit to work with and on raw matter. Plasticity is the manifestation of a "new materialism," which refuses any separation between brain and thought, matter and spirit.[46] And this is a theological materialism because it is a matter of ultimate concern, life.

The *écart infime* must be thought synaptically, plastically, and as *éclosion*. In this sense, the gap is a border, a threshold. The gap extends infinitely along the border, but it is not itself uncrossable, just ineliminable. In vision, the gap or border is between the eye seeing a thought coming and the eye of the thought that gazes upon the seer. Malabou writes provocatively about "the impossible face-to-face encounter between the eye on the edge of discourse that looks and the eye that tries to look to see the thought."[47] What is important is that the thought is born along a border that constitutes an *écart infime* between the seer and the object of thinking, what Malabou calls "the eye of language . . . at the edge of discourse."[48]

If Christianity is coextensive with the West, then there is no possibility of rigorously separating philosophy and theology. Most forms of theology would be dedicated to preserving and continuing some form of Christianity, even if at times in the name of overcoming it. Most forms of (Western) philosophy would be dedicated to preserving Western logic and discourse, if not Western culture and hegemony, whether or not they are aware of how deeply Christian this logic and discourse are. Why would a radical theology think or desire to let go of Christianity, even the deconstruction of Christianity? So long as this is not a repression, a *Verwindung*, or twisting free of, Christianity remains the only creative alternative for (Western) thinking.[49]

A task to which a radical theology can contribute is to create a new brain for our species, based on this insight into the plasticity of form, both material and immaterial. This is also an urgent political and perhaps even a post-political task. Here theology would remain, as Bergson claims, "a machine for making gods," but these gods would be plastic gods and the theological machine would be a brain: "it is there that the possibility of religion persists: the religious bond (scrupulous, respectful, modest, reticent, inhibited) between the value of life, its absolute 'dignity,' and the theological machine, the 'machine for making gods.'"[50] Nancy's deconstruction of Christianity can be read as messianic, as an attempt to save the West by associating it with the radical self-surpassing of the tradition, or alternatively as plastic, as the opening of opening itself, the "eclosure of eclosure itself and the spacing of space itself."[51] Is it possible to render a decision given those alternatives? And, would any such decision not be theological? That is, theology itself concerns the possibility of choosing or not choosing between a messianic and a plastic version of the deconstruction of Christianity.

Lacan claims that "only theologians can be truly atheistic, namely those who speak of God," because God is the locus of speech and "as long as things are said, the God hypothesis will persist."[52] But, so long as theism and atheism remain questions of conscious belief, they remain superficial compared to a psychoanalytic understanding of the unconscious and derivative of more primary human motivations and desires. In chapter 6, I appealed to Deleuze (and Guattari) in my understanding of the production of an unconscious event that creates a law beyond law. In chapter 7, I applied this understanding of the event to radical theology by considering contemporary discussions of Paul in relation to Deleuze. In this chapter, I have shifted from the event to the concept of plasticity to develop a political critique of messianism and to interrogate the notion of the deconstruction of Christianity.

In a way, plasticity gets us beyond deconstruction, but in another sense there is no beyond of deconstruction to get beyond. Plasticity offers a new way to render thought and philosophy, one that cuts across the presumption that one must read thinkers in either-or terms. Deleuze, as well, provides resources for such conjunctions: Derrida *and* Deleuze, Deleuze *and*

Agamben *and* Badiou *and* Žižek *and* Negri *and* Malabou *and* Nancy. Such thinking may appear incompatible and monstrous, but it is also a product of the freedom of radical theological thinking, which is freed from theological *and* philosophical *and* political orthodoxy. To think profoundly is to think theologically, to think about what ultimately matters, and this is also a political task, because to truly interpret the world is to change it. In the wake of Nietzsche, the task of the theologian is to transvalue our (theological, political, and liberal) values. As Carl Schmitt declares: "today everything is theology, except what the theologians declare to be such."[53]

CONCLUSION

SIX THESES ON POLITICAL THEOLOGY

BY WAY OF A CONCLUSION, I WANT TO SET OUT SIX THESES CONCERNING political theology. These theses sum up the overall purpose of the book and serve to illustrate once again what is at stake in thinking radically about political theology. These theses do not follow the chapter progression but rather provide an overview of the scope and theme of political theology for which the chapters offered more fine-grained descriptions and interventions.

I

Today we can see a deconstruction or breakdown of any strict opposition between the religious and the secular, and this theoretical conclusion is coincident with a resurgence of religion in cultural, political, academic, and sociological terms. One name for this situation has been suggested as "postsecular," although I would qualify the postsecular as signifying more properly a postsecular*ist* situation or orientation. Postsecularism means that there is no way to ascertain a secure secularist and nonreligious viewpoint or to rigorously exclude religion from it. One way to define European modernity is as the attempt, which is ultimately unsuccessful, to achieve such a secularist viewpoint and to instantiate it in viable social and political frameworks. From this perspective, the postsecularist would accord with the postmodern. That is, postmodernism names, however problematically, the inability to completely set apart the modern from the nonmodern. And postsecularism is a corollary to postmodernism, because the possibility of secularism is intrinsic to the identity of modernism.

II

If one cannot sustain a rigorous distinction between the religious and the secular, then it follows that we cannot maintain a strict distinction between political philosophy and political theology, as I have discussed in chapter 4. In *Political Theology*, Carl Schmitt famously claims that "all significant concepts of the modern theory of the state are secularized theological concepts."[1] Now, according to the temporalization or periodization of modernity, secular concepts succeed and replace theological concepts, which is the more conventional reading of modernity. But Schmitt says that these concepts should be seen as secularized theological concepts "not only because of their historical development . . . but also because of their systematic structure."[2] So there is a structural relationship between secular and theological concepts in addition to the historical relationship, and this structural opposition is breaking down even as the temporal succession has been called into question. Therefore, any serious theoretical understanding of the political must grapple with the problem or question of political theology. We cannot excise theology from politics to secure a valid political philosophy or program, which is what modernity was based on. Modernity grounds reason, ethics, aesthetics, and politics in an autonomous secular sphere, which possesses validity precisely insofar as it excludes theological or religious criteria. But this project is what postmodernism and postsecularism undermine.

III

The fundamental ideology of modern secularism is liberalism, which functions both politically as liberal democracy and economically as liberal capitalism. Liberalism is the target of radical critiques from the Left and the Right, although it attained a pyrrhic victory in the late twentieth century with the downfall of the U.S.S.R. Liberalism sustains modernism and secularism, and it legislates the freedom of individual choice in the market (free-market capitalism) and in the government (representative democracy). The reason that modernism is being called into question as postmodernism and that secularism has been critiqued by what can be called a "postsecular" or "postsecularist" understanding is because liberalism itself is breaking down. The end of modernity is the end of liberalism, both economically and politically. Today, neoliberalism still exists, but mainly as a façade, a power-play to uphold the financial and military interests of the strongest. Representative democracy has been corrupted and corroded by lobbyists, special interests, media apparatuses, and paperless electronic voting with secret proprietary source codes. Liberal capitalism has been surpassed by a virulent, savage capitalism that Naomi Klein calls corporatism, which increasingly consumes the means of productive capital itself as it flails about desperately in search of ever more short-term profit.[3]

IV

For many Americans, the only alternative to liberalism seems to be a conservative or neoconservative political worldview. During the latter half of the twentieth century, a number disillusioned radicals and liberals drifted toward conservative positions with varying degrees of zealousness. The critique of modern liberalism advanced by intellectuals such as Carl Schmitt and Leo Strauss seemed to leave no alternative to conservatism or pessimism, especially as the horrors committed in the name of Marxism became more and more apparent. Marxism was proclaimed dead in the wake of communism's collapse, but many of the most interesting, important, and powerful contemporary political philosophy has been done in a broadly post-Marxist, Continentalist context, including works by Badiou, Laclau, Mouffe, Negri, Rancière, Agamben, Žižek, and Derrida. Many people appalled by the cynicism of neoconservatism take refuge in a nostalgic liberalism, but unfortunately this position only serves to maintain the status quo and masks the radical alternative.

V

There is the possibility for a radical political theology, which means the refusal of conservative or neoconservative options in politics and in theology after the demise of liberalism. Most varieties of political theology take some form of liberal or at best liberation theology, or alternatively some form of neoorthodox theology. At the same time, we can trace a speculative genealogy back from the work of Paul Tillich and view a somewhat under-the-radar tradition of radical theology in the United States as a radicalized Tillichianism. I see the Death of God theologies of the 1960s associated with figures like Thomas J. J. Altizer, William Hamilton, Richard Rubenstein, and others as a twisting free from orthodoxy and an opening up of theological thinking to an engagement with contemporary culture and philosophy. The next generation of radical theologians combined insights into the death of God with interpretations of French poststructuralist, deconstructive, and postmodern philosophies, generating an American postmodern theology in the 1980s. These American postmodern theologians included Mark C. Taylor, Carl Raschke, Charles Winquist and Edith Wyschogrod, and for many of them, deconstruction is "the death of God put into writing," as Raschke puts it.[4] In the 1990s, newer and more conservative forms of postmodern theology appeared, with the translation of and engagement with works by Jean-Luc Marion and the emergence of Cambridge Radical Orthodoxy. At the same time, during the '90s a Continental philosophy of religion formed that was deeply responsive to Derrida's so-called turn to religion. This movement was primarily identified with Merold Westphal, Richard Kearney, and John D. Caputo, who brought Derrida to Villanova for three celebrated "Religion and Postmodernism" conferences. Derrida's engagement with explicitly religious themes coincides with his more direct treatment of political ideas, and after this connection, other Continental theorists have been engaged from the standpoint of theology, philosophy of religion, and theoretical religious studies, many of whom have also written about religion in important ways. Such thinkers include Badiou, Žižek, Negri, Agamben, Gianni Vattimo, and Jean-Luc Nancy. The point is not whether any specific thinker is a believer or an atheist, but more importantly how the relationship between religion and politics can be understood and configured, and what tools are offered for theoretical as well as practical transformation. Today, there are some thinkers (including myself and Jeffrey W. Robbins, and in a slightly different way, Creston Davis)[5] who identify with the tradition of radical theology and also follow this political "turn," and who attempt to theorize the intrinsic relationship between the religious and the political within the world today. This trajectory is neither an embrace nor an exclusion of transcendence, but thinks beyond liberalism and eschews conservatism as well as nostalgia for liberal and traditionalist theologies and political theories.

VI

My last thesis is in the form of a question, if not a promise: If liberalism comes to an end, what about democracy? Is liberal democracy the only form of democracy, and does it perish with liberalism, or is there a possibility for radical democracy, as I tried to suggest in chapter 5? Our challenge is to think the possibility of a radically democratic politics and practice, which would be necessarily a religious or quasireligious politics and practice insofar as religion is inescapable. If the political retains any hope, then our hope may be a democratic hope, a hope for radical democracy. The hope for radical democracy is a potentiality, a form of freedom that requires plastic forms to bring it into being.

Otherwise politics becomes technical management and manipulation or the worship of a new or old form of political sovereignty. There do not appear to be many good reasons to hope, and one of the bitter lessons of the Left over the past few decades has been a pessimistic resignation to the unmitigated victory of capitalism. But, capitalism itself is reaching very real limits to growth, including global climate systems change and depletion of finite natural resources, including oil, water, and minerals. If we can maintain a politics, will it or could it be a form of democracy, or does democracy die with liberalism? Does the end of capitalism offer us only new forms of fascism? I would like to hope that democracy could survive the death of liberalism (and capitalism). I would also like to hope that politics survives and continues. However, the financial, economic, and ecological collapse that we are undergoing may in an extreme case bring an end to politics as such, because in a catastrophic scenario the polis or city might not survive, and the polis is the condition of sorts for what we call human culture or civilization. In conclusion, what can we think, what can we hope, and how can we act, in light of the possibility of imminent global collapse? Is there a radical theological thinking that would be responsive to this apocalyptic situation?

We need to experiment radically with new ways of thinking and living, because the current paradigm is in a state of exhaustion, depletion, and death. Potentiality as read through Negri and Agamben and Malabou's notion of plasticity are names for such a new way of thinking. Another is materialism, or the possibility of taking the material world seriously as a work against idealist denial and other-worldliness. Theology seems to be intrinsically tied to transcendence and other-worldly value, and it calls that value God. But a radical theology that affirms the death of God is freed from transcendence, and rather than constituting a form of nihilism as many theological critics charge, radical theology is an affirmation of thinking and living under the conditions of reality and materiality. We seek to transform the world, not to exchange it for another one that conforms to our desires. The urgency is the awareness that overpopulation, resource exploitation, and global climate change may bring an end to human civilization within the next century. Our contemporary form of life is unsustainable, and our forms of thought are not nourishing or sustaining either. A radical political theology may not appear nourishing, but it is a necessary theoretical intervention into our current way of life.

NOTES

Introduction:

The Freedom of Radical Theology After the Death of God

1. *The Analects of Confucius*, trans. Simon Leys (New York: W.W. Norton, 1997), 60.

2. A good survey of the history of religion in the United States is George M. Marsden, *Religion and American Culture* (Boston: Wadsworth, 2000).

3. George M. Marsden, *Understanding Fundamentalism and Evangelicalism* (Grand Rapids, MI: Eerdmans Publishing, 1991), 172.

4. One of the best ways to read the history of the civil rights movement is through the lens of Taylor Branch's monumental trilogy, focusing largely but not exclusively on Martin Luther King: *Parting the Waters: America in the King Years 1959–63* (New York: Simon & Schuster, 1989); *Pillar of Fire: America in the King Years 1963–65* (New York: Simon & Schuster, 1998); and *At Canaan's Edge: America in the King Years 1965–68* (New York: Simon & Schuster, 2006).

5. See Branch, *Pillar of Fire*, 404.

6. See Kevin Phillips, *American Theocracy: The Perils and Politics of Radical Religion, Oil and Borrowed Money in the 21st Century* (New York: Penguin, 2006), particularly chapters 4–6. My reading of the rise of the Religious Right accords

with Phillips's to a great extent, although I differ from his interpretation of minor aspects of the religious history of the United States prior to the 1960s. Phillips does an excellent job of explaining the historical development of religious conservatism in the United States, and he ties these views to dangerous attitudes concerning disturbing financial and economic situations such as the peaking of world oil production and the weakened status of the U.S. dollar. For another source in addition to Phillips and Marsden that addresses this understanding of the Religious Right in relation to the aftermath of the Civil War, see David Goldfield, *Still Fighting the Civil War: The American South and Southern History* (Baton Rouge: Louisiana State University Press, 2002).

7. See Sigmund Freud, *Moses and Monotheism*, trans. Katherine Jones (New York: Random House, 1967),160–164, for a discussion of the notion of the return of the repressed.

8. See Rousas John Rushdoony, *The Institutes of Biblical Law* (Nutley, NJ: The Craig Press, 1973). I will return to the notion of biblical law and compare Christian Reconstruction to aspects of Islamic fundamentalism in chapter 6.

9. Gary North and Gary DeMar, *Christian Reconstruction: What It Is, What It Isn't* (Tyler, TX: Institute for Christian Economics, 1993), xii.

10. See Jeff Sharlet, *The Family: The Secret Fundamentalism at the Heart of American Power* (New York: HarperCollins, 2008), 348. On Dominionism more generally, see Michelle Goldberg, *Kingdom Coming: The Rise of Christian Nationalism* (New York: W.W. Norton, 2006).

11. See the ties between conservative Christianity and the Republican party documented by Theocracy Watch, www.theocracywatch.org.

12. For more on some of these imminent dangers, particularly the peaking of global oil production, see Phillips, *American Theocracy*, chapters 1–3, 8–10. See also, Kenneth S. Deffeyes, *Beyond Oil: The View From Hubbert's Peak* (New York: Hill and Wang, 2005); Michael T. Klare, *Blood and Oil: The Dangers and Consequences of America's Growing Dependency on Imported Petroleum* (New York: Metropolitan Books, 2004); and Michael C. Ruppert, *Crossing the Rubicon: The Decline of the American Empire at the End of the Age of Oil* (Gabriola Island, British Columbia: New Society Publishers, 2004).

13. Naomi Klein, *The Shock Doctrine: The Rise of Disaster Capitalism* (New York: Metropolitan Books, 2007), 6.

14. Ibid., 15.

15. Ibid., 102.

16. On the Death of God theology, see Gabriel Vahanian, *The Death of God: The Culture of our Post-Christian Era* (New York: George Braziller, 1966); Thomas J. J. Altizer,

The Gospel of Christian Atheism (Philadelphia: Westminster Press, 1966); Thomas J. J. Altizer and William Hamilton, *Radical Theology and the Death of God* (Indianapolis: Boobs-Merill, 1966). See also Michael Grimshaw's account, "Did God Die in *The Christian Century?*"*Journal for Cultural and Religious Theory* 6.3 (2005).

17. See Mark C. Taylor, *Erring: A Postmodern A/theology* (Chicago: University of Chicago Press, 1984); Carl A. Raschke, *Alchemy of the Word* (1979), republished as *The End of Theology* (Aurora, CO: Davies Group Publishers, 1999); and Charles E. Winquist, *Epiphanies of Darkness* (Minneapolis: Fortress Press, 1986).

18. Jeffrey W. Robbins, "Terror and the Postmodern Condition: Toward a Radical Political Theology," in *Religion and Violence in a Secular World: Toward a New Political Theology*, ed. Clayton Crockett (Charlottesville: University of Virginia Press, 2006), 196.

19. Ibid., 197.

20. Ibid., 199. This orthodox theological framework has been challenged somewhat by recent representatives of Latin American liberation theology, including Marcella Althaus-Reid and Ivan Petrella. According to Althaus-Reid in her edited book on *Liberation Theology and Sexuality* (Burlington, VT: Ashgate Publishing, 2006), "the fact is that over time Latin American Liberation Theology also developed its own orthodoxy," although she and others are opening up this orthodoxy by "doing a theology of liberation grounded on people's own sexual life and struggle" (1). See also Ivan Petrella, *Beyond Liberation Theology: A Polemic (Reclaiming Liberation Theology)* (London: SCM Press, 2008). Petrella calls for a relinking of liberation theological struggles around the theme of poverty, beyond their disruption and distraction into constraining categories mapped by identity politics.

21. Ibid., 204–205. Process theology does reject theological orthodoxy, and while it has sometimes been less explicitly political, its focus on nature and ecology provides important resources for political and economic engagement. A struggle for process theology, in addition to its occasional overadherence to Whitehead's philosophy as applied to metaphysics and theology by Charles Hartshorne and John B. Cobb, is the temptation to have it both ways, to place divinity in time and thus overcome traditional theological problems like omnipotence but still find creative ways to assert faith in such a God in a way that links up with traditional Christian ideas and practices, without the result becoming a vague and fuzzy feel-good spirituality. Certainly many process theologians do not fall into this category: see especially the work of Catherine Keller, an eco-feminist and process theologian whose work engages with postmodern themes and theorists, and whom I address in chapter 3, in particular her stunningly original *The Face*

of the Deep: A Theology of Becoming (London: Routledge, 2003). Although less explicitly political in their implications than Keller's work, two very good recent books from a process theology perspective are Roland Faber, *God as Poet of the World: Exploring Process Theologies* (New York: Westminster John Knox Press: 2008) and Whitney Bauman, *Theology, Creation and Environmental Ethics: From Creatio Ex Nihilo to Terra Nullius* (London: Routledge, 2009). For the engagement of a couple of the most influential process theologians with critical issues of economics and politics, see John B. Cobb's constructive work with the economist Hermann Daly, *For the Common Good: Redirecting the Economy Toward Community, the Environment, and a Sustainable Future* (Boston: Beacon Press, 1994); and David Ray Griffin's courageous although controversial work concerning the events of 9/11, including *The New Pearl Harbor: Disturbing Questions About the Bush Administration and 9/11* (Northampton, MA: Olive Branch Press, 2004).

22. See Creston Davis, John Milbank, and Slavoj Žižek, eds., *Theology and the Political: The New Debate* (Durham, NC: Duke University Press, 2005). For example, Antonio Negri critiques Giorgio Agamben in his essay on "The Political Subject and Absolute Immanence" (231–239). While Negri criticizes Agamben's understanding of the political subject as too negative and too marginal, he absolves Agamben of the charge of theology, associating theology with "verticalization" and transcendence (236). One question I am raising here is whether it is possible to imagine a fully immanent theology, or whether theology necessarily refers to transcendence. This question will be more explicitly developed in chapter 3.

23. Friedrich Nietzsche, *The Gay Science*, trans. Walter Kaufmann (New York: Vintage Books, 1974), 181.

24. See Jürgen Habermas, *The Philosophical Discourse of Modernity*, trans. Frederick Lawrence (Cambridge, MA: MIT Press, 1987).

25. See Carl A. Raschke, *The Next Reformation: Why Evangelicals Must Embrace Postmodernism* (Grand Rapids, MI: Baker Academic, 2004).

26. Nietzsche, *The Gay Science*, 181.

27. Mark C. Taylor, *Confidence Games: Money and Markets in a World Without Redemption* (Chicago: University of Chicago Press, 2004), 30.

28. Ibid., 30

29. Ibid., 30.

30. See ibid., 126–127.

31. Taylor traces the connection between John Calvin's understanding of God's absolute sovereignty and providence and Adam Smith's invisible hand of the market. The metaphor of the invisible hand derives from Calvin's emphasis on the providential hand of God (*Confidence Games*, 84). In *After God* (Chicago: University

of Chicago Press, 2007), Taylor argues that "After God, the divine is not elsewhere but is the emergent creativity that figures, disfigures, and re-figures the infinite fabric of life" (xviii). I agree with Taylor for the most part, and I will develop a compatible reading later in the introduction, focusing more explicitly upon the concept of freedom. But at the same time, Taylor's captivation by the technological fabric of global capitalism and his dismissal of Marxist political theory severely limits the effectiveness of his theological intervention. He claims that contemporary critics of "late capitalism" such as Antonio Negri, Michael Hardt, and Frederic Jameson presume "a Marxist perspective in which cultural processes can always be reduced to a supposedly material economic base" (*Confidence Games*, 29). This is a very crude assessment that ignores the subtleties of some of the most observant Marxist and post-Marxist theories, including thinkers mentioned here. Taylor is one of the best thinkers of religion and culture of his generation, but his thought is somewhat idealistic and ideological despite his desires to the contrary and despite the complexity of most of his work. I will develop my understanding of ideology and its connection to theology in chapter 1.

32. Friedrich Nietzsche, *On the Genealogy of Morals*, trans. Walter Kaufmann (New York: Random House, 1967), 161.

33. Ibid., 161 (emphasis in original).

34. Charles E. Winquist, *Desiring Theology* (Chicago: University of Chicago Press, 1995), ix.

35. See Richard Dawkins, *The God Delusion* (Boston: Houghton Mifflin, 2008); Sam Harris, *The End of Faith: Religion, Terror and the Future of Reason* (New York: Norton, 2005); Daniel Dennett, *Breaking the Spell: Religion as a Natural Phenomenon* (New York: Penguin, 2007); and Christopher Hitchens, *God is Not Great: How Religion Poisons Everything* (New York: Hachette Publishing, 2007). I contend that these new secularists are too reactionary and risk becoming mirror images of the so-called intolerant faiths they seek to resist.

36. Charles H. Long, *Significations: Signs, Symbols and Images in the Interpretation of Religion* (Aurora, CO: Davies Group, Publishers, 1999), 7.

37. Geoffrey Bennington and Jacques Derrida, *Jacques Derrida* (Chicago: University of Chicago Press), 155.

38. Immanuel Kant, *Groundwork of the Metaphysics of Morals*, trans. H. J. Paton (New York: Harper, 1956), 116.

39. Ibid., 119 (emphasis in original).

40. Ibid., 121.

41. Ibid., 131.

42. Nietzsche, *The Gay Science*, 264 (emphasis in original).
43. Friedrich Nietzsche, *Beyond Good and Evil*, trans. Walter Kaufmann (New York: Random House, 1966), 29 (emphasis in original)
44. Ibid., 25 (emphasis in original).
45. Ibid., 25 (emphasis in original).
46. Ibid., 53.
47. Jacques Derrida, *The Gift of Death*, trans. David Wills (Chicago: University of Chicago Press, 1995), 108.
48. Ibid., 109.
49. Ibid., 115.
50. See Martin Heidegger, *Aristotle's Metaphysics Θ 1–3: On the Essence and Actuality of Force*, trans. Walter Brogan and Peter Warnek (Bloomington: Indiana University Press, 1995).
51. Giorgio Agamben, *Potentialities: Collected Essays in Philosophy*, trans. Daniel Heller-Roazen (Stanford: Stanford University Press, 1999), 180.
52. As John D. Caputo puts it in *On Religion* (London: Routledge, 2001), deconstruction and deconstructive theology concerns "thinking the possibility of the impossible, of the possible as the 'im-possible,' and to think of God as the 'becoming-possible of the impossible'" (10).

1. THE PARALLAX OF RELIGION: THEOLOGY AND IDEOLOGY

1. See also Clayton Crockett, ed., *Secular Theology: American Radical Theological Thought*, ed. (London: Routledge, 2001).
2. Wilfred Cantwell Smith, *The Meaning and End of Religion* (1962; New York: Harper & Row, 1978), 46.
3. Tomoko Masuzawa, *The Invention of World Religions* (Chicago: University of Chicago Press, 2005), 327.
4. Ibid., xiii.
5. See Talal Asad, *Genealogies of Religion: Discipline and Reasons of Power in Christianity and Islam* (Baltimore: Johns Hopkins University Press, 1993); Jonathan Z. Smith, *Imagining Religion: From Babylon to Jonestown* (Chicago: University of Chicago Press, 1982); Jacques Derrida, "Faith and Knowledge: The Two Sources of 'Religion' at the Limits of Reason Alone," in *Religion*, ed. Jacques Derrida and Gianni Vattimo (Stanford: Stanford University Press, 1998); Dipesh Chakrabarty, *Provincializing Europe: Postcolonial Thought and Historical Difference* (Princeton: Princeton University Press, 2000); and Arvind Mandair, *Religion and the Specter of the West* (New York: Columbia University Press, 2009).

6. See Russell T. McCutcheon, *The Discipline of Religion: Structure, Meaning, Rhetoric* (London: Routledge, 2003), ix, 147.

7. Masuzawa, *The Invention of World Religions*, 328.

8. Partha Chatterjee, *The Politics of the Governed: Reflections on Popular Politics in Most of the World* (New York: Columbia University Press, 2004), 128.

9. Ibid., 129.

10. Chakrabarty, *Provincializing Europe*, 237.

11. See the impressive book by Ananda Abeysekara, *The Politics of Post-Secular Religion: Mourning Secular Futures* (New York: Columbia University Press, 2008). Abeysekara deepens the political significance of Derrida's work by formulating the aporias of democracy, sovereignty, and community as a complex and convincing postcolonial political theory.

12. Hent de Vries, introduction to *Political Theologies: Public Religions in a Post-Secular World*, ed. Hent de Vries and Lawrence E. Sullivan (New York: Fordham University Press, 2006), 88.

13. Gianni Vattimo, *The End of Philosophy*, trans. Jon R. Snyder (Baltimore: Johns Hopkins University Press, 1988), 172.

14. Ibid., 173.

15. See Gianni Vattimo, *Belief*, trans. Luca D'Isanto (Stanford: Stanford University Press, 1999).

16. Vattimo, *The End of Philosophy*, 179.

17. De Vries, "Introduction," 8.

18. Ibid., 20.

19. William E. Connolly, *Why I Am Not a Secularist* (Minneapolis: University of Minnesota Press, 1999), 5 (emphasis in original).

20. Ibid., 39.

21. William E. Connolly, *Capitalism and Christianity, American Style* (Durham, NC: Duke University Press, 2008), 94.

22. Ibid., 108.

23. Talal Asad, *Formations of the Secular: Christianity, Islam, Modernity* (Stanford: Stanford University Press, 2003), 191.

24. Ibid., 192.

25. Ibid., 25.

26. Ibid., 5.

27. Ibid., 200.

28. Slavoj Žižek, *The Parallax View* (Cambridge: MIT Press, 2006), 4.

29. Ibid., 7.

30. Ibid., 10.

31. Louis Althusser, *Lenin and Philosophy and Other Essays*, trans. Ben Brewster (New York: Monthly Review Press, 2001), 109.

32. Ibid., 116.

33. Ibid., 121.

34. Antonio Negri, *Time for Revolution*, trans. Matteo Mandarini (New York: Continuum, 2003), 253.

35. Ellen Meiksins Wood, *Empire of Capital* (London: Verso, 2003), 4 (emphasis in original).

36. Ibid., 5.

37. See Immanuel Wallerstein, *The Modern World-System: Capitalist Agriculture and the Origins of the European World-Economy in the Sixteenth Century* (New York: Academic Press, 1974) and *The Modern World-System II: Mercantilism and the Consolidation of the European World Economy 1600–1750* (New York: Academic Press, 1980).

38. Immanuel Wallerstein, *The Decline of American Power: The U.S. in a Chaotic World* (New York: The New Press, 2003), 46.

39. Ibid., 58.

40. Ibid., 63.

41. Ibid., 63.

42. See Philip Goodchild, *Capitalism and Religion: The Price of Piety* (London: Routledge, 2002).

43. Philip Goodchild, *Theology of Money* (London: SCM Press, 2007), 84.

44. See Kevin Phillips, *American Theocracy: The Peril and Politics of Radical Religion, Oil and Borrowed Money in the 21st Century* (New York: Viking, 2006), 21. On peak oil, see also Kenneth S. Deffeyes, *Beyond Oil: The View From Hubbert's Peak* (New York: Hill and Wang, 2005), as well as the analyses offered by The Oil Drum, www.theoildrum.com.

45. See Phillips, *American Theocracy*, chapter 7, 218–262.

46. See Niusha Boghrati, "Iran's Oil Bourse: A Threat to the U.S. Economy?" *Worldpress.org*, April 11, 2006, www.worldpress.org/Mideast/2314.cfm (accessed September 11, 2007).

47. See Connolly, *Capitalism and Christianity*, 79.

48. Jacques Derrida, "Faith and Knowledge: The Two Sources of Religion at the Limits of Reason Alone," trans. Samuel Weber, in *Religion*, ed. Jacques Derrida and Gianni Vattimo (Stanford: Stanford University Press, 1998), 58.

49. Ibid., 59.

50. Slavoj Žižek, *The Parallax View*, 105.

51. Slavoj Žižek, "Towards a Materialist Theology," *Angelaki: Journal of the Theoretical Humanities* 12, no. 1 (2007): 26.

2. SOVEREIGNTY AND THE WEAKNESS OF GOD

1. Jeff Sharlet, *The Family: The Secret Fundamentalism at the Heart of American Power* (New York: HarperCollins, 2008), 91.
2. Ibid., 195.
3. Ibid., 30.
4. Ibid., 57.
5. Sharlet, *The Family*, 256.
6. Pierre Manent, *An Intellectual History of Liberalism*, trans. Rebecca Balinski (Princeton: Princeton University Press, 1995), xvii.
7. Ibid., 7.
8. Thomas Hobbes, *Leviathan*, ed. Richard Tuck (Cambridge: Cambridge University Press, 1996), 341.
9. Ibid., 185.
10. Ibid., 114.
11. Ibid., 120.
12. Ibid., 120.
13. Ibid., 121.
14. Ibid., 249.
15. See Philip Goodchild, *A Theology of Money* (London: SCM Press, 2007).
16. See Ernst H. Kantorowicz, *The King's Two Bodies: A Study in Mediaeval Political Theology* (Princeton: Princeton University Press, 1957).
17. Jacques Derrida, *Rogues: Two Essays on Reason*, trans. Pascale-Anne Brault and Michael Naas (Stanford: Stanford University Press, 2005), xii (emphasis in original). See also Jacques Derrida's 2001–2002 seminar, *The Beast and the Sovereign, Volume I*, trans. Geoffrey Bennington (Chicago: University of Chicago Press, 2009), which includes a specific discussion of Hobbes's *Leviathan*.
18. Ibid., 10.
19. Ibid., 13.
20. Ibid., 13.
21. Ibid., 16.
22. Ibid., 17.
23. Ibid., 81.
24. Ibid., 102.
25. Ibid., 87.

26. Ibid., 87.

27. Ibid., 114.

28. Jean-Luc Nancy, *Dis-Enclosure: The Deconstruction of Christianity*, trans. Bettina Bergo, Gabriel Malenfant, and Michael B. Smith (New York: Fordham University Press, 2008), 31.

29. Ibid., 32.

30. Ibid., 41.

31. Ibid., 41.

32. John D. Caputo, *The Weakness of God: A Theology of the Event* (Bloomington: Indiana University Press, 2006), 85.

33. See Jacques Derrida, *Rogues*, 110.

34. John D. Caputo, "Without Sovereignty, Without Being: Conditionality, the Coming God, and Derrida's Democracy to Come," in *Religion and Violence in a Secular World*, ed. Clayton Crockett (Charlottesville: University of Virginia Press, 2006), 143.

35. Caputo, *The Weakness of God*, 39 (emphasis in original).

36. Ibid., 90.

37. Ibid., 209.

38. Ibid., 252.

39. Ibid., 250.

40. Ibid., 272.

41. Catherine Keller, *The Face of the Deep: A Theology of Becoming* (London: Routledge, 2003), xv.

42. Ibid., 14.

43. Ibid., 164.

44. Ibid., 168.

45. Ibid., 198.

46. Ibid., 227 (emphasis in original).

47. Catherine Keller, *God and Power: Counter-Apocalyptic Journeys* (Minneapolis: Augsburg Fortress Press, 2005), xi.

48. Ibid., 50–51 (emphasis in original).

49. Ibid., 30.

50. Ibid., 151.

51. Laurel Schneider, *Beyond Monotheism: A Theology of Multiplicity* (London: Routledge, 2007), 167 (emphasis in original).

52. Jacques Lacan, *On Feminine Sexuality, The Limits of Love and Knowledge 1972–1973: Encore, The Seminar of Jacques Lacan, Book XX*, ed. Jacques-Alain Miller, trans. Bruce Fink (New York: W.W. Norton, 1998), 22–23.

53. Alain Badiou, *Deleuze: The Clamor of Being*, trans. Louise Burchill (Minneapolis: University of Minnesota Press, 2000), 11. See Alain Badiou, *Being and Event*, trans. Ray Brassier (London: Continuum, 2006).

54. Caputo, "Without Sovereignty, Without Being," 154.

55. Giorgio Agamben, *Potentialities: Collected Essays in Philosophy*, trans. Daniel Heller-Roazen (Stanford: Stanford University Press, 1999), 179 (emphasis in original).

56. Ibid., 180.

57. Ibid., 246–47.

58. Ibid., 182.

59. Ibid.

60. Ibid., 183.

61. Ibid., 184 (emphasis in original).

62. Ibid., 270.

63. Ibid., 271. Recall the subtitle of Taylor's book: "Money and Markets in a World Without Redemption."

64. Walter Benjamin, "Theses on the Philosophy of History," in *Illuminations: Essays and Reflections*, ed. Hannah Arendt, trans. Harry Zohn (New York: Schocken Books, 1968), 254, 263 (emphasis in original).

65. In addition to Caputo, *The Weakness of God*, see Jacques Derrida, "Force of Law: The Mystical Foundation of Authority," trans. Mary Quaintance, in *Acts of Religion*, ed. Gil Anidjar (London: Routledge, 2001); Jacques Derrida, *Specters of Marx: The State of the Debt, The Work of Mourning, and the New International*, trans. Peggy Kamuf (London: Routledge, 1994); Giorgio Agamben, *The Time That Remains: A Commentary on the Letter to the Romans*, trans. Patricia Dailey (Stanford: Stanford University Press, 2005); Slavoj Žižek, *The Puppet and the Dwarf: The Perverse Core of Christianity* (Cambridge, MA: MIT Press, 2003); and Hent de Vries, *Religion and Violence: Philosophical Perspectives from Kant to Derrida* (Baltimore: Johns Hopkins University Press, 2001). See also Walter Benjamin, "Critique of Violence," in Walter Benjamin, *Selected Writings, Vol. 1, 1913–1926*, ed. Marcus Bullock and Michael W. Jennings (Cambridge: Harvard University Press, 1996).

66. Judith Butler, "Critique, Coercion, and Sacred Life in Benjamin's 'Critique of Violence,'" in *Political Theologies: Public Religions in a Post-Secular World*, ed. Hent de Vries and Lawrence E. Sullivan (New York: Fordham University Press, 2006).

67. Ibid., 204.

68. Ibid., 206.

69. Ibid., 208.

70. Ibid., 210 (emphasis in original).

71. Ibid., 211.

72. Ibid., 216.

73. Ibid., 218.

74. Ibid. Butler's reading of Benjamin is indebted to Eric Santner's extraordinary book *On the Psychotheology of Everyday Life: Reflections on Freud and Rosenzweig* (Chicago: University of Chicago Press, 2001). Butler reads Benjamin along similar lines that Santner interprets Rosenzweig and Freud, where God is not a transcendent Being or super-ego, but rather an ethical (or meta-ethical) force: "God is above all the name for the pressure to be alive to the world, to open to the too much pressure generated in large measure by the uncanny presence of my neighbor" (9); and this counters traditional forms of sovereign power. Santner discusses Rosenzweig's proximity to Benjamin, including Derrida's reflections on Benjamin in "Force of Law," on 56–60.

3. Baruch Spinoza and the Potential
for a Radical Political Theology

1. Gilles Deleuze, *Bergsonism*, trans. Hugh Tomlinson and Barbara Habberjam (New York: Zone Books, 1991), 96.

2. Ibid., 100.

3. Ibid. (emphasis in original).

4. Ibid.

5. Gilles Deleuze, *Difference and Repetition*, trans. Paul Patton (New York: Columbia University Press, 1994), 211–212.

6. Ibid., 207.

7. Ibid., 209.

8. Deleuze, *Bergsonism*, 15.

9. Antonio Negri, *The Savage Anomaly: The Power of Spinoza's Metaphysics and Politics*, trans. Michael Hardt (Minneapolis: University of Minnesota Press, 1991), 191.

10. Ibid., 214.

11. Ibid., 202.

12. See Deleueze and Guattari's claim that Spinoza was "the Christ of philosophers. . . . Spinoza, the infinite becoming-philosopher: he showed, drew up, and thought the 'best' plane of immanence" (Gilles Deleuze and Félix Guattari, *What is Philosophy?*, trans. Hugh Tomlinson and Graham Burchell (New York: Columbia University Press, 1994), 60.

13. Yirmiyahu Yovel, *Spinoza and Other Heretics: The Marrano of Reason* (Princeton: Princeton University Press, 1989), 20. See also my discussion of Spinoza in rela-

tion to Kant, Derrida, and John D. Caputo in "Post-Modernism and its Secrets: Religion Without Religion," *CrossCurrents* 52, no. 4 (2003): 500–503.

14. Ibid., 22, 26.

15. Jonathan I. Israel, *Radical Enlightenment: Philosophy and the Making of Modernity 1650–1750* (Oxford: Oxford University Press, 2001), 159.

16. Baruch Spinoza, *Ethics, Treatise on the Emendation of the Intellect and Selected Letters*, trans. Samuel Shirley (Indianapolis: Hackett Publishing Company, 1992), 31.

17. Ibid., 33.

18. Ibid., 48.

19. Ibid., 49.

20. See Spinoza, *The Principles of Descartes' Philosophy*, trans. Halbert Hains Britan (La Salle, IL: Open Court, 1974).

21. *Ethics*, 37.

22. Etienne Balibar essentially follows Deleuze's lead in *Spinoza and Politics*, trans. Peter Snowdon (London: Verso, 1998) when he claims that "the whole of Spinoza's philosophy . . . can be understood as a highly original philosophy of communication" (99).

23. Gilles Deleuze, *Spinoza: Practical Philosophy*, trans. Robert Hurley (San Francisco: City Lights Books, 1988), 199.

24. Ibid., 128.

25. Gilles Deleuze, *Expressionism in Philosophy: Spinoza*, trans. Martin Joughin (New York: Zone Books, 1992), 54–55.

26. Ibid., 56.

27. See Spinoza's distinction between obedience to God, which is required by revelation, and intellectual knowledge of God, which is known by reason, in his *Theological-Political Treatise*, trans. Samuel Shirley (Indianapolis: Hackett Publishing Company, 1998), 158.

28. See Gilles Deleuze, *Nietzsche and Philosophy*, trans. Hugh Tomlinson (New York: Columbia, 1983), 57: reactive forces "decompose: they separate active force from what it can do; they take away all or almost all of its power."

29. See Antonio Negri, *Marx Beyond Marx: Lessons on the Grundrisse*, trans. Harry Cleaver, Michael Ryan, and Maurizio Viano (New York: Pluto Press, 1991), 45–46.

30. Antonio Negri, *The Savage Anomaly: The Power of Spinoza's Metaphysics and Politics*, trans. Michael Hardt (Minneapolis: University of Minnesota Press, 1991), 62.

31. Ibid., 122.

32. Ibid., 200.

33. Ibid., 62.

34. Ibid.
35. Ibid., 63.
36. Ibid., 202.
37. Michael Hardt and Antonio Negri, *Multitude: War and Democracy in the Age of Empire* (New York: Penguin Press, 2004), 329.
38. Ibid., 330.
39. Ibid., 336.
40. Ibid., 351.
41. Ibid., 352.
42. See John Milbank, *Theology and Social Theory* (Oxford: Blackwell, 1990), 37.
43. Graham Ward, *Christ and Culture* (Oxford: Blackwell, 2005), 89.
44. See Jacques Derrida, *Rogues: Two Essays on Reason*, trans. Pascale-Anne Brault and Michel Naas (Stanford: Stanford University Press, 2005).
45. Friedrich Nietzsche, *Twilight of the Idols* in *The Portable Nietzsche*, ed. Walter Kaufmann (New York: Penguin, 1968), 486.
46. Gilles Deleuze, *Cinema 2: The Time-Image*, trans. Hugh Tomlinson and Robert Galeta (Minneapolis: University of Minnesota Press, 1989), 172.
47. Ibid., 171.
48. Ibid., 172.

4. Carl Schmitt, Leo Strauss, and the Theo-Political Problem of Liberalism

1. Carl Schmitt, *Political Theology: Four Chapters on the Concept of Sovereignty*, trans. George Schwab (Chicago: University of Chicago Press, 1985), 36.
2. Ernst H. Kantorowicz, *The King's Two Bodies: A Study in Mediaeval Political Theology* (Princeton: Princeton University Press, 1957), 58.
3. See Max Weber, *Economy and Society: An Outline of Interpretive Sociology*, ed. Gunter Roth and Claus Wittich, 2 vols. (New York: Bedminster Press, 1968).
4. See Marcel Gauchet, *The Disenchantment of the World: A Political History of Religion*, trans. Oscar Burge (Princeton: Princeton University Press, 1999).
5. See Schmitt, *Political Theology*, 36–37. See also Schmitt, *Political Theology II*, trans. Graham Ward and Michael Hoelzl (London: Polity Press, 2008).
6. On the development of Schmitt's thought, see Gopal Balakrishnan, *The Enemy: An Intellectual Portrait of Carl Schmitt* (New York: Verso, 2000).
7. Heinrich Meier, *Carl Schmitt & Leo Strauss: The Hidden Dialogue*, trans. J. Harvey Lomax (Chicago: University of Chicago Press, 1995), xv.
8. Ibid., 50.

9. Heinrich Meier, *Leo Strauss and the Theologico-Political Problem*, trans. Marcus Brainard (Cambridge: Cambridge University Press, 2006), 84.

10. Ibid., 85.

11. Leora Batnitzky, *Leo Strauss and Emmanuel Levinas: Philosophy and the Politics of Revelation* (Cambridge: Cambridge University Press, 2006), 5.

12. Ibid., 14 (emphasis in original).

13. Carl Schmitt, *The Crisis of Parliamentary Democracy*, trans. Ellen Kennedy (Cambridge, MA: The MIT Press, 1985), 35.

14. Schmitt, *Political Theology*, 62.

15. Carl Schmitt, *The Concept of the Political*, trans. George Schwab (Chicago: University of Chicago Press, 1996), 70.

16. Leo Strauss, "Notes on *The Concept of the Political*," trans. J. Harvey Lomax, in Schmitt, *The Concept of the Political*, 83–107 (quote on 84).

17. Ibid., 101. See also Meier, *Carl Schmitt & Leo Strauss*, 47: "Ultimately, for Schmitt the affirmation of the political is nothing but the affirmation of the moral. But Schmitt sees the affirmation of the moral as itself based in the theological."

18. Ibid., 106.

19. Ibid., 107.

20. See Leo Strauss, *What is Political Philosophy?* (Westport, CT: Greenwood Press, 1959), 28–29.

21. Meier, *Carl Schmitt & Leo Strauss*, 47.

22. See Naomi Klein, *The Shock Doctrine: The Rise of Disaster Capitalism* (New York: Metropolitan Books, 2007).

23. Karl Polanyi, *The Great Transformation: The Political and Economic Origins of Our Time* (Boston: Beacon Press, 1957), 72.

24. Ibid., 73.

25. Ibid., 242.

26. See Kevin Phillips, *American Theocracy: The Peril and Politics of Radical Religion, Oil, and Borrowed Money in the 21st Century* (New York: Viking, 2006).

27. Polanyi, *The Great Transformation*, 71.

28. Samir Amin, *The Liberal Virus: Permanent War and the Americanization of the World*, trans. James H. Membrez (New York: Monthly Review Press, 2004), 9.

29. See Amin, *The Liberal Virus*, 39.

30. Jean-Bertrand Aristide, *Eyes of the Heart: Seeking a Path for the Poor in the Age of Globalization* (Monroe, ME: Common Courage Press, 2000), 49.

31. Ibid., 11.

32. Ibid., 5.

33. Peter Hallward, *Damming the Flood: Haiti, Aristide, and the Politics of Containment* (London: Verso, 2007), 235–249.

34. Ibid., 100.

35. See Polanyi, *The Great Transformation*, 40–41.

36. John Locke, *A Letter Concerning Toleration*, in *John Locke on Politics and Education*, ed. Howard R. Penniman (Toronto: D. Van Nostrand Company, 1947), 24. See also the critique of Locke which suggests that his effort to demarcate separate spheres for religion and politics necessarily fails, in my editorial introduction, coauthored with Creston Davis, to the special issue of *Angelaki* that Creston Davis and I coedited on "The Political and the Infinite: Theology and Radical Politics," *Angelaki* 12, no. 1, (2007): 1–10.

37. Talal Asad, *Formations of the Secular: Christianity, Islam, Modernity* (Stanford: Stanford University Press, 2003), 183 (emphasis in original).

38. Ibid., 191 (emphasis in original).

39. See Ibid., 192.

40. Leo Strauss, *Persecution and the Art of Writing* (Chicago: University of Chicago Press, 1988), 25.

41. Ibid., 177.

42. On the paradoxical nature of belief, with attention to its ideological and political implications, see the work of Slavoj Žižek, including *On Belief* (London: Routledge, 2001). On the relevance of ideas of the unconscious in Freud, Lacan, and Žižek for radical theology, see my book *Interstices of the Sublime: Theology and Psychoanalytic Theory* (New York: Fordham University Press, 2007).

43. See Sam Harris, *Letter to a Christian Nation: A Challenge to Faith* (New York: Bantam, 2007) and Christopher Hitchens, *God is Not Great: How Religion Poisons Everything* (New York: Hachette Books, 2007).

44. Jacques Derrida, "Taking a Stand for Algeria," in Jacques Derrida, *Acts of Religion*, ed. Gil Anidjar (London: Routledge, 2002), 306.

45. Asad, *Formations of the Secular*, 200.

46. See *Secular Theology: American Radical Theological Thought*, ed. Clayton Crockett (London: Routledge, 2001), especially the introduction, 1–9, and chapter 1, "Theology and the Secular" by Gabriel Vahanian, 10–25.

5. Elements for Radical Democracy: Plasticity, Equality, Governmentality

1. For a similar approach to these issues, see Jeffrey W. Robbins, *Radical Democracy and Political Theology* (New York: Columbia University Press, 2011). Robbins and

I both critique the theoretical understandings of political theology that are dominated by Carl Schmitt, and we argue that a serious engagement with political theology does not foreclose democracy; but democracy must be radicalized, as I suggest and offer conceptual tools for in this chapter.

2. Jeffrey Stout, *Democracy and Tradition* (Princeton: Princeton University Press, 2004), 289.

3. Ibid., 293.

4. Naomi Klein, *The Shock Doctrine: The Rise of Disaster Capitalism* (New York: Metropolitan Books, 2007), 288.

5. Ibid., 322.

6. Ananda Abeysekara, *The Politics of Postsecular Religion: Mourning Secular Futures* (New York: Columbia University Press, 2008), 2.

7. Jean-Bertrand Aristide, *Eyes of the Heart: Seeking a Path for the Poor in an Age of Globalization* (Monroe, ME: Common Courage Press, 2000), 36.

8. Carl Schmitt, *Political Theology: Four Chapters on the Concept of Sovereignty*, trans. George Schwab (Chicago: The University of Chicago Press, 1985), 36.

9. See Gopal Balakrishnan, *The Enemy* (London: Verso, 2000), 180.

10. Baruch Spinoza, *Theological-Political Treatise*, 2nd ed., trans. Samuel Shirley (Indianapolis: Hackett Publishing, 1998), 3.

11. Ibid., 64.

12. Matthew Stewart, *The Courtier and the Heretic: Leibniz, Spinoza, and the Fate of God in the Modern World* (New York: W.W. Norton, 2006), 101.

13. Ibid., 215.

14. See Etienne Balibar, *Spinoza and Politics* (London: Verso, 2008), 17

15. Baruch Spinoza, *Political Treatise,* trans. Samuel Shirley (Indianapolis: Hackett Publishing Company, 2000), 44.

16. Ibid., 44.

17. Rocco Gangle, "Sovereignty and State-Form," in *The Sleeping Giant Has Awoken: The New Politics of Religion in the United States*, ed. Jeffrey W. Robbins and Neal Magee (New York: Continuum, 2008), 141.

18. Pierre Manent, *An Intellectual History of Liberalism*, trans. Rebecca Balinski (Princeton: Princeton University Press, 1995), 116.

19. Claude Lefort, *Complications: Communism and the Dilemmas of Democracy*, trans. Julian Bourg (New York: Columbia University Press, 2007), 190.

20. Carl Schmitt, *Political Theology: Four Chapters on the Concept of Sovereignty* (Chicago: University of Chicago Press, 2005), 5.

21. Ibid., 12.

22. Antonio Negri, *The Savage Anomaly: The Power of Spinoza's Metaphysics and Politics*, trans. Michael Hardt (Minneapolis: University of Minnesota Press, 1991), 202.

23. Michel Foucault, *Security, Territory, Population: Lectures at the Collège de France 1977–1978*, trans. Graham Burchell (New York: Palgrave Macmillan, 2007), 110. See also Giorgio Agamben's genealogical extension of Foucault's notion of governmentality back into theological understandings of economy in *Il Regno e la Gloria* (Rome: Neri Pozza, 2007).

24. Ibid.

25. Ibid., 165.

26. Ibid., 266.

27. Ibid., 326.

28. Ibid., 354.

29. Ibid., 356.

30. Ibid.

31. Jacques Rancière, *The Hatred of Democracy*, trans. Steve Corcoran (London: Verso, 2006), 13.

32. Ibid., 36.

33. Ibid., 45, 33.

34. Ibid., 49.

35. Ibid.

36. Ibid., 97.

37. Ibid.

38. Alain Badiou, "A Speculative Disquisition on the Concept of Democracy," in *Metapolitics*, trans. Jason Barker (London: Verso, 2005), 78 (emphasis in original).

39. Ibid., 85 (emphasis in original).

40. Ibid., 93.

41. Ibid., 94.

42. Catherine Malabou, *La plasticité au soir de l'écriture: Dialectique, destruction, déconstruction* (Paris: Éditions Léo Scheer, 2005), 25. The English translation is *Plasticity at the Dusk of Writing: Dialectic, Destruction, Deconstruction*, trans. Carolyn Shread (New York: Columbia University Press, 2009).

43. Ibid., 94.

44. Ibid., 107.

45. See, for example, Jean-Pierre Changeux, *Neuronal Man: The Biology of Mind*, trans. Laurence Garey (Princeton: Princeton University Press, 1997); Jean-Pierre Changeux and Paul Ricoeur, *What Makes us Think?*, trans. M. D. Bevoise (Princeton:

Princeton University Press, 2000); and Antonio Damascio, *Looking for Spinoza: Joy, Sorrow, and the Feeling Brain* (Orlando: Harcourt Books, 2003).

46. Catherine Malabou, *Que faire de notre cerveau?* (Paris: Bayard, 2004), 32. The English translation is *What Should We Do with Our Brain?*, trans. Sebastian Rand (New York: Fordham University Press, 2008).

47. Ibid., 161.

48. On destructive plasticity, see Catherine Malabou, *Les nouveaux blessés: De Freud à la neurology, penser les traumatisms contemporains* (Paris: Bayard, 2007), 48–49. *The Newly Wounded* concerns our traumatic brain injuries, whether from war or disease, and their ability to render us completely other than who we are.

49. Walter Benjamin, *Illuminations: Essays and Reflections*, trans. Harry Zohn (New York: Schocken Books, 1968), 263.

6. Law Beyond Law:
Agamben, Deleuze, and the Unconscious Event

1. Jacques Derrida, *Rogues: Two Essays on Reason*, trans. Pascale-Anne Brault and Michel Naas (Stanford: Stanford University Press, 2005), 92.

2. "President Signs Military Commissions Act of 2006." Available online at http://www.whitehouse.gov/news/releases/2006/10/20061017–1.html.

3. Carl Schmitt, *Political Theology: Four Chapters on the Concept of Sovereignty*, trans. George Schwab (Chicago: University of Chicago Press, 1985), 5.

4. Ibid., 9.

5. Carl Schmitt, *The Concept of the Political*, trans. George Schwab (Chicago: University of Chicago Press, 1996), 39.

6. See John Locke, *The Second Treatise of Government* (Indianapolis: The Liberal Arts Press, 1952), 84; Jean-Jacques Rousseau, *The Social Contract and Discourses*, trans. G. D. H. Cole (London: J. M. Dent & Sons, 1973), 200–202.

7. Rousseau, *The Social Contract and Discourses*, 136.

8. See Giorgio Agamben, *State of Exception*, trans. Kevin Attell (Chicago: University of Chicago Press, 2005), 34–35.

9. Ibid., 86.

10. Rousas John Rushdoony, *The Institutes of Biblical Law* (The Craig Press, 1973), 4.

11. Gary North and Gary DeMar, *Christian Reconstruction: What It Is, What It Isn't* (Tyler, TX: Institute for Christian Economics, 1991), xi, 37.

12. Ibid., 51.

13. Chris Hedges, *American Fascists: The Christian Right and the War on America* (New York: Free Press, 2006), 11.

14. See Khaled Abou El Fadl, *The Great Theft: Wrestling Islam from the Extremists* (New York: HarperCollins, 2005).

15. See Wael Hallaq, *The Origins and Evolution of Islamic Law* (Cambridge: Cambridge University Press, 2005).

16. Tamara Sonn, "Phases of Political Islam," in *Religious Fundamentalism in the Contemporary World*, ed. Santosh Saha (Lanham, MD: Lexington Books, 2004), 95.

17. See Abu A'la Mawdudi, *Islamic Law and Constitution*, trans. Khurshid Ahmad (Lahore: Islamic Publications, 1967).

18. Abou El Fadl, *The Great Theft*, 83.

19. Ibid., 29.

20. Sonn, "Phases of Political Islam," 101.

21. Olivier Roy, *Globalized Islam: The Search for the New Ummah* (New York: Columbia University Press, 2004), 32–33.

22. See Irving Kristol, *Neo-Conservativism: The Autobiography of an Idea* (Chicago: Ivan R. Dee, Publisher, 1999), 6–9.

23. Agamben, *State of Exception*, 39.

24. Ibid., 51.

25. Ibid., 59.

26. Ibid., 86.

27. Ibid., 87.

28. Ibid., 88.

29. Ibid.

30. Jacques Derrida, "Force of Law: The Mystical Foundation of Authority, trans. Mary Quaintance, in *Acts of Religion*, ed. Gil Anidjar (London: Routledge, 2001), 233.

31. Ibid., 243.

32. Ibid., 242.

33. Alain Badiou, *Saint Paul: The Foundation of Universalism*, trans. Ray Brassier (Stanford: Stanford University Press, 2003), 79.

34. Ibid.

35. Ibid., 83.

36. Ibid., 84.

37. Ibid., 81 (emphasis in original).

38. Ibid., 88.

39. See Jacques Lacan, *Écrits: The First Complete Edition in English*, trans. Bruce Fink (New York: W.W. Norton, 2006), 232–34.

40. See Jacques Lacan, *Seminar XVII: The Other Side of Psychoanalysis*, ed. Jacques-Alain Miller, trans. Russell Grigg (New York: W.W. Norton, 2007).

41. See Alain Badiou, *Metapolitics*, trans. Jason Barker (New York: Verso, 2005); Alain Badiou, *Being and Event.*, trans. Oliver Feltham (New York: Continuum, 2006); Slavoj Žižek, *Tarrying With the Negative: Kant, Hegel, and the Critique of Ideology* (Durham, NC: Duke University Press, 1995); Slavoj Žižek, *The Parallax View* (Cambridge, MA: The MIT Press, 2006).

42. Jacques Lacan, *The Four Fundamental Concepts of Psychoanalysis*, ed. Jacques-Alain Miller, trans. Alan Sheridan (New York: W.W. Norton, 1978), 20.

43. See Jacques Lacan, *The Seminar of Jacques Lacan Book XX: One Feminine Sexuality, the Limits of Love and Knowledge 1972–1973*, ed. Jacques-Alain Miller, trans. Bruce Fink (New York: W.W. Norton, 1998). On Freud and Lacan and their significance for theological thinking, see my *Interstices of the Sublime: Theology and Psychoanlytic Theory* (New York: Fordham University Press, 2007).

44. Gilles Deleuze, *The Logic of Sense*, trans. Mark Lester (New York: Columbia University Press, 1990), 22.

45. Ibid., 9.

46. Ibid., 148.

47. Ibid., 151.

48. Ibid., 149.

49. Gilles Deleuze and Félix Guattari, *Anti-Oedipus: Capitalism and Schizophrenia*, trans. Robert Hurley, Mark Seem, and Helen R. Lane (Minneapolis: University of Minnesota Press, 1983), 26.

50. Ibid., 29.

51. Ibid., 53.

52. Ibid., 6.

53. Ibid., 36.

54. Ibid.

55. See Gilles Deleuze, *Pure Immanence: Essays on a Life*, trans. Anne Boyman (New York: Zone Books, 2001).

56. Peter Hallward, *Out of This World: Deleuze and the Philosophy of Creation* (London and New York: Verso, 2006), 2. Although I am critical of Hallward's interpretation of Deleuze, which follows too closely upon his influential reading of Badiou in *Badiou: A Subject to Truth* (Minneapolis: University of Minnesota Press, 2003), I want to affirm the incredible importance of Hallward's book on Haiti, *Damming the Flood: Haiti, Aristide, and the Politics of Containment* (London: Verso, 2007), which is a searing engagement with contemporary politics and a damning critique of neoliberalism.

57. Ibid., 162.

58. Gilles Deleuze, *Cinema 2: The Time-Image*, trans. Hugh Tomlinson and Robert Galeta (Minneapolis: University of Minnesota Press, 1989), 216.

59. Gilles Deleuze and Félix Guattari, *A Thousand Plateaus: Capitalism and Schizophrenia*, trans. Brian Massumi (Minneapolis: University of Minnesota Press, 1987), 369, 493.

60. Ibid., 509.

7. Radical Theology and the Event: Deleuze with Paul

1. In *The Weakness of God: A Theology of the Event* (Bloomington: Indiana University Press, 2006), John D. Caputo invokes Deleuze's paradoxical thinking of the event and Deleuze's discussion of *Alice in Wonderland* in relation to Caputo's reading of the Bible (see 109, 204–205), although overall Caputo's notion of the event is more influenced by Derrida, and while Caputo has a chapter specifically devoted to Paul ("St. Paul on the Logos of the Cross"), he does not discuss Deleuze explicitly in relation to Paul.

2. Alain Badiou, *Saint Paul: The Foundation of Universalism*, trans. Ray Brassier (Stanford: Stanford University Press, 2003), 2.

3. In the prologue, Badiou singles out two secondary works on Paul, one by a Catholic, Stanislas Breton, *Saint Paul*, trans. Joseph Ballon (New York: Columbia University Press, 2011), and one by a Protestant, Günther Bornkamm, *Paul* (Minneapolis: Fortress Press, 1995). In situating his contribution, Badiou writes: "A Catholic, a Protestant. May they form a triangle with the atheist" (3). Now, any book that seriously considers Paul's political significance today would have to have at least four sides or corners to take into account the 1987 lectures by Jacob Taubes, published as *The Political Theology of Paul*, trans. Dana Hollander (Stanford: Stanford University Press, 2004).

4. Witness the conference at Syracuse University, "St. Paul Among the Philosophers: Subjectivity, Universality and the Event," April 12–14, 2005, featuring Alain Badiou, Slavoj Žižek, along with New Testament and St. Paul scholars and historians. See my review, from which the first part of this chapter partially draws, "St. Paul and the Event," *Journal for Cultural and Religious Theory* 6.2 (2005), and the book that resulted from this conference, *St. Paul Among the Philosophers*, ed. John D. Caputo and Linda Martín Alcoff (Bloomington: Indiana University Press, 2009).

5. See Slavoj Žižek, *The Indivisible Remainder: An Essay on Schelling and Related Matters* (London: Verso, 1996), especially chapter 2, "Schelling-for-Hegel: The Vanishing Mediator," 92–186.

6. Jacques Derrida, "Faith and Knowledge: The Two Sources of 'Religion' at the Limits of Reason Alone," in *Religion*, edited by Jacques Derrida and Gianni Vattimo (Stanford: Stanford University Press, 1998), 33 See also Jacques Derrida, *Monolinguism of the Other; or, The Prosthesis of Origin*, trans. Patrick Mensah (Stanford: Stanford University Press, 1998.

7. See Dominique Janicaud, et.al., *Phenomenology and the "Theological Turn": The French Debate* (New York: Fordham University Press, 2000).

8. See my constructive elaboration of a radical theology developed out an encounter with Continental philosophy and psychoanalytic theory in *Interstices of the Sublime: Theology and Psychoanalytic Theory* (Fordham: Fordham University Press, 2007).

9. See Friedrich Nietzsche, *The Antichrist* in *The Nietzsche Reader*, ed. Walter Kaufmann (New York: Penguin Books, 1976), 565–656.

10. Jacob Taubes, *The Political Theology of Paul*, 40.

11. Ibid., 53.

12. Martin Heidegger, *The Phenomenology of Religious Life*, trans. Matthias Fritsch and Jennifer Anna Gosetti-Ferencei (Bloomington: Indiana University Press, 2004), 63.

13. Ibid., 83.

14. Ibid., 55.

15. Martin Heidegger, *Being and Time*, trans. John Macquarrie and Edward Robinson (New York: Harper & Row, 1962), 373.

16. Gilles Deleuze, *Difference and Repetition*, trans. Paul Patton (New York: Columbia University Press, 1994), 64–65.

17. Ibid., 78.

18. Ibid., 79.

19. Ibid., 85.

20. Ibid., 86.

21. Ibid.

22. Ibid., 88.

23. Ibid., 87.

24. Ibid. Deleuze also privileges Hölderlin as an alternative to Hegel, whose philosophy he strongly opposes. I wonder, however, whether it would be possible to rehabilitate Hegel for a Deleuzian reading of history, to render a Deleuzian reading of Hegel, something like: "From the Science of Logic to the Logic of Sense." Such a project, however, is far beyond the scope of this chapter and this book.

25. Ibid., 90.

26. Ibid., 93.

27. Ibid., 95.

28. Ibid.

29. Ibid., 117.

30. Ibid. Deleuze does not distinguish between differentiation and differenciation until chapter 4, by way of explaining the relationship between the virtual and the actual. Differentiation translates the French *différentier*, which is a more formal mathematical term, and concerns virtual differences. Differenciation translates the French *différencier*, which is the more common word that means what we call in English differentiation, and Deleuze associates this word with the actualization of differences (see 207). This is a crucial distinction in *Difference and Repetition*, but these two terms and processes are not yet separated out in chapter 2, where Deleuze uses the more general word (in French) differenciation. See also my discussion of this term in relation to that of the virtual in the introduction to this book.

31. Ibid., 119.

32. Ibid., 66.

33. Giorgio Agamben, *The Time That Remains: A Commentary on the Letter to the Romans*, trans. Patricia Dailey (Stanford: Stanford University Press, 2005), 65–66.

34. Ibid., 67.

35. Gilles Deleuze, *The Logic of Sense*, trans. Mark Lester (New York: Columbia University Press, 1990), 22. Sense is associated with language, and the event is tied to sense. Agamben's reading of Paul attends to the "experience of a pure event of the word that exceeds every signification," that is, a "revelation of language itself" (*The Time That Remains*, 134). This experience of the pure word is similar to what Deleuze means by sense in *The Logic of Sense*, and both Agamben and Deleuze relate sense or the experience of a pure word directly to event, although as I will discuss later, Agamben remains more faithful to a chronological temporality and its inherent teleology than Deleuze, whose pluri-directionality of sense disrupts linear chronology.

36. Ibid., 10.

37. Quoted in ibid., 5.

38. Ibid., 151.

39. Ibid., 241.

40. Ibid., 35.

41. See Badiou, *Saint Paul*, 88: "Law returns as life's articulation for everyone, path of faith, law beyond law. This is what Paul calls love."

42. See John Dominic Crossan and Jonathan L. Reed, *In Search of Paul: How Jesus's Apostle Opposed Rome's Empire with God's Kingdom* (New York: HarperCollins, 2004).

43. See Jacques Derrida, "*Différance*," in *Margins of Philosophy*, trans. Alan Bass (Chicago: University of Chicago Press, 1978).

44. See Gilles Deleuze, *Cinema 2: The Time-Image*, trans. Hugh Tomlinson and Robert Galeta (New York: Columbia University Press, 1989).

45. Deleuze, *The Logic of Sense*, 22.

46. Ibid., 1.

47. Ibid., 151.

48. Ibid., 149.

49. Ibid.

50. Ibid.

51. Ibid.

52. Agamben, *The Time That Remains*, 103.

53. See ibid., 23–24, where Agamben discusses Paul's injunction to disciples to be "weeping as not weeping." This tensor or tensive relationship occurs in Deleuzian time, which is "time contracted itself," but at a micro or molecular level, not in an overarching, molar, or macro level. We could also consider Deleuze's time as micro-messianic, or messianic in a minor sense.

54. See Gilles Deleuze and Félix Guattari, *What is Philosophy?*, trans. Hugh Tomlinson and Graham Burchell (New York: Columbia University Press, 1994), 60.

55. See Edith Wyschogrod, *Saints and Postmodernism* (Chicago: University of Chicago Press, 1990).

56. Gilles Deleuze, *Essays Critical and Clinical*, trans. Daniel W. Smith and Michael A. Greco (Minneapolis: University of Minnesota Press, 1997), 37.

57. Ibid., 39.

58. Ibid., 37.

59. Taubes, *The Political Theology of Paul*, 79.

60. Ibid. 85.

61. Ibid., 87.

62. See Deleuze's opposition of two orders in his reading of Klossowski in the appendix to *The Logic of Sense*, the order of God versus the order of the Antichrist. The title, Antichrist, may be too literally Nietzschean, but here Deleuze understands God as the master of the disjunctive syllogism, who preserves himself from its operations, whereas the order of the Antichrist occurs when "the disjunctive syllogism accedes to a diabolical principle and use, and simultaneously the disjunction is affirmed for itself without ceasing to be a disjunction; divergence or difference becomes objects of pure affirmation" (*The Logic of Sense*, 296). Later in *The Fold*, Deleuze subjects God explicitly to this thinking of disjunction as disjunction, or pure difference, which means in Leibnizian terms that God passes through the

possibles and the imcompossibles. Contrasting Whitehead with Leibniz, Deleuze claims that with Whitehead, "God desists from being a Being who compares worlds and chooses the richest compossible. He becomes Process, a process that at once affirms incompossibilities and passes through them." See *The Fold: Leibniz and the Baroque*, trans. Tom Conley (Minneapolis: University of Minnesota Press, 1993), especially chapter 6, "What is an Event?" 76–82, quote on 81. We could elaborate an alternative Deleuzian reading of Christ, specifically in terms of his divinity, along these lines, but it is beyond the scope of the present chapter.

63. See the expressions and formulations of Radical Orthodoxy, including John Milbank, *Theology and Social Theory: Beyond Secular Reason* (Oxford: Blackwell, 1990); Catherine Pickstock, *After Writing: On the Liturgical Consummation of Philosophy* (Oxford: Blackwell, 1998); and Conor Cunningham, *Genealogy of Nihilism: Philosophies of Nothing and the Difference of Theology* (London: Routledge, 2002). See also their essays in *Theology and the Political: The New Debate*, ed. Creston Davis, John Milbank, and Slavoj Žižek (Durham: Duke University Press, 2005).

64. See Jacques Derrida, *Rogues: Two Essays on Reason*, trans. Pascale-Anne Brault and Michael Naas (Stanford: Stanford University Press, 2005), 143.

65. See Alain Badiou, *Infinite Thought: Truth and the Return to Philosophy*, trans. Oliver Feltham and Justin Clemens (London: Continuum, 2003), introduction: "some human beings *become* subjects: those who act in *fidelity* to a chance encounter with an *event* which disrupts the *situation* they find themselves in" (6).

66. Deleuze, *Cinema 2*, 172.

8. PLASTICITY AND THE FUTURE OF THEOLOGY: MESSIANICITY AND THE DECONSTRUCTION OF CHRISTIANITY

1. See Marcel Gauchet, *The Disenchantment of the World: A Political History of Religion*, trans. Oscar Burge (Princeton: Princeton University Press, 1997).

2. Jacques Derrida, *Specters of Marx: The State of the Debt, The Work of Mourning, and the New International*, trans. Peggy Kamuf (London: Routledge, 1994), 59.

3. Ibid.

4. Ibid., 167.

5. Mark C. Taylor, *After God* (Chicago: University of Chicago Press, 2007), 43.

6. Richard Rorty and Gianni Vattimo, *The Future of Religion*, ed. Santiago Zabala (New York: Columbia University Press, 2005), 53.

7. Ibid., 50.

8. Ibid., 51.

9. See Tomoko Masuzawa, *The Invention of World Religions* (Chicago: University of Chicago Press, 2005), 145.

10. Ibid. 301.

11. Mohammed Arkoun, *Islam: To Reform or to Subvert?* (London: Saqi Books, 2006), 13.

12. Giorgio Agamben, *The Time That Remains: A Commentary on the Letter to the Romans*, trans. Patricia Dailey (Stanford: Stanford University Press, 2005), 67.

13. Ibid., 66.

14. Jean-Luc Nancy, *Dis-Enclosure: The Deconstruction of Christianity*, trans. Bettina Bergo, Gabriel Malenfant, and Michael B. Smith (New York: Fordham University Press, 2008), 140. This essay was originally published in English as Jean-Luc Nancy, "The Deconstruction of Christianity," in *Religion and Media*, ed. Hent de Vries and Samuel Weber (Stanford: Stanford University Press, 2001), 112–130.

15. Ibid., 141.

16. Ibid., 145.

17. Jacques Derrida, *On Touching—Jean-Luc Nancy*, trans. Christine Irizarry (Stanford: Stanford University Press, 2005), 54.

18. See Ibid., 60: "Let us never forget that Christian, in fact, Lutheran, memory of Heideggerian deconstruction (*Destruktion* was first *destructio* by Luther, anxious to reactivate the originary sense of the Gospels by deconstructing theological sediments."

19. See Martin Heidegger, *The Phenomenology of Religious Life*, trans. Matthias Fritsch and Jennifer Anna Gosetti-Ferencei (Bloomington: Indiana University Press, 2004).

20. Alain Badiou, *Saint Paul: The Foundation of Universalism*, trans. Ray Brassier (Stanford: Stanford University Press, 2003), 45.

21. Catherine Malabou, *La Plasticité au soir de l'écriture: Dialectique, destruction, déconstruction* (Paris: Éditions Léo Scheer, 2005), 25n1. English translation: *Plasticity at the Dusk of Writing: Dialectic, Destruction, Deconstruction*, trans. Carolyn Shread (New York: Columbia University Press, 2009).

22. For a consideration of the transcendental imagination in Heidegger and Kant, as well as a theological reading of the Kantian sublime, see my *A Theology of the Sublime* (London: Routledge, 2001).

23. Catherine Malabou, *The Future of Hegel: Plasticity, Temporality and Dialectic*, trans. Lisabeth Durling (London: Routledge, 2005), 112.

24. Ibid., 113. See also Cyril O'Regan, *The Heterodox Hegel* (New York: State University of New York Press, 1994).

25. Malabou, *The Future of Hegel*, 119.

26. Ibid., 128.

27. Derrida, *On Touching*, 60.

28. Jacques Derrida, *Of Grammatology*, trans. Gayatri Chakravorty Spivak (Baltimore: Johns Hopkins University Press, 1976), 68.

29. Here Malabou's reading of Hegel conflicts with the standard reading according to which the progression of spirit is essentially circular. Furthermore, Malabou, along with Žižek and others, provides a new way of engaging with Hegel's contemporary significance, beyond the stereotypical postmodern critique of Hegel as a totalizing thinker. See *Hegel and the Infinite: Religion, Politics and the Dialectic*, edited by Slavoj Žižek, Creston Davis and myself (New York: Columbia University Press, 2011).

30. Catherine Malabou, *Que faire de notre cerveau?* (Paris: Bayard, 2004), 14. English translation: *What Should We Do with Our Brain?* trans. Sebastian Rand (New York: Fordham University Press, 2008). All translations, however, are my own.

31. See Dean Hamer, *The God Gene: How Faith is Hardwired into our Genes* (New York: Anchor, 2005); Pascal Boyer, *Religion Explained: The Evolutionary Origins of Religious Thought* (New York: Basic Books, 2001).

32. Gilles Deleuze, *Cinema 2: The Time-Image*, trans. Hugh Tomlinson and Robert Galeta (Minneapolis: University of Minnesota Press, 1989), 17.

33. Malabou, *Que faire de notre cerveau?*, 83.

34. Ibid., 38–39.

35. Nancy, *Dis-Enclosure*, 160.

36. Ibid.

37. See Alain Badiou, *Polemics*, trans. Steve Corcoran (London: Verso, 2006), 207 (emphasis in original).

38. Margaret Atwood, *Surfacing* (1972; New York: Random House, 1998), 160.

39. Nancy, *Dis-Enclosure*, 160.

40. Ibid.

41. Ibid., 161.

42. Malabou, *Que faire de notre cerveau?*, 149.

43. Leonard Lawlor, *The Implications of Immanence: Toward a New Concept of Life* (New York: Fordham University Press, 2006), 43.

44. Ibid., 53.

45. Ibid., 146.

46. See Catherine Malabou, *Les nouveaux blesses: De Freud à la neurologie, penser les traumatismes contemporains* (Paris: Bayard, 2007), 342.

47. Catherine Malabou, "An Eye at the Edge of Discourse," trans. Carolyn Shread, *Communication Theory* 17 (2007): 22.

49. Ibid., 16.

50. On *Verwindung*, see Gianni Vattimo, *The End of Modernity*, trans. Jon R. Snyder (Baltimore: Johns Hopkins University Press, 1988), especially chapter 10, "Nihil-

ism and the Post-Modern in Philosophy," 164–81. Vattimo contrasts *Verwindung* with *Überwinding* in Heidegger, and claims that rather than a straightforward overcoming, *Verwindung* constitutes an acceptance that is a convalescence, which Vattimo also translates as "secularization" (179).

51. Jacques Derrida, "Faith and Knowledge: The Two Sources of 'Religion' at the Limit of Reason Alone," in *Religion*, ed. Jacques Derrida and Gianni Vattimo (Stanford: Stanford University Press, 1998), 51.

52. Nancy, *Dis-Enclosure*, 160.

53. Jacques Lacan, On *Feminine Sexuality: The Limits of Love and Knowledge Book XX Encore*, ed. Jacques-Alain Miller, trans. Bruce Fink (New York: W.W. Norton, 1998), 45.

54. Carl Schmitt, letter to Armin Mohler, published in Jakob Taubes, *Ad Carl Schmitt: Gegenstrebige Fügung* (Berlin: Meuve, 1987), 34–35.

CONCLUSION:
SIX THESES ON POLITICAL THEOLOGY

1. Carl Schmitt, *Political Theology: Four Chapters on the Concept of Sovereignty*, trans. George Schwab (Chicago: University of Chicago Press, 1985), 36.

2. Ibid.

3. See Naomi Klein, *The Shock Doctrine: The Rise of Disaster Capitalism* (New York: Metropolitan Books, 2007).

4. Carl Raschke, "The Deconstruction of God," in *Deconstruction & Theology* (New York: Crossroad, 1982), 3.

5. Robbins, like myself, studied with Winquist at Syracuse University and claims the heritage of radical theology started there by Gabriel Vahanian. See Jeffrey W. Robbins, *Between Faith and Thought: An Essay on the Ontotheological Condition* (Charlottesville: University of Virginia Press, 2003), as well as John D. Caputo and Gianni Vattimo, *After the Death of God*, ed. Jeffrey W. Robbins (New York: Columbia University Press, 2007). John D. Caputo's retirement from Villanova to take a position in the Religion department at Syracuse marks his shift from philosophy to theology, and he has also embraced this tradition of radical theology in the United States. Davis studied with John Milbank at the University of Virginia and emerges out of the Radical Orthodoxy tradition, but he is also drawn to it and eventually toward a nuanced American radical theology because of its resources for theo-political critique of liberal capitalism. See Creston Davis, John Milbank, and Slavoj Žižek, eds., *Theology and the Political* (Durham, NC: Duke University Press, 2005), as well as Slavoj Žižek and John Milbank, *The Monstrosity of the Christ*, ed.Creston Davis (Cambridge, MA: MIT Press, 2009).

INDEX

Index